POUGHKEEPSIE, N.Y.

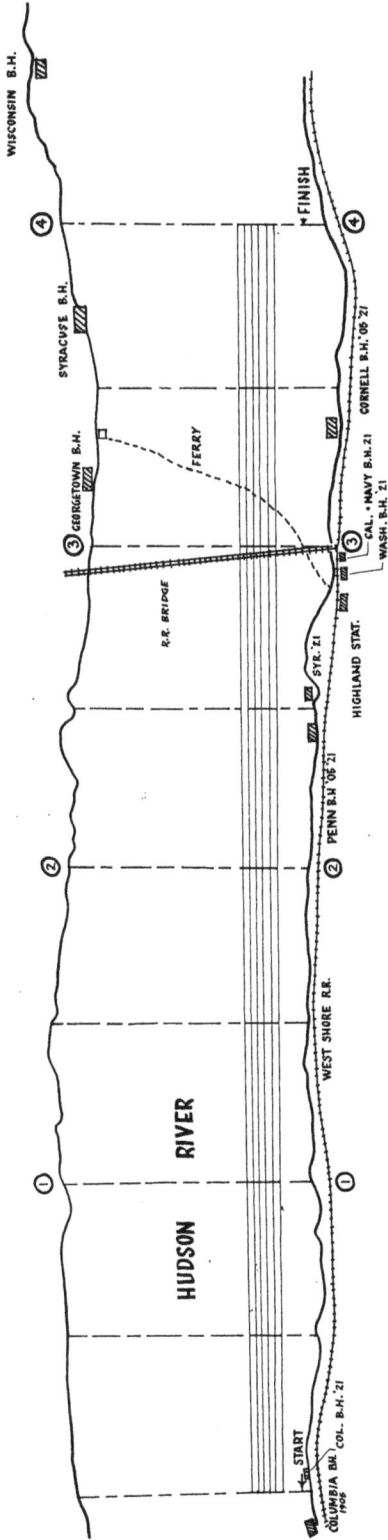

WISCONSIN B.H.

SYRACUSE B.H.

GEORGETOWN B.H.

FERRY

R.R. BRIDGE

HUDSON RIVER

HUDSON   RIVER

START

COLUMBIA B.H. 1909

COL. B.H. '21

WEST SHORE R.R.

PENN B.H. '06 '21

HIGHLAND STAT.

SYR. '21

WASH. B.H. '21

CAL. • NAVY B.H. '21

CORNELL B.H. '06 '21

FINISH

HIGHLAND, N.Y.

① ② ③ ④

HUDSON RIVER I.R.A. REGATTA COURSE

DOWN TO THE WATER

MARK OF THE OARSMEN

MALCOLM R. ALAMA
THE AUTHOR

A Narrative History

of Rowing at Syracuse University

Sponsored and published by
Syracuse Alumni Rowing Association
(SARA)
Syracuse, New York
1963

Estabrook Printing, Inc.

College youths who race down the water in frail-looking boats propelled by their own exertions are a different breed of men from those we normally expect to find in athletics. So are their teachers. These men do not expect or receive personal glory. There isn't any. Their success as a crew depends on all of them, not on one or two. Even at that, they take a risk. Their months' accumulation of training, hardships and aspirations are often crystallized into either victory or defeat, sometimes in less than twenty minutes of a big race. Henry W. Clune better expresses than the author the texture of a crew in his March fourteenth, 1935 column in the *Rochester* (N.Y.) *Democrat and Chronicle*:". . . But no racing shell goes finely without eight young men at the sweeps, each perfectly disciplined, each for the moment dedicated to the hard job at the oar, each willing to sacrifice for the common good of all. And the youth of today, well trained, well disciplined, and with a fine and noble sense of sacrifice . . . is the citizen of tomorrow who may stem the raging torrents of disorder and discontent. . . ."

To learn about and become acquainted with those oarsmen of Syracuse and their deeds vicariously was the author's privilege. He has glimpsed briefly into their lives and humbly recorded their deeds. At the same time, he is a much richer man for it. This record, he is sure, leaves to the future, a deep-rooted and noble tradition of sacrifice and of love for the nonpareil of all college sports. This is their story, those men who went down to the water and willingly extended themselves.

An important part of that heritage, of course, is the Syracuse Alumni Rowing Association (S.A.R.A.) whose enthusiastic support of crew at the University enriches campus life. Once an oarsman, always a crewman is its credo. Deeds rather than words are its program. Success of crew with its educational value is its ultimate objective.

During research, faded and torn and smudged newspaper clippings provided some of the data. Unfortunately, they were not always sufficient nor accurate enough to provide all the necessary material. Books, magazines, personal letters, notes, scrapbooks, all were examined. Personal interviews were frequently held. In some cases, the author was forced to draw heavily upon what he considered most reasonable, for many items of allegedly historical value were not always in agreement. In all cases, however, truth was the goal.

Since the book was started, the author was blessed by the help of many, but especially by the untiring zeal and understanding of Drs. Bruce Chamberlain and Anthony Ladd; and Sidney Mang. Their patience and enthusiasm, their hours of research and checking, all helped make this a labor of love. Praise must be given the S.A.R.A. Historical Committee for its efforts.

No author engaged in some phase of history can do without the assistance of many others, directly or indirectly.

Foreword – May 2011

So much has changed in the nearly 50 years since Mark of the Oarsmen was originally published. Thin blades have given way to spoon oars and in turn to hatchets. Cumbersome wooden shells have been replaced by sleek composites. Training has become extremely sophisticated. Who had ever heard of an "erg" in 1963? And of course, the women - now competing for decades at the highest levels of rowing for college and country.

But much of what Gordon Hoople wrote in his foreword then remains true today. The men...and now women...who compete in the sport of rowing remain a breed apart. They continue to exhibit remarkable spirit, dedication, integrity and honor. As such they and their sport continue to reflect excellence on the organizations they represent - notably our Alma Mater Syracuse University.

Dr. Hoople noted then that the program had escaped extinction on several occasions and while crew has survived over the past half-century, the need for strong alumni backing and involvement remains if it is to continue.

Those who know and love sports understand that history is critical to their appreciation. In no sport is this truer than in rowing. The Syracuse Alumni Rowing Association, of which I am privileged to have been a founder, has always understood the importance of history to keeping crew alive at Syracuse. That is why we commissioned the book.

Now, as SARA members from ensuing generations are working on a sequel documenting the years since Mark of the Oarsmen was written, it seems a good time to make the original available to the thousands more who have worn the Orange and those who have supported them.

I sincerely hope that Mark of the Oarsmen will inspire many more men and women not only to keep the tradition of rowing alive at Syracuse University but to help it grow and prosper.

May 2011   Bruce E. Chamberlain M.D. '41
                                          SARA Co-Founder

FOREWORD

"Ready all . . . Row!"

For over one hundred years college oarsmen have
waited, tense and eager, to hear those words to start a race
for which they have practiced many months. This has happened scores upon scores of times at Syracuse University.
The drama of these moments and what follows immediately
after deserves telling. This book does it well.

This is the story of from three thousand to four
thousand college oarsmen who in one way or another contributed to the history of rowing at Syracuse University.
Some of these faded from the crew picture after a few days
or weeks of an attempt to become a freshman oarsman. However, many others struggled and sweated through four years
of rowing to make this history possible. It records somewhat
more than sixty years of rowing at Syracuse. It details many
triumphs but it tells of defeats as well.

This story is not an even one. The reader will be impressed by the recital of the many times Syracuse rowing
faced extinction. Despite setbacks, crew has persisted and
set a record of which all Syracusans may be proud.

Malcolm Alama's history is in proper perspective, for
he correlates it with parallel current events and the unfold-

Therefore, sincerest appreciation goes to all these: Governor W. Averell Harriman, Dr. Edward N. Packard, Jr., M. Charles Hatch, Jr., Hubert Stratton, James Trace, John Riedel, Dr. Thomas Kerr, Dr. Uri Doolittle, Kenneth Fairman of Princeton University; John Marcham of Cornell University; Robert Stone, Louis Dworshak, Frank Early, Gerald van de Water, Mrs. David Wright of the Onondaga County Historical Society; Bill Reddy of the *Syracuse Post Standard;* Russell S. Swanson, President of S.A.R.A., William Hunter Smith of the Syracuse Public Library; Miss Elizabeth Girard of Betts Memorial Branch, Syracuse Public Library; Coach Loren Schoel, Coach Victor Michalson, Coach Eugene Perry, Dr. Dayton Lierely, Charles E. Mills, Jr., Selwyn Kershaw, William Wallace, Michael D. Gustina, A. Ward West, and especially my wife, whose encouragement and assistance were in large part responsible for the completion of the book.

January 25, 1963   Malcolm R. Alama

ing of the history of crew in other colleges throughout the United States. While it is primarily a history of rowing at Syracuse, these accounts of contemporary rowing elsewhere are neatly woven into the narrative. For instance, nowhere is there an account of the records of the Intercollegiate Rowing Association (IRA) as fully detailed as in this volume. Thus, this is a book which should interest all and especially those who have have any connection with rowing.

No apology is needed for the amount of space allotted to James A. Ten Eyck. He epitomized all that is good and fine about rowing. How many coaches of rowing have continued to coach winning crews at the age of 87? Of all the marks of oarsmen at Syracuse his is by far the greatest.

Rowing is the king of all sports. It breeds men set apart from others. It is one of the few strictly amateur sports now extant. No scandal has marred its history. No coward, no weakling, no scoundrel can become an oarsman. Men of this ilk have not got what it takes! Crew demands dedication of the highest order for it takes sterling purpose to row thirty or more strokes a minute for ten to fifteen minutes on end. This tale gives one a picture of strong determined men giving their all for one reason, their loyalty to Alma Mater. It makes a regal story. I commend it to all those who have a respect for or a loyalty to Syracuse University.

March 1963   GORDON D. HOOPLE, M.D.
                                 Chairman, Board of Trustees
                                 Syracuse University

PART I

Down to the Water

CHAPTER I

— CRACK!!! — Crack!! — crack! —

echoed the referee's pistol shot up and down the valley, and thirty-two men, naked to the waist, strained at their oars and pulled. In a blur of motion, they sent four cigar-shaped boats over the river as one.

With the boats away, the starting signals for the spectators—B-o-o-m! B-o-o-m!—of aerial bombs—accompanied the din of shrill train and yacht whistles, with the crowd's high-pitched shrieks. Seven successive explosions mushroomed out into snowy puffs above the outline of the Palisades.

It was June. The year, 1904.

It was on the Hudson. Near Poughkeepsie, New York.

The men rowed in the freshman race.

The first event of the Intercollegiate Rowing Association regatta.

Excitement in the race beckoned early—20 strokes beyond departure. While foam from the oars of Cornell, Columbia and Pennsylvania streamed out behind in concentric circles, Syracuse fought desperately to stay afloat.

The crisis arrived, when swells from the referee's boat rolled menacingly down the third lane, almost capsizing the boat of the small upstate university. Its men strained muscles in trying to bring their craft about, while Cornell spurted into the lead.

Meanwhile ashore, the crowd on the chugging and puffing observation train that ran alongside the races on the west bank yelled out encouragement to favorites, unmindful of soft rain that fell on bowlers and straws and dampened milady's hour-glass fashions of the era.

If by chance the partisan crowd expected the misfortune to force Syracuse out of the race, it was, indeed, disappointed. Quickly recovering poise and boat, the spindly coxswain and his eight companions swung back into unison and grimly set out to catch up.

Given the lead, Cornell, meanwhile, majestically paced the pack with an average 30-stroke cadence in the first half-mile. Pennsylvania was second, and Syracuse, rowing furiously, was coming up. The light blue of Columbia remained far behind. The boats kept these positions as they neared the railroad bridge, half-way mark of the freshman two-mile race.

Here, adversity again struck Syracuse. A patch of water heaved near the shell, striking Arnold Armstrong, bow oar, flush in the back. Instinctively he ducked under without interrupting his rowing, but a serious consequence followed.

Impact of the wave braked the shell's forward progress, slowing it down to a point where Coxswain Leon Cornwall, with pounding heart, recognized their precarious position.

"More power, men!" he screamed. "Give me more power. Hurry! Now—now!"

Catching the urgency of his appeal, the crew swiftly responded. Stroked by Darius "Dri" Davis, they began to increase the stroke to 32 without interrupting their rhythm. With the resultant smooth resurgence of power moving the boat in an angular blot of motion, they closed up a quarter of a boat length on Cornell in less than 600 feet. Now, the battle was joined.

Inch by inch, they crept up on Cornell.

Stroke by stroke, they narrowed the gap.

Blade by blade, Cornell desperately resisted.

To those on shore, the two appeared to be in mortal combat. To the sixteen in the boats, it was hell.

Someone was to falter, thought the crowd. Surely, humans weren't capable of withstanding such strain. Too much—much too much for flesh and bone! Neither crew, however, gave signs of washing out as their shells nosed into the area of the bridge.

—Clackclack — Clackclack — Clackclack — sounded the wooden handles of rudder ropes as they were pounded by excited coxswains on the sideboards of their shells.

Their frantic movements were justified, it seemed, for there was one axiom of the Hudson that all coxswains believed in with equanimity: To come from beneath the bridge in front gave any crew great psychological advantage, perhaps enough with which to remain out in front, or at least, with which to make a successful bid for victory.

"More—more, men!" shouted Cornwall. "More!"

"Come on—come on!" barked Cornell's coxswain.

Before disappearing under the bridge, the two appeared as glued together indistinctly and wrapped against the backdrop of the span in a moving montage of heads, arms, oars, legs and racing boats.

The responsibility of separating them visually belonged to a pair of black eyes found in a solitary figure on the bridge. Unobservable to the crowd, he was the official lookout for the races, and he was standing at his post.

It was his job to notify everyone up and down the Hudson by aerial bombs the position of each crew according to its lane, when each rowed through the open archway of the steel span. At the moment, his eyes anxiously scanned the water below.

"In all my years," wildly he thought, "I've never seen a dead heat like this before. They're so close together!"

Leaning farther over, he shaded his eyes from the rain. One eye, he squinted next as he desperately tried to measure a marginal difference between the two boats.

Cornell led. Yes, no doubt about it, he thought. He peered down below once more. No—wait a moment! Make sure, he cautioned himself. Be sure about it. He hesitated. Bygawd, next he thought, shaking his head. He was wrong! In a halved leap of time, he reversed himself. By six inches, perhaps. Yes—yes, but enough, yes enough!

Racing over to the wooden fireworks frames, he tipped glowing punk to the fuses of his arsenal and fired off his bombs—

—B-o-o-m! B-o-o-m! B-o-o-m!

Syracuse was ahead.

And as the sounds of the bombs raced up and down the valley cupped by mist-hidden escarpments, the deep roar of astonishment swelled up in volume from the crowd on the banks and on the train.

Unbelievable!

The Syracuse freshmen, vigorously renewed by their baptism of fire, burst forth on the other side of the bridge, holding the lead. Spacing beautifully, they swung into the final mile, making lengthy runs between strokes of their

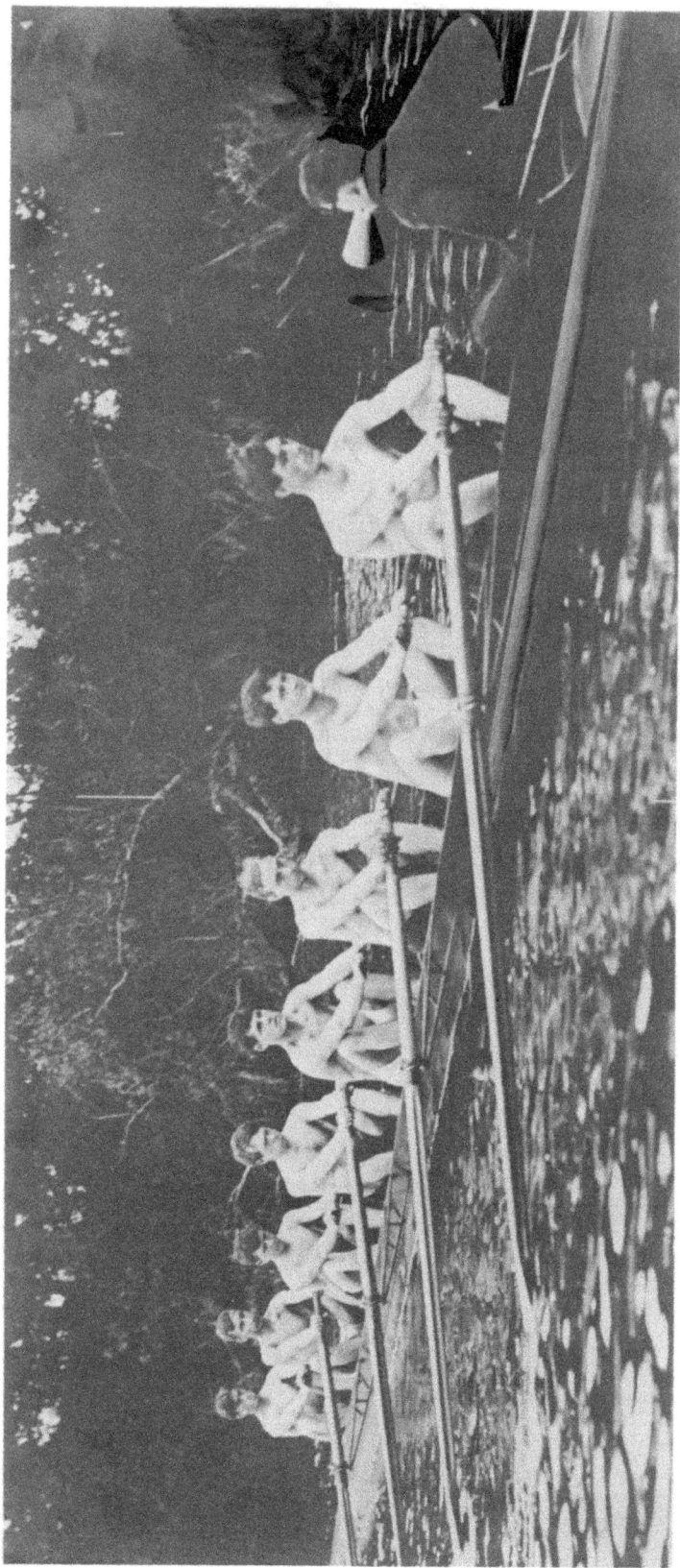

1904 FRESHMAN CREW, first Syracuse crew to win on the Hudson: Str. Darius Davis, Willard Andrews, Andrew Hale, Leon Rice, Herbert Robinson, Dwight Stone, Henry Spencer, A. M. Armstrong, Cox, Leon Cornwall.

oars. Steadily, they merged oars with muscles, and power with pride.

A sliver of sunshine, as if in tribute, momentarily pierced through the overcast and struck the river, while behind the Syracuse boat, the resulting combination of inky water at random splashed with color, formed endless pools of orange flame.

In the short distance to the finish, the crew savagely lengthened its lead, as if from sweat and fury they swept away the frustrations and disappointments, the ridicule and heartaches which plagued them and those who came to the Hudson before them.

Cornell finished two lengths behind them, followed by Pennsylvania and trailed by Columbia.

To the freshmen of Syracuse went the honor of capturing their University's first trophy on the river. They now looked hopefully to the varsity to duplicate it, while 80,000 spectators settled down for the last race of the Intercollegiate Rowing Association's Regatta.

CHAPTER II

WHEN AND WHY

Syracuse came to the Hudson in the beginning was interesting history.

Cornell, Columbia and Pennsylvania in 1895 banded together and held their first race, later calling themselves the Intercollegiate Rowing Association (IRA), sponsoring a regatta for each of the following years. To mingle with this group came Syracuse in 1901.

The reason?

Students in general, and the Chancellor in particular, sought to possess a sense of belonging with others in the world of rowing.

At face value, however, rowing was truly a precarious endeavor for so small a school. Madness, thought others in Syracuse.

The sport was expensive, a luxury generally reserved for larger and richer schools. And since it was considered the blue-ribbon event of collegiate athletics, those affluent schools unblushingly sponsored rowing and willingly absorbed financial losses.

With Syracuse, it was a far different story. She wasn't able to underwrite athletic deficits of any kind. She was only thirty-two years old at the time, a fledgling in the aristocracy of higher learning. Without sizable endowment upon which to draw, she was kept alive in large part by tuition of students.

Frankly, while IRA members and others publicly claimed that rowing constituted nothing more than clean and beneficial exercise for their students—a reason undisputed—there was another motive, the public reason notwithstanding: Rowing offered a splendid opportunity of carving a niche in national collegiate athletics.

Syracuse subscribed to both, but its quest for the second one, thus far eluded its oarsmen in three previous journeys to the Hudson. Hope for the 1904 regatta wasn't promising, either. The same handicaps, which faced other Syracuse crews, continued to face them:

Money. None.

Manpower. An acute shortage.

Oarsmen. Inexperienced.

Whereas, the history of when and why Syracuse came to the Hudson was fascinating, how the ability of its varsity crew was compared with others in 1904 proved astonishing!

If paucity of men for the shells was a major problem, there was an identical shortage of partisan and public support. Even professional gamblers laid 10 to 1 odds that the varsity wasn't able to finish first, and 2 to 1 that it wasn't able to finish in the first three. The 10 to 1 odds went begging—even back home in Syracuse!

While Syracuse was largely ignored by everyone, there was a supporter—a vociferous one—who loudly proclaimed his faith in both of her crews. A breeder of fine French coach horses, he was Rollin M. Stone from Marcellus, a hamlet near Syracuse.

A fine figure of a man, measuring over half a dozen feet in height, Stone was of trim physique, and sported a Vandyke beard shoring up an angular jaw. At age 55, he was genial, smiled often without apparent provocation. Stone's faith in Syracuse was biased, perhaps.

Son Robert was captain of the varsity crew, and another son, Dwight, stroked No. 3 oar in the freshman boat.

Besides all this, Stone was a deacon of the Presbyterian Church, and he kept an eye out for righteous business. To demonstrate his belief, he slipped Robert $25 before the races and suggested the money be placed on underdog Syracuse. Matter of faith, nothing else, he told his son.

Two weeks before the races, Stone came to Poughkeepsie to inspect the competing crews. And on the day before the races, he more than willingly gave his unqualified opinion of Syracuse crews to a young New York reporter.

"Now—I don't want to seem overconfident," he told him, "but I tell you, the freshmen are not the only crew who's going to do well, today."

"Who else?"

The elder Stone replied that he expected the varsity crew to win their race, too.

"You mean, sir, that the varsity boat of Syracuse will win?"

Stone paused before answering, detecting a whiff of the Turkish cigarette dangling from the lips of the young man. Whew! he thought, screwing up his face, the cigarette smelled like burnt goose feathers!

"What were you going to say, sir?"

Stone's attention returned to the reporter's face.

"Well—the only way I can gauge them," he confided, "is from my experience with horses—which may sound peculiar—"

The reporter stopped scribbling.

"Yessir, it does."

Stone, hastening to explain, placed thumbs in the pockets of his vest and continued.

"But I've watched them, carefully, and those big fellows of Syracuse got it in them—yessiree, they've got it in them!"

Disbelief flooded the reporter's face.

"May I ask, sir, if you mean Syracuse will win both the varsity and the freshman races, today?"

"Yes, I certainly do."

"May I quote you, sir?"

A hardness came into Stone's eyes, and he stared into the young man's eyes.

"What's so unusual about that?" he asked him.

"Oh—you know, sir," stammered the reporter, "no one gives Syracuse much chance today, do they?"

"I do," replied Stone. "Certainly you may quote me. I give them the best chance in the world, young man!"

And the reporter quoted the Marcellus horse breeder. Since Stone's optimism for Syracuse was like a raft of hope in a surrounding sea of confidence for Cornell, the interview rated nine lines of type in a New York newspaper.

Meanwhile, behind boathouse doors, Charles Courtney, the Cornell coach, wrestled with a problem.

Stone unabashedly told the newsman, in substance, that the Syracuse crews were to win because they possessed that unmeasured marrow of human endeavor—heart, or the courage, and desire to overcome all obstacles and win. With crews of Courtney, as well, lack of heart was rarely a factor. Rather, because its oarsmen were endowed with it and were given superb training, Cornell remained at the pinnacle of collegiate rowing for many years.

To Courtney, either a youth hungered for victory so acutely that he willingly sacrificed the full measure of his strength in pursuit of it, or quietly, he was dropped from the squad early in the season.

Courtney was one of those few coaches who enjoyed the gift of accurately sizing up young men; he quickly evaluated an oarsman; one not measuring up to the standard, he chopped ruthlessly off the roster.

No, definitely, it wasn't the human factor bothering the rotund coach with the walrus moustache. His problem was inextricably tied up with a human equation: How to race an eight-oared race and a four-oared race with but ten proven oarsmen?

The Cornell predicament came about when A. R. Coffin, varsity captain who stroked the boat to Hudson supremacy the previous year of 1903, was felled earlier that week with fever. Another oarsman, W. H. Forbes of the 1903 championship four-oared crew, developed blood poisoning from a leg gash and was sent back to Ithaca.

What was Courtney to do? All that morning, he sought an answer.

Outside the boathouse, the public began to catch whisperings of Courtney's dilemma, and the betting was no longer fluid, firming up something like this: Cornell, even money; Wisconsin, 3 to 1, both Georgetown and Pennsylvania, 4 to 1; Columbia, 6 to 1; and on Syracuse, the odds skyrocketed up to 25 to 1!

While Courtney grappled with his problem, Coach Ten Eyck of Syracuse faced one of his own.

The New York newspapers unfairly heaped criticism

upon two of Ten Eyck's men. So abusive were they, the coach feared for his men's morale. He tucked the newspapers out of sight.

Unknown to the Syracuse crews, the public learned in the newspapers that varsity stroke, Edward Packard, Jr., who was two inches short of six feet and carried 152 pounds around on his slight frame, leaned too far over while rowing, "that he is likely to fall out of the shell and interfere in the smoothness of the rowing unison."

Clarence Dempster, Packard's mate at No. 5 oar, was the second target of the metropolitan papers. He was criticized severely for "not being varsity material," because his habit of jerking his head at the end of each stroke caused him, the papers said, to tire easily.

Some of the readers at Poughkeepsie became inquisitive on race day and asked Ten Eyck about his men's peculiarities. The Syracuse mentor hesitated a moment before answering the barrage of questions.

"I let my men keep their peculiarities in a boat to a greater extent than most coaches," he told them. "My idea of that is to allow greater harmony by letting every man do the thing in his own way—so long as it doesn't interfere with the others."

The questioners muttered, "Most unorthodox," shook their heads and sadly turned away.

Ten Eyck's jaws worked up and down on a bulge of tobacco, his face opaque as they abandoned him.

CHAPTER III

THE HUDSON WAS

chosen as a site in 1895 by Charles Tremaine of Cornell, Thomas Reath of Pennsylvania and Frederick Sill of Columbia, who later was the founder and headmaster of Kent School in Connecticut. The course was laid out the following Spring by Sill and by Walter "Doc" Peet, Columbia's first crew coach.

The course began three miles north of the Poughkeepsie Bridge, near a place called Krum Elbow, and measured downstream four miles to the finish line.

Square-bottomed stakeboats, one each for the competing crews, were anchored fore and aft of the starting line, eight feet apart and 325 feet from the western shore.

At one point, one-quarter mile south of the bridge, mark boats bearing ball signals were anchored on each side of the course on a perpendicular line with piers of the second bridge span. The finish line itself was marked by two boats bearing ball signals and flags.

Those aerial bombs—skyrockets—announcing the beginning of the races and the crew positions at the three-mile mark in the varsity races were provided by the Pain Manufacturing Company of New York.

Order of finish was indicated by the college colors of the crews, suspended from the middle span of the bridge, the upper flag denoting the winner.

By race time of 1904, the shadows of early evening were deepening over the scene on the Hudson; and although thoroughly drenched, the spectators remained enthusiastic.

In contrast, the oarsmen of Syracuse were quiet. Earlier that afternoon, they chewed beefsteaks and sipped hot tea for their forthcoming exertions. After shouting hearty congratulations to the freshmen, they returned to silence.

Ten Eyck desperately tried to relieve the tension at the boathouse, quietly reeling off positions of the six varsity crews in the race: the dark blue and gray of Georgetown, first lane; light blue of Columbia, second; Syracuse, third; Penn's blue and red, fourth; Cornell, fifth; and Wisconsin's cardinal, sixth, out in midstream.

Before dispatching them to the stakeboats, Ten Eyck once more spoke to them.

"If there's a chance to nurse Cornell or the others," he instructed, "I want you to do it."

His eyes wandered over the circle of young faces before him. Packard stared moodily. Stone chewed his lips. "Monk" Miller, the coxswain, nervously worked his jaws up and down as if on hinges. The others stared obliquely.

"No doubt those other fellows," Ten Eyck continued, "will be more tired than you. You're well-trained. Spread your strength over the four miles—and don't faint," he reminded them. "If you do, you're a deadweight—just a passenger." [1]

He cautioned:

"Remember what I've told you about spreading your

[1] Robert R. Stone, West Simsbury, Connecticut, in letter to author, dated March 5, 1962.

stamina. Spread it out as you do butter on bread—evenly across the entire slice."

Pointing a gnarled finger for emphasis, he added:

"Make sure, now, that you've enough left over to reach that edge—!"

They shuffled down off the dock into their shell, measuring each movement carefully so as not to injure the boat's taut skin. When they were settled, the flimsy-appearing craft supported their weight, three-quarters of a ton.

From his launch, Ten Eyck departed with these words:

"Just row the race you want to—you've got the guts, and I know d___ well, you'll do it!"

When Syracuse arrived at the stakeboats, four other crews were impatiently waiting for the officials to appear, their boats bobbing up and down at the mercy of the waves. Too, part of the blame for delay belonged to Wisconsin, which was very late.

Cornell came up to the line, swinging in that mechanical motion that always characterized Courtney's crews, and the crowd sent up cheer after cheer. Others received ovations, too, but none quite so tumultuous as those given the Ithacans. Finally, the Badgers appeared, followed by the boat containing the following race officials:

Referee Richard Armstrong, Yale. Timekeeper Everett J. Wendall, Harvard. Stewards: Francis S. Bangs, Columbia; Thomas Reath, Pennsylvania; Frank Irvine, Cornell.

Lined up for the start, the crews anxiously awaited the signal.

"Are you ready, all?" asked Armstrong.

Then came the interminable five seconds wait as specified by race rules, followed by the upstretched arm and the sound of the pistol.

Pandemonium broke loose from the spectators, the yachts and barges as the six boats moved forward; and the people roared when Cornell immediately took the lead. Courtney's men were serving notice early that any challenger this day must reckon with them.

Syracuse, forty strokes later, challenged her.

Rowing at a rapid clip of 33 strokes per minute, the Syracuse boat matched its puddles, glued even to the prow of the Cornell shell, matching her stroke for stroke. There wasn't a resemblance of a check in the Syracuse boat as it gained momentum.

Ten Eyck's men were ahead by three-quarters of a length at the first half-mile.

Courtney's men increased their stroke.

The view of the Syracuse boat was a blend of movement, smooth and frictionless. Digging deep, Packard, the stroke, recovered in strength, sweeping with his mates. They gradually increased the stroke back up to 33 in answer to Cornell.

All oars caught (entered the water simultaneously), and all eight released (emerged from the water) as the boat went forward. This was what a rowing coach always seeks— perfect and instantaneous co-ordination of men and materials.

A section in the wide tableau of the observation train, which contained Cornell rooters, was immobile. The people were bewildered, except for a few optimists nudging companions about the deplorable state of Cornell's position.

The Big Red, the few comforted themselves, was deliberately holding its awesome power in reserve. And a few moments later, in apparent confirmation, the nudgers now slapped their companions on the backs, with smiles of I-told-you-so smearing their faces. The reason for their excitement was evident.

Moving suddenly, Cornell caught up with Syracuse.

Now watch Courtney's boat go!

The Cornell rooters forgot about Packard. But he replied quickly, drawing forth the tremendous stamina Ten Eyck told him the crew possessed, and increased the stroke from 33 to 34 to 35 and then to a torrid 36.

From the shore, the two boats appeared to be gummed together, but when Packard increased the beat, the spectators saw Syracuse inch ahead, until at the two-mile mark, open Hudson separated the two.

Syracuse played cat-and-mouse with Cornell.

Packard eased off the stroke by three.

Cornell moved up even with Syracuse.

Packard increased the stroke by three.

Cornell doggedly remained parallel.

Packard pushed the stroke up to 38, a grueling task for any crew at that stage of the race. The boat raced ahead of the 1903 champions of Cornell.

Courtney's boat fell back, the men frantically watching their invincibility ebbing away downstream.

"Well, boys," Miller shouted from his coxswain seat, "you can spurt if you want to—but you don't need to—!"

Still, Syracuse spurted, drawing steadily away from Cornell, its high stroke astonishing the experts ashore, who earlier predicted Ten Eyck's men were unable to sustain such a pace.

Unaccompanied across the line, Syracuse was three lengths of water ahead of Cornell. Penn barely lost second place to the Big Red. Columbia finished fourth; Georgetown, fifth; and the Badgers, last.

The area was carpeted with a bedlam of noise caused by shrieking whistles of trains, yachts, cruisers, tugboats, barges, Coast Guard cutters and ferryboats; ear-splitting skyrockets upstream; hoarse shouts and grating screams of joy of spectators from the shore, from those on the observation train, and from those on nearby anchored crafts which lined both sides of the finish area. These were the tumultuous signs of tribute accorded new champions.

Enveloped in all this was Ten Eyck, who, out of sheer nervous and excitable joy, collapsed heavily in his launch. Tears of happiness welled up in his eyes. The moment was his glory.

Waves of victory overlapped in other instances. Coach Ellis Ward of Penn, Ten Eyck's friend, whose brother raced against the Syracuse coach in the 1860s steered his launch alongside another and asked its occupants to convey his congratulations to Ten Eyck.

"I'm glad he won," shouted the side-whiskered coach. "And I'm glad it was him who brought Courtney down from his high horse—!"

Dismounted by Syracuse, Courtney at the same time came under heavy criticism for the way he solved his equation. He placed the Foote brothers, Edward and George, in both the four-oared and eight-oared races. Given little other choice, Courtney gambled, and he lost.

It was to Courtney's credit that he never alibied, never apologized and didn't downgrade Syracuse's victory, later confiding to a friend that the Ten Eyck crew earned its victory with a well rowed race.

Down at Syracuse headquarters, joy knew no bounds. The dressing room was a confusion of wild whooping and exuberance. Into this melee of noise stepped Hurlbut Smith, trustee of the University, chairman of the Syracuse Navy and brother of Lyman Smith, Syracuse typewriter tycoon. He offered his congratulations.

Cornered by bobbing heads, swinging arms and a babble of voices, Ten Eyck spied Smith.

"You've helped me," he shouted out, "and now, I hope I've done my share!"

"More than your share," generously agreed Smith.

The name of Syracuse University blossomed forth across the sports pages of the nation as result of the victories. New York papers, particularly, lavished heretofore unknown praise upon the two crews. They gave much space to the race in their front sections, which was most unusual at a time, when news of sports was generally relegated to back pages.

The *New York Herald:*

Syracuse is the new giant of intercollegiate rowing. . . . If the Syracuse crews at Poughkeepsie yesterday had stepped out of their boats on to the water and, lifting the shell on their shoulders, had run over the course and crossed the finish line first they would not have surprised the onlooking dumb-with-amazement crowd more than they did by winning the freshmen and varsity races. . . .

The *New York Times:*

The unexpected victory of Syracuse was very marked here in a great increase in all manifestations of interest in racing in general. . . . Today, Syracuse deserved to win. . . .

The *New York Tribune:*

A new boating star has arisen over the waters of the Hudson, and its name is Syracuse. . . .

One of the country's big newspapers wrote that victory

for Syracuse was a victory for the farmer's boy.

The great significance of the Poughkeepsie victory was by no means lost on Chancellor James Roscoe Day when he stepped down from a train the next morning in Syracuse, after a trip to Elmira (N.Y.). He purchased all the New York papers before a reporter asked him what he thought the victory meant to the University. An expansive smile covered his heavy-set face.

"I think it will mean a new gymnasium," he candidly replied. "It's a splendid advertisement for the University, and I believe it will do much for our athletics."

With that, the Chancellor stepped into his carriage and rode off.

Hurlbut Smith also talked to a *Syracuse Journal* reporter on his return to the city:

> Those victories are worth a million dollars to Syracuse, and I hope our Syracusans fully appreciate them. That varsity race was a good one to look upon, and I will not forget it, if I live to be a hundred. . . . .

Ten Eyck and his men arrived back in Syracuse early that next morning after the races; because of the hour, few were on hand to welcome them. The oarsmen walked over to the Onondaga Hotel and breakfasted. The celebration for them was held that night.

During the day, news of the Syracuse victories spread about and electrified the city. A milling crowd of 25,000 people gathered at 8 o'clock in downtown Hanover Square to pay homage.

The noisy demonstrators were led by Albert Petrie '03, decked out in reams of orange ribbon and waving aloft a large imitation of a broom—symbolic of a clean sweep on the Hudson.

Petrie's broom renewed a time-honored gesture of supreme triumph handed down to present-day college rowing. His symbol was deep-rooted in tradition of the open seas and stretched backwards to 1652.[2]

His visual concept of victory was perpetuated later by American submarines in both world wars, when upon returning from successful patrols, they also carried brooms atop their conning towers.

The joyous citizens of Syracuse—the students long departed for the summer—paraded through the streets, hauling Ten Eyck, Dr. Day and the oarsmen in carriages and followed by a procession of snorting, huffing and juggling automobiles. Snaking past hastily-decorated stores, the marchers wound down through Warren Street to Onondaga, over to Genesee Street and later made the long climb on University Avenue to the campus, where they lighted a bonfire. Fireworks, later, were fired off.

"Speech—speech—speech—" chanted the swaying crowd in front of the Administration building.

Vainly, Jacob "Jake" Gramlich '04, Navy Commodore and himself a former oarsman, atempted to put the crowd in order. His efforts for quiet futile, he finally introduced Professor Delmar Hawkins, who in turn, presented Chancellor Day. Dr. Day spoke and the *Syracuse Post-Standard* reported his words:

> For the first time in the history of my connection with this college, I feel as if I amounted to nothing. I feel ex-

[2]Rear Admiral, USN (Ret.) E. M. Eller, director of U.S. Naval History, in a letter to author, dated 21 March 1962: "It is said that when the celebrated Dutch Admiral Van Tromp defeated an English fleet in 1652, he cruised with a broom at her masthead to signify that he had swept his enemy off the sea. When the positions were reversed the following year, the British commander flew a long streamer symbolic of a lash to show that he had whipped his adversary from the water."

ceedingly small when I congratulate the University in having as the coach of such a gallant band Mr. James Ten Eyck (Cheers). When we engaged this man, we said to him, here is your material. It is not large, it may be crude and present many difficulties to the beginner, but here is the opportunity. He went to work. . . . To use a phrase that you sometimes indulge in, he "sawed wood", and I leave it to you to see how large a stick he has sawed off (Prolonged cheering).

Lyman C. Smith, described by Dr. Day as the founder of the Syracuse Navy, spoke after the Chancellor:

"In four years, the Syracuse Navy has achieved what no other Navy has achieved in a decade. We have here the nucleus of the greatest college in the United States, and I expect to see the reputation which we have recently won on th water not only sustained in all other branches of our athletics, but even increased."

"Ten Eyck—speech—speech!" demanded the crowd.

Someone from the crew entourage held aloft the two ornate trophies from Poughkeepsie. They were the Steward's Cup donated four years earlier by Francis S. Bangs of Columbia for the winning freshman crew, and the Varsity Cup given in 1898 by Dr. Louis Seaman '72, of Cornell. The latter trophy, valued at $2500, stood thirty inches tall with a ten-inch diameter base. The Bangs Cup is still awarded freshmen IRA winners in present days.

By this time, the platitudes said, the flowery language finished, Ten Eyck gave in to the urgings of the crowd and strode to the front of the assembly. Gesturing for quiet after a boisterous and deafening ovation, he spoke:

"I hope you do not expect a speech. The Chancellor said I could saw wood and that is what I can do if it is here to saw. I am proud of the crew men," Ten Eyck told them, "because you are proud. The credit is due to the men by my side. I may have started the ball rolling, but they kept it up.

"Syracuse's rowing future holds the promise of great things after winning these races. In that, we shall, doubtless, be handicapped no longer by the difficulties which have so greatly handicapped us this year."

The crowd stirred uneasily.

"In the first place," Ten Eyck continued, "we have suffered from lack of money and of a critical lack of facilities—"

Shouts of "We'll fix that!" "How much do you need?" and "Who's to blame?" swept up from the crowd.

Ten Eyck repeated the familiar list of difficulties—that the varsity crew was made up last year's freshman eight— two of the crew weren't good enough to make the freshman boat last year—and there were only two of last year's experienced men in the championship varsity boat.

"We only had 14 men trying out for the varsity," he admitted with a shake of his head. "No one of these 14 ever put an oar in the water before coming to Syracuse!"

The crowd remained reverently hushed and listened. When the coach finished, they roared their tribute to him, at the same time demanding to see the varsity eight.

With fatherly gesture, Ten Eyck introduced each one of them "as my man—"

Bow oar—Augustus Squires, Binghamton
No. 2—Jay Salisbury, Liverpool
No. 3—Oscar Kimberly, Niagara Falls
No. 4—Ross Anderson, Cicero
No. 5—Clarence Dempster, Ellisburg
No. 6—Robert Stone, Captain, Marcellus
No. 7—Francis Rice, Madison
Stroke—Edward Packard, Syracuse
Coxswain—Charles Miller, Herkimer

24

VARSITY CREW, 1904, IRA CHAMPIONS

Later that evening at a smoker held downtown by the University Club in the Larned Building, D. Raymond Cobb, a local attorney, presented a loving cup on behalf of the alumni to Ten Eyck. And Hurlbut Smith gave a purse of $200 from citizens to the smiling coach.

A few days afterwards, the village of Marcellus was ablaze with welcome for its oarsmen of the Rollin Stone family. The little hamlet held a parade, and the Stone men rode in a carriage ornamented with orange bunting. After the parade, a bonfire thirty feet high was set afire in front of the Stone residence, and fireworks costing $500 were set off.

An impressive amount of praise came to the stroke, Edward Packard, in the following days. For example:

New York World:

No small meed of praise should fall to Stroke Packard, of the Syracuse Varsity. He set a pace and kept it that simply beat the Cornell crew to a standstill, and though the lightest rower in the shell, he pulled mightily with a swing that won the admiration of the thousands of spectators.

New York Tribune:

Packard made a name for himself in boating history to-day. He is only a sophomore in Syracuse.

Modesty and intense loyalty to his mates and to Coach Ten Eyck caused him to write a letter on July 13:

My dear Coach: I want to write you a word in way of defense. I think you laid it on a little too thick after the race concerning my performance. The way the papers took it up one would think that Packard rowed an eight-oared shell alone and won. You know as well as I do that if a stroke hits it up to 35 and keeps it there, it is because the other seven men are rowing 35 also. And so I think praise should be distributed more evenly. At any rate *you* cannot get too much praise. "Punish yourselves," yelled at us at the close of a race, did more good than individual faultfinding.

. . . I can remember the very day that the Varsity began to crawl out of the slump she took. . . . I also want to give you my word for the splendid training. Hard as nuts and up to the top notch of physical condition you brought us up on the day of the race. Every man was well and in good spirits, which counts for much. . . . We rowed the race, coach, as you had taught us. . . . You have heard the applause of the crowd many times, but I have not, and as a result you get this lengthy letter thrust upon you. Whatever praise I have received has been brought about by your work, and so, it all comes back on you. . . .

Probably, the best description of Packard's style of stroking was found a week later in the *Poughkeepsie Courier:*

Yet every man in the boat kept perfect time, and the stroke himself was a marvel to watch. At every sweep of the oar his body bent over so far that his chest seemed almost to be flattened against the bottom of the boat. Such strenuous work seemed almost too much to last for a four-mile pull, but Packard never let up for an instant, and he has stamped himself as one of the most remarkable and capable strokes that ever sat in a 'Varsity crew. . . .

As the community recovered from its victory binge in the days following, other things were happening on the page of history.

At the time, the University consisted of five colleges—Liberal Arts, Applied Science, Fine Arts, Law and Medicine—and embraced an enrollment of 2,200; the New York City subway system opened; the Russo-Japanese War commenced; and later that November, Teddy Roosevelt was re-elected President.

It was a moment in history when Syracuse became of age on the scene of intercollegiate sports. How this miracle came about was described. How rowing came to the campus in the early years is a story of dramatic interest—an unfolding pageant thirty-two years long.

CHAPTER IV

MUSCULAR SPORTS AT

the University in the formative years were frowned upon
by the first three chancellors who sincerely believed they
interfered with academic life. They seriously doubted that
athletics were a focal point of student loyalty ,an outlet for
young energies, and a way to health and leadership. One
dean even admitted that "athletic sports do more harm
than good."

The major roadblock in the years of beginning was
Chancellor Alexander Winchell, a man of science preoccupied with study and teaching. First administrator of
the University, he heatedly opposed athletics of all kinds.
His forte was geology, and his papers on fossils were trademarks in the study of past alluvial ages.

Strong opposition to athletics on campus by the administration continued down through the years; thus, rowing
at Syracuse remained in the deep-freeze for more than a
quarter of a century.

By no means did this imply that the students accepted
the decision against rowing as inevitable during those years.
They agitated; they argued; and they pressured. Those supporting crew first attacked by pen.

Two years after the founding of the University, in 1872,
and 21 years after the first Harvard-Yale crew race, the student newspaper boldly explored the question with an edi-

torial headlined in capital letters "SHALL WE BOAT" setting forth three reasons why the "acquatic sport" should be introduced on Piety Hill:

Availability of Onondaga Lake.

Boat Clubs were formed by Cornell and nearby Hobart College.

A sense of pride.

Unfortunately, the effect of the editorial on campus wasn't assessed, inasmuch as it appeared shortly before the term ended for the summer. But when the fall term opened, the *University Herald,* a student publication, picked up the cudgel again and printed columns of rowing news from other colleges and universities.

The campaign failed.

Meanwhile, two enterprising freshmen entered the picture. Charles Holden and George Hine formed a partnership, which although not affluent, was at least rich in enthusiasm and ingenuity. They went downtown and solicited merchants and citizens in the business section of Syracuse. Successful and with their pockets bulging, they went to Rochester, where they purchased a four-oared boat.

Now that the University was part-owner of a boat for rowing, where was the craft to be housed?

The partners solved that, too. Someway, somehow—history is mute about the details—they constructed a wooden shack to serve as a boathouse. Cost was $700, and the structure placed on land in the vicinity of what then was known as Salina Landing, an area to the north of the city.

Commendable as the effort was, the shack wasn't satisfactory. A major detriment was the hardship involved in getting to it. To reach it, one needed to board a downtown trolley near campus, exchange near the business section for a horsedrawn Liverpool Stage, ride to Liverpool, and then trudge through Syracuse's major industry—the salt works. Oftentimes, too, the shack was surrounded by spring floods; but worst of all, the section reeked with a fishlike odor!

The next year, 1873, enthusiasm for rowing burst out anew. when the Commodore of the Cornell Navy visited campus and urged the students to send a crew to the Memorial Day regatta at Ithaca.

Elated at the suggestion, students enlisted pathetically green but spirited candidates, who at once went into training. Practice progressed until someone remembered some thing important: Who was to pay the bill?

The burning question was forcefully asked on May 20 by the *Herald:*

> Now the question occurs who is to pay the expenses of this crew? . . . If boating is to flourish here, we must put our hands in our pockets and push things. . . .

Evidently none pushed, for the training ceased.

But they reckoned without the intrepid duet of Holden and Hine, who saved the day for rowing in Syracuse.

By this time, too late for the May 30th meet at Cornell, they planned a more grandiose undertaking. Forming a Boating Association of Syracuse University, they went into business again. Once more, they needed money. And again. they canvassed the merchants.

Part of the money they raised—$400—was set aside for prizes. Then, they announced a regatta of their own for June 25th on Onondaga Lake, a body of water, which 79 years later became the site of the famous IRA regatta.

Lured by the gold offered them by Holden and Hine, professional citizen boat clubs from New York, Albany,

Buffalo, Rochester and Union Springs eagerly entered the races.

Back in the Chancellor's office, Dr. Winchell continued to oppose rowing, particularly this new effort, and hurriedly dashed off letters to enlist support of influential friends in Syracuse; and while he furiously penned his opposition, Holden and Hine captured the imagination of the community.

Countywide support was very much in evidence, when thousands turned out for the races and excitedly watched Union Springs win the single sculls match, and the Gramercy Club of New York capture the eight-oared race.

The regatta stimulated the interest of students in rowing even more, and the following autumn they met for the purpose of organizing a Syracuse Navy. Meanwhile, Hine dropped out of school, and Holden sent Elwyn Plaisted in his place to represent him at the meeting. As usual, Holden dangled a deal before the eyes of the group.

Terms were succinct: If the group organized, the shack and two boats purchased earlier were to be given the students. The property, according to information given Plaisted by Holden, was valued at $900. However, there was a mortgage on the shack, first payment due the following January of 1874. The land, upon which the shack rested. was leased for ten years.

While the students pondered over these terms, a committee was appointed to enlist more members in the Navy, with Edwin Redhead of Fulton (New York) serving as chairman. In turn, Redhead appointed Plaisted, Chester Congdon of Duluth (Minn.), and Frederick Esmond of Syracuse as a committee for drawing up a constitution. They were instructed to present the constitution at the next meeting, 17 days hence.

At the meeting, the group unanimously accepted the constitution, when William Wood of New Dorchester (Massachusetts), moved that "we go into boating." In this way did the Syracuse Navy become a reality.

Officers elected to serve were: President, A. F. Berrian: Vice President, James Gilbert; Secretary, Nathaniel Wheeler; Treasurer, Wood; Commodore, Congdon; and Vice Commodore, William Dunlop.

It was quite a blow to the group when they discovered that sincere interest in rowing was pretty much confined to those few who formed the Navy. Only nine other students besides the officers joined:

Milton Buck, John Nichols, William Gilbert, H. F. Thomsen, Charles Wall, Edwin Nottingham, S. H. Wilhelm, D. E. Anthony and Charles Holden.

The fifteen, who joined the first Syracuse Navy, represented little more than ten per cent of the University's study body of that day, and they didn't take action on Holden's magnanimous offer. Disillusioned and discouraged, the group eventually died, and rowing languished through the years.

A wide panorama of history flowed into textbooks before rowing was again mentioned in all seriousness on the campus of the University.

Around this period in the University's early history, the first colors of Syracuse were adopted—rose pink and pea green The following year, they were changed to rose tint and azure. Eventually, they became pink and washed-out blue. But students, a quarter of a century later, were to say something vigorously about these colors of their University.

In 1899, they protested loudly about the colors and changed them.

Meanwhile, Syracuse University and rowing awaited their master builder.

CHAPTER V

THAT MASTER BUILDER

was James Roscoe Day, who became Chancellor in 1894. An architect with vision, he was a preacher of the Methodist cloth; and by his persistence, all phases of the University began to change.

A heavy-set man, he was a figure of great talents and in order to reach some objectives he employed the rare gift of persuasion. This asset he used to carry out his vision: enlarging the physical plant of the University; increasing enrollment; and upgrading the academic structure. But a part of his dream consisted of his desire to improve the athletic status of college life. Fortunately, he leaned towards rowing.

To successfully introduce the sport on campus, the Chancellor faced three requirements:

Student interest.

Money.

A coach.

In that order.

Keen observer of men and unusual catalyst that he was, Dr. Day sometimes moved in quiet, unobtrusive ways. Five years sped away before he considered the time opportune to bring rowing to the University.

About the time Admiral Dewey hoisted his flag over Manila Bay in 1899, Dr. Day and others met in the Yates

CHANCELLOR JAMES ROSCOE DAY
(That master builder)

Hotel, organizing the Lake Side Yacht and Boat Club. The group's purpose was to promote yachting and water sports on Onondaga Lake. Lyman Cornelius Smith was chosen Commodore and Dr. Day and F. M. Power were appointed to the governing board.

The new club announced plans for construction of an $18,000 boat house on a boulevard road on the west side of the Lake.

Syracuse newspapers, the next day, carried stories about the meeting, the details of which they attributed to "a spokesman." The anonymous speaker said the club's other purpose than to promote yachting was to form and maintain a college crew at the University:

> Onondaga Lake affords an excellent place for rowing and there is no reason why Syracuse University shouldn't train a crew on Onondaga Lake as well as Cornell University on Cayuga Lake. . . .

Students, four days after that meeting, went wild with enthusiasm, when the Chancellor announced at chapel that Mr. Smith offered to donate an eight-oared shell to the University.

Students in 1899 wasted no time. Assisted by alumni, they quickly formed a second Navy; and John Alexander Robinson Scott, the gymnasium director, was picked as chairman.

It was a meeting packed with excitement and the fervor of a beginning; discussions on such topics as raising money, date of tryouts, and what style of rowing was to be adopted—Yale or Harvard—occupied most of the attention. During the formal part of the meeting, Smith was asked to visit Courtney at Cornell and learn all he might absorb about rowing.

Upon arrival at Ithaca, the typewriter tycoon was met by Courtney at the train station. Then in his 17th year as coach on the heights above Cayuga waters, Courtney was gracious and of great assistance to Smith. Ironic as it later proved, Smith was accorded the friendliest hospitality by a coach, who in the years to come, was the disturbing centrifugal force against Syracuse rowing hopes and aspirations on the water.

Courtney, who was to coach 146 Cornell crews in his lifetime, of which 101 were to be winners, detailed for Smith the rudimentary needs of crew: enthusiastic support by students and the administration, as well as money, and a coach of dedication. As time leaped past, Courtney understood the values of these from his own experience.

Returning to Syracuse, Smith suggested that Scott might like to visit Courtney and observe practice sessions, too. On the last day of March, the Navy officially adopted its constitution, and Scott departed for Ithaca.

Courtney, during their discussion, suggested that the Syracuse Navy obtain a rowing machine and put candidates to work on it before putting them in a shell on water. Then, the conversation drifted to the position of coach and likely candidates for the position. Scott suggested Louis Emerick, a former Cornell crew member under Courtney in his undergraduate years. The portly figure agreed with him.

Back on the Syracuse campus, Dr. Day announced that Clarence Seamens of Brooklyn, a University trustee, agreed to purchase rowing machines; and two weeks later, Smith added two four-oared gigs to his previous gift of an eight-oared shell.

Meanwhile, speculation was rampant as to whom might

be appointed the coach. Mentioned most frequently was Frederick Colson, captain of the 1898 championship Cornell crew. Although many others supposed Emerick was to obtain the position, Syracuse newspapers quite authoritatively pronounced it was to be Colson.

Neither one was hired.

Amid the bustle of preparation for spring sports, the University's Athletic Board unwittingly solved the problem of securing for the crew a coach by hiring a Cornell graduate to coach football.

Edwin Regur Sweetland was born on a farm in Dryden, (N.Y.), a locality some fifty miles south of Syracuse, and during four years at Cornell, won four letters. Before graduating, Sweetland starred in football, baseball, track and crew.

Coaching football at Syracuse at that time, was only a part-time position, and supporters of crew anxiously wondered, why not offer Sweetland the job of coaching crew?

Sweetland, when approached with the suggestion, quickly accepted the offer, happy in the knowledge that the extra $500 for tutoring oarsmen augmented his thin pay envelope as director of gridiron activities.

A Navy organized, boats available, a coach hired and enthusiasm for the sport growing daily, meant everything was in readiness for introduction of crew at Syracuse early in 1900.

Forty men reported to Sweetland for the first tryouts,

and they were put to work on the rowing machines installed in the gymnasium. For three months they labored
on the machines before the winter broke up enough in
March to allow them outdoors.

Sweetland on the 30th dispatched an advanced party
of seven to chop up the thin layer of ice still covering
Seneca River, the outlet to the Lake. Later, Sweetland and
his first squad boarded the Syracuse and Baldwinsville trolley and rode out for their first workout in the open air.

Eager as they were to test the oars, the men shivered
and shook more from the frigid winds than from any anticipation they felt for the first workout. Adding to their
misery, they were forced to wade out through icy water to
the outlet, carrying above their heads one of the four-oared
gigs donated by Smith; there, they floated it, and the first
boatload of benumbed and frozen University oarsmen prepared to swing their oars.

John Hill, because of his small size, served as coxswain,
and his companions included Willard Pangmon, No. 2 oar,
Clinton Goodwin, No. 1 oar. Sweetland was stroke oar, a
position he held in the other four boat trials.

In the mauve-misted twilight of the cold wintry day,
the gig moved off, the inexperienced men jerkily going
through the motions of co-ordinating oars in the water.

The first practice session was truly a humble beginning, the gig veering back and forth on its way up to the
Lake and return, a half-mile distance. After thirty minutes
of getting the feel of the oars, they began to smooth out their
movements, increasing their strokes to a still erratic 18
strokes and grimly rowing another full mile.

Others working out:

Boat 2—James Middleton, Harvey Connell, Robert Farrington

Boat 3—Dayton, Royal Woolsey, Lanckton, Charles Creegan

Boat 4—Lynn Jennison, Duane Phelps, George Connell, Creegan

Boat 5—Case, Arthur Davis, William Costello, Creegan

Sweetland devoted the remainder of daylight, after the runs, to instructing his men on feathering, or rotating oars, in the swing, without splashing or otherwise impeding progress of the gig.

On April 4, came the first cut. Sweetland dropped off two from the squad, this leaving only 18 of the original 40, who reported for the squad early in January. Normal attrition took care of many; academic failures others; but there was probably a more valid reason for the larger number who left on their own accord.

Chilled by the cold, aching from newly-strained muscles, the oarsmen faced each practice day clothed in still sweaty and damp garments from the previous days. After practice, they changed in a small shack, which offered only a pot-bellied stove, much too small for any satisfying warmth. They showered under primitive conditions: a sloshing of cold lake water from wooden bucks administered by obliging fellow oarsmen. Dressing hastily, teeth still chattering, they dashed to catch the trolley and the long trip back to their lodgings.

On top of these handicaps, Sweetland was a rough taskmaster. He firmly advocated strenuous workouts and was sparse on sympathy and understanding of his youths. Sometimes, the men behind his back called him, "Iron Jaw."

But for those who survived, the sport of rowing opened up new and wide vistas of understanding, knitting them

together as close as brothers. One of those experiences responsible for drawing them closer happened on a windy
day. Rowing from the outlet to the Old Club House on the
west side of the Lake, the varsity boat sank, about half a mile
from the point of destination, when a wave splashed over.
At the time, Sweetland was coaching another boat some
distance afar.

Nine men floundered wildly in the freezing water,
until one shouted, "Come on, fellows—we ccccan ssswimmm
ashore!" And off he swam.

Lynn Wykoff, crew captain, figured otherwise.

"Come back—come back! Don't follllowww him. Stay
wwwith the shell—she'll float us alllll!" he chattered.

Luckily, they swam to the half-submerged shell and
with arms and legs numbed from the icy water managed to
push the boat to the west shore. Upon beaching the boat,
they turned it over with great effort, dumping out the
water. With anxious eyes on the Lake for Sweetland, they
climbed back in the boat and resumed their rowing.

Sweetland eventually missed them, and when he came
to the area of the mishap, he saw the crew rowing towards
their goal. Not one to display emotion, Sweetland allowed
himself a flicker of a smile to cross his grim-set lips. He
seemed to know what happened.

Two months later, on May 6, some of the crew met in
a small restaurant sandwiched in between a shoe parlor and
a saloon. When they got there, the leader sat high on a
stool, harpooning syrupy baked beans on the prongs of his
fork. His curly blonde hair reflected the bluish light of the
gas flame.

He looked at his companions, sideways. Before speaking, he wiped away the remains of his meal with a slice of thick bread that he stuffed in his mouth until his cheeks puffed out. He chewed noisily, and when he released the last of the bread, he cleaned off his lips with a swipe of an arm.

"Well, boys," he exclaimed with gusto, "what're we going to do about it?"

The rest stirred.

"Well—speak up! Dontcha agree with me, or not?"

A chorus of conforming voices spoke out.

"Well, now," the leader said with a shake of his head, after the vocal vote of confidence, "I'll go and see that reporter from the paper and tell him how some of us feel— keep it under your hats!"

On May 7, the *Syracuse Telegram*:

> Not one dollar except the salary of the coach has been spent on the crew this season. The University promised Sweetland that the men would have a training table. The men go out on the water early in the afternoon and do not get back until 8 o'clock at night. It is then too late to get anything more than a lunch at their boardinghouses. In many cases all they can get is a bowl of bread and milk. . . . Bread and milk is generally not supposed to be very good diet for a man who works hard. Another complaint: When they come in cold and wet after their workout, they have to change their clothes in a room in the boathouse. . . . They have to dress in the cold and hang up their rowing suits . . . and the next day put them on wet as when they took them off. . . .

The reporter wrote that the oarsmen expressed to him a veiled threat that unless the problems were solved, they might not continue to row.

Other universities, he said they told him, provided training tables for their crews: Penn paid $11 a week per oarsman for board at a training table, while Cornell paid

41

$9 per week per man. Here at Syracuse, they complained, it cost themselves $3 for board.

With deep regrets, the Athletic Board was unable to provide a training table for the men due to lack of funds, and as if in confirmation, turned down the IRA's first invitation to the Hudson; but as an alternative in keeping with its pocketbook, the Board arranged a race with the Francis Boat Club of Ithaca for that June 15th on Onondaga Lake.

The new Yacht Club House on race day was aglow with flags and pennants as hundreds lined the shore and others were conveyed on private launches, an observation train and on steamers.

Losing its maiden race, the first organized crew gave an excellent account of itself. Having practiced but 30 times on the Lake that season, the men gave evidences of greenness and inexperience. Despite this handicap, they led most of the race until the last 150 yards from the finish.

In that first race were:

Bow—Harvey Connell
No. 2—Lynn Jennison
No. 3—Ancil Brown
No. 4—Clinton Goodwin
No. 5—Harry Elden
No. 6—Lynn Wykoff
No. 7—Royal Woolsey
Stroke—D. Forest Phelps
Coxswain—John Hill

On the same day, many miles to the east, stood a man of erect carriage, calm visage, wearing a baggy suit. He was watching the first crew of the U. S. Naval Academy. It was his crew, he was the coach, and his young Midshipmen de-

THE SYRACUSE NAVY, 1900, at the Lakeside Yacht and Boat Club.

43

feated mighty Yale for their very first victory on the water in collegiate rowing. His name was James A. Ten Eyck, and he was chomping tobacco that day. He could not know it, of course, but his path was coming closer and closer to Syracuse University.

When the Syracuse Navy snapped shut its books for the first season of crew (1899-1900), only $38.16 remained in its treasury! However, something important happened that previous May of 1899. The students changed the University's colors. Dissatisfaction is sometimes the mother of change, and a field meeting with Hamilton College at Clinton (N.Y.), proved fertile ground for it.

Syracuse was victorious in the meet, but its colors of pink and blue, adopted in 1873, came under derisive comment. Returning home, the irate students chose a faculty member to serve with their committee in search of a suitable new color. Subsequent research revealed that a primary color, Orange, was not yet adopted as a single color by any higher institution of learning. Consequently, they adopted Orange, and later, the faculty and trustees approved of the choice. From that day forth, Syracuse athletes were known as Orangemen.

At the time Orange was chosen, the city of Syracuse boasted of a 90,000 population, the Erie Canal and the New York Central Railroad ran through the center of the city, and William McKinley was President of the nation.

CHAPTER VI

THE ROWING SITUATION

in 1901 at Syracuse was in a state of constant change, ebbing and flowing as the ocean caresses and then spurns the beaches of continents throughout the world. One moment the picture was rosy; the next, gloomy.

With a depleted treasury, the Navy refused Sweetland's request for a salary increase; at the same time, few men reported or showed any interest for rowing that spring. Thirty-two men from a student body of 1700 was nothing to indicate a burning desire on the part of the campus for rowing. For comparison, 60 reported at Cornell; 48 at Harvard and 90 at Columbia.

Rowing received a shot of adrenlin for its hopes when the alumni club of New York subscribed $700 towards cost of a proposed boathouse. The gift was made possible by the herculean effort of the Rev. Karl Schwartz, who solicited the club members for the money; land for it was given by the Maple Bay Company through owners Arthur Peck, William Hoffman and Fred Schaefer. The property was situated on a bank near the outlet to the Lake.

C. Van Merrick of the local architectural firm of Merrick and Randall was hired to draw up specifications for the structure. Soon, he disclosed that the boathouse was to be 80 feet long and 26 feet wide and a section of the structure reserved for storage of boats.

45

Another followed these gifts when Alexander Brown, an executive of L. C. Smith Premier Typewriter Company, gave a new launch for the coach. Valued at $1,500, the craft was fashioned by Thomas Milton, Brewerton (N.Y.) boat builder. Brown's brother, Edward, was district manager of Standard Oil, and in turn, he promised a year's supply of gasoline to feed the boat's 20-horsepower engine.

Others generously gave of what they possessed to help out the crew at the crucial moment. Students at a mass meeting in the Hall of Languages raised $322; and before the day's end, another $28 were collected.

Along with the good fortune, of course, came misfortune. Sweetland became ill with typhoid fever, and Charles Smallwood, Cornell alumnus registered in the Syracuse Law School, took over the crews, temporarily. No sooner than returning to duty, Sweetland was next called home by the death of his mother. It was one thing after another.

On April 30, fire brought calamity, when it destroyed the boatbuilding factory of E. Waters & Sons of Troy (N.Y.). Inside the building was a new papier-maché shell for Syracuse. The gasoline torch held by George Waters, while applying the finishing touches to the Syracuse order, exploded and $600 worth of shell went—p-o-o-f!—into nothingness. Shells for Pennsylvania and the Potomac Boat Club of Washington, D.C. were saved, but the builder told Syracuse he needed at least 60 days before building another for them.

Navy Commodore O. D. Blanchard appealed to Hobart and Pennsylvania for loan of a shell. Both refused.

What to do? Time was running out.

One choice was left the Navy. Crew members went to work and patched over the bones of its long-discarded and unseaworthy shell, pasting on layers of paper with adhesive, covered next by several coats of shellac. When finished, the papier-maché boat was still of doubtful condition for hard racing.

As if this hardship wasn't enough, the Navy indirectly became embroiled in a dispute with the Lakeside Railway trolley company over fares charged the oarsmen for transportation to practice.

The sequence of misundestandings came about when the trolley line asked the University football team to play a home game off campus on its picnic grounds on the west side of Onondaga Lake. The request was denied.

Forgotten by the University, the subject was kept alive by the trolley company, which in a fit of pique, childishly argued that it gave cash gifts for the crew in 1900, and in addition to this, provided free transportation to the oarsmen that first year. Was there no gratitude? the firm implied.

Stung by the rebuttal, the Navy, in anger, switched a June race with the Francis Club of Cornell from the west side to the east side of the Lake. Dr. H. W. Burchard, E. L. French and J. A. R. Scott were sent by the Navy to discuss with the Rapid Transit Company and the Rome, Watertown and Ogdensburg Railroad, the possibility of operating their excursion trains at the forthcoming race.

While the argument raged, directors of the Syracuse Yacht and Boat Club quietly applied pressure on the Navy, suggesting that its hasty decision be reconsidered. The water, they explained, was rougher on the east side, anyway.

In time, cooler heads took over and satisfactorily ironed out the dispute.

And still more controversy raged. The Big Red of Cornell charged that Syracuse used professionals in its football game the previous autumn, as well as being unnecessarily rough in its game with them.

Of course, Syracuse denied the allegations.

Despite the denial, however, Cornell ruptured athletic relations with Syracuse, canceling football, baseball and spring sports. Because of this, the Navy feared the race with the Francis Club might be postponed.

This was not the case. The races were held, and an imposing number of men of stature acted as officials at the races:

Referee, Schuyler Fisher, Cornell
Timers, Daniel Lanigan and Austin Barnes, Cornell; and
    C. L. Becker, Syracuse
Starter, Lyman C. Smith, Syracuse
Judges, Howlett Durston, Yale, Willis Peck and Howard
    Tracey, Cornell

Edward "Ned" Ten Eyck, world champion sculler in 1897, served as judge for the single scull race that opened the events in which Clinton Goodwin raced John Francis, Jr., the junior champion of the Amateur Rowing Association of America. The latter was coached by Jim Ten Eyck, who was no longer at Navy. However, before the races, Francis and his Alma Mater disagreed over personal matters. Therefore at Syracuse, the young man refused to represent Cornell. Instead, he wore the colors of the Laureate Boat Club of Troy (N.Y.).

The Syracuse oarsmen were unsuccessful against the visitors. Goodwin lost to young Francis by a large margin;

the freshman lost; and the varsity, after a game attempt, was defeated by superior conditioning and training of its opponents.

While victory eluded its grasp, the Syracuse Navy won in quite a different way. It realized a profit of $99.10 after expenses. Following on the heels of the profitable venture came Syracuse's second invitation to the IRA.

Come to the Hudson.

This time, the Syracuse Navy accepted.

The big problem facing the oarsmen was how to get there. Penniless, the crews now looked to the Hudson with sinking hearts. But they reckoned without the sincerity behind the invitation, for Cornell, Columbia and Pennsylvania sought the Orangemen, eagerly. And the IRA catapulted Syracuse into the big time of intercollegiate sports by generously paying its transportation. Since there was no other money available, the Syracuse crews remained home until 48 hours prior to the races.

People always remembered regatta day of June second, 1901, as being the hottest day on record up to that year at Poughkeepsie. In the city, the mercury hovered persistently to the 100-degree bar, while on the river, itself, the heat remained two degrees lower. Whew! thought everyone, how could the oarsmen row in that heat?

Goodwin carried the Syracuse colors in the single sculls race, but he rowed against time. His scheduled opponent, again Francis, disagreed with Cornell once more and refused to row. Francis loaned Goodwin his shell, and the Syracusan raced the mile and one-half in nine minutes, 31 seconds.

Syracuse's freshmen made a gallant attempt in their

1901 FRESHMAN CREW: G. H. Wildman, Str., C. B. Ellis, R. R. Stone, E. J. Brady, R. M. Hawn, F. Sowers, G. W. Fowler, C. F. MacMurray, Cox, M. W. Nelson. Inset: Coach Edwin R. Sweetland

50

race, but unskilled handling of their patched and water-
logged boat, and inexperience with tidewater and swells
from passing steamers on the Hudson brought them close
to disaster. One swell filled up the boat high enough to brim
the coxswain's seat; but to their credit, the freshmen gave it
all they possessed.

Always in imminent danger of sinking, they slowed
down and temporarily left the race under the bridge.
Emptying the shell of water with their hands, they again
shoved off, furiously stroking 34 and closing up in the
stretch drive. They finished three lengths behind winning
Pennsylvania at the end.

The four-oared race was won by Cornell.

In the varsity race, Captain Wykoff kept his boat within
reasonable distance of fourth-place Georgetown, but at the
three-mile mark, it was the same old refrain. Swells from
the referee's boat cascaded down into the boat. almost sinking it. The wave was violent enough to swing the boat cross-
wise, and while the shell was pounded by the swell, the
rudder protruded grotesquely in mid-air!

Cornell, of course, won handily, and a strong myth of
her invincibility spread about the campuses of colleges and
universities. Once more, Courtney's crews ruled the Hudson.

With a surprising gesture, Courtney took time out from
accepting accolades to say magnanimously, "I'm willing to
be quoted when I say the Syracuse freshmen would have
beaten Penn and Columbia had they been properly boated."
He claimed the Syracusans lost their chance by the "slow-
ness of the boat itself, not by the fault of their rowing."

Whereupon, Courtney resumed his favorite sport: attempting to persuade the IRA to transfer its regatta from the treacherous Hudson to the calm of Cayuga Lake or to some other lake. More specifically, he argued:

> Upon the Hudson no matter the time of day, the tide makes some courses better than others. One course, for fairness, should be absolutely as good as any other. And the Hudson course couldn't be properly policed.

While Courtney expounded the virtues of lake racing, George Bond, the Syracuse Navy representative, told a reporter:

> The alumni are proud of Syracuse's work today. The men went through as tough an ordeal as falls to the lot of most athletes and came out with honor. This is a good beginning. We'll come back here until we win one of these races!

On January tenth, 1902, athletics on Piety Hill were recognized officially when Sweetland assumed the complete management of all muscular sports. He refused an offer of a position on the faculty with the title of professor of athletics, but he was given assurance of employment as coach for an indefinite period.

Early that year, his oarsmen defeated the Laureate Boat Club of Troy, while the freshmen defeated Cascadilla, a preparatory school for Cornell.

On May 30, in a triangular race for second varsity boats of Cornell, Harvard and Syracuse held on Cayuga Lake, Sweetland's crew finished second to Cornell, but ahead of the Cantabs.

The next month, the eager and spirited crews of Piety Hill industriously practiced for the Poughkeepsie races, sensing perhaps, that their efforts on the Hudson were responsible for future rowing on campus. When Sweetland drove them without mercy, they responded admirably with

GEORGE H. BOND
A great friend of Syracuse rowing
Athletic Governing Board, University Trustee

LYMAN C. SMITH
Founder and benefactor of the Syracuse Navy

HURLBUT W. SMITH
Hired Ten Eyck to coach crew
Chairman of the Navy 1904

53

full measure of flesh and bone. But the oarsmen seemed to be concerned more about their showing for the University and themselves than about any honor they might bring to Sweetland.

Despite Sweetland's own belief that his men respected him, again they referred to him, outside of hearing range, as "Iron Jaw". To put it bluntly, they tolerated him for the sake of their University. Other than that, they directed their loyalty and camaraderie to the sport and to their own group.

The specter of defeat on the Hudson haunted Sweetland's men on June 21 at the regatta. The varsity once more finished fifth out of six boats; the freshmen duplicated their fourth position out of five entries as in 1902; and Cornell, Sweetland's Alma Mater, continued to command the Hudson by lofty right of sweeping both races.

Fortunately, Syracuse entered a new era of rowing that December. Once more, Sweetland asked for additional money as coach of crew. Once more, due to strained financial conditions of athletics, the Syracuse Navy was unable to fulfill his demand.

Sweetland immediately resigned.

PART II

Riding the Crest

CHAPTER VII

STUDENTS PAID $100

tuition a year and obtained room and board for $5 weekly
in 1903, the year the Wrights flew the first airplane. With
the brothers conquering air, crew supporters were trying
to keep the sport alive on campus.

The Navy was in dire circumstances. A barren treasury,
without a coach, its outlook appeared dark; but in a bright
burst of optimism and faith, candidates reported for the
squad anyway, working without supervision on the machines on the second floor of the women's gymnasium.

It was at this particular moment that Dr. Day reasoned
that first things came first, and highest priority went to obtaining financial help for all athletics. Undaunted, he enlisted the financial support of University friends, and with
others interested in continuing sports on campus, he raised
money.

With all athletics assured of continued life for a time,
at least, next he turned to the task of obtaining for crew a
coach. He called upon another friend from the Smith family, Hurlbut Smith.

When the two met in the Chancellor's office in 1903,
the door ajar, Dr. Day was seen talking animatedly with
Smith. Friend that he was, Smith understood almost by
clairvoyance the reason for his friend's enthusiasm: the
Chancellor sought a coach possessing the traits that often

inspire men to victory; one who considered dedication to guiding men more important than money. A figure of a man flashed to Smith's mind.

And as they discussed the prospect, the Chancellor's door clicked shut, sealing off from posterity the words they spoke.

Later, on the appointed day they met, Smith searched James Ten Eyck's face as they talked, noting the furrowed lines in the leathery skin of fifty summer tans, the sorrel-eyes and the oak of a man in peak health.

"Mr. Ten Eyck," said Smith, "Dr. Day and I remember you when you coached young Francis in Syracuse in 1901. Now, we wonder if you were interested in coming back to Syracuse to stay—teaching our young men in rowing?"

"Well, Mr. Smith," Ten Eyck replied quietly, parceling out his words, "I certainly do appreciate no end the offer and the kind consideration you've showed me. I feel rowing's got a great future at Syracuse. And believe me, I say this because I liked the spirit of your men at the Francis Club races."

Smith nodded, recalling the hopeless efforts of the youthful Syracusans against a stronger, better-trained opponent on that particular day.

"Mr. Ten Eyck, the Chancellor wishes to put Syracuse rowing on the lips of the college world—make its name synonymous with victory on the Hudson. Do you believe you might do this, or how do you feel about this idea?"

Ten Eyck's eyes flashed as he nodded his head in agreement.

"—but besides that," Smith hastened to explain, "he wants, above all, a leader of young men, who will put into practice the ideals of Christianity. He's a strong Methodist, you know!"

Ten Eyck's gaze arched around Smith's figure, his eyes unrecording the figure of the speaker, but his mind absorbing and sifting the bits of information fed it by the conversation. Suddenly, he felt a surge of excitement course through his body.

"Well—Mr. Smith," he answered, "I'd like nothing better than to accept your kind offer. But you and Dr. Day must remember that it'd take some time before we can boat a crew that's going to win a big race on the river—"

Sagacious Smith smiled in agreement. He swung his body forward and outstretched his hand to Ten Eyck; and the two clasped hands, forging a future rein of many golden years of rowing.

Ten Eyck's first job was to look over his candidates, harden them up and shape a freshman crew for the immediate future. Astute and cunning, he knew a fact of life at Syracuse, however: Syracuse wanted a winner, and it wanted one as soon as possible.

In order to accomplish this, Ten Eyck figured, a training program must be instituted immediately. An oarsman needed three things, he knew:

Strong legs and arms, and co-ordination of these.

Good wind and stamina.

Guts.

Give him a man with the first two attributes, and Ten Eyck could teach him the fundamentals and the finesse. The last was something inherent in the young man, not something even Ten Eyck could teach. Only Ten Eyck's innate ability enabled him to discover a man with this quality.

To whip the men into shape, Ten Eyck energetically led the pack on long, arduous hikes up and down the hills of Syracuse. At the same time, he evaluated the physical condition of the men. The fibre of what constituted intestinal fortitude was to be revealed later in the men under the rigors of racing.

On the first day the men worked out on the rowing machines, Ten Eyck studied them, his eyes roving over. back and across the group.

"What's your name, young man?" he brusquely asked a short-statured freshman standing nearby.

"Packard, sir—I mean Edward Packard."

"Packard—you ever rowed before?" Ten Eyck asked him.

The youth hesitated briefly before answering.

"No, sir, I can't say I have."

"Want to row?"

"Yes, sir, I do."

"Good—" Ten Eyck declared with satisfaction. "Come here. Sit down at the machine," he ordered.

Packard commenced flexing his arms, and Ten Eyck squatted down beside him, quietly explaining the elementary points of pulling an oar. Later, he informed Packard:

"You're the freshman stroke, young man."

Packard gulped in amazement.

The new teacher was cut from the same pattern as was

JAMES A. TEN EYCK, SR., new rowing coach at Syracuse.

Courtney of Cornell. Another gifted coach, Ten Eyck instinctively knew men. His judgments were uncanny. For example, his first estimate of young Packard proved correct, for in the next four years, the freshman was never to occupy any other seat than the stroke position. He justified Ten Eyck's faith in him, when in the following year he led the Syracuse varsity to its first Poughkeepsie victory.

Training progressed satisfactorily according to Ten Eyck's standards, but the time arrived when he wanted his men to row under competition. Therefore, he encouraged them to compete in the new interclass races on the Lake early in May.

In fact, the races were the only ones offered them before the Poughkeepsie events. The Athletic Department, shamefully believing that rowing wasn't to survive the spring, neglected to schedule any competition for them!

A few of those rebellious oarsmen, who met in the restaurant in 1900 to voice their complaint about paying for their own meals saw the day when crew was given its own training table. Upon arrival, Ten Eyck established a table at the Yacht Club, and for the first time in the short history of crew at Syracuse, training rules were observed.

The wonderful rapport between Ten Eyck and his young men and his paternal influence on them probably were, in part, responsible for the lore that grew up about him through the unfolding years to come. Whether all of the anecdotes attributed to him were true is not at all important. For where does fiction and reality really divide into separate channels in the minds of the young, who idolize the elder? Importantly, though, in Ten Eyck, young Syracusans of crew were exposed to the texture of a man's man.

At the same time, it would be remiss to assume that Ten Eyck was entirely a paragon of virtue. He wasn't. He was only human. And of course there was another dimension of his character, the one that conformed to his constant demand for perfection.

Ten Eyck loved a winner, above all. Most things considered, he believed, the purpose of rowing in competition was to win. Therefore, from time to time, men were required to yield willingly without question the last ounce of physical endurance.

With his men, Ten Eyck was patient to the point of repeating again and again how to correct a flaw. However, he held little tolerance for an oarsman if the same young man continued to make the identical mistake in a hotly-contested race. Ten Eyck saw these things, for he watched every movement in one of his boats. His eyes, during a race, were usually transfixed on the shell as are the sculptured orbs of the granite figures on Mt. Rushmore. They swept over everything, everyone; and to the mind, they sent back for storage, and later retrieval, all those impressions, especially the repeated mistakes.

To his credit, Ten Eyck waited for the erring youth to return to the boathouse; quietly took him aside, a distance away from his mates and tongue-lashed him as did a Roman excoriate a galley slave in the days of Empire.

Later, his wrath subsided, Ten Eyck again called back the youth to him and assuaged his hurt feelings by explaining once more where he erred.

In this way, the coach demonstrated the unique faculty for driving a student to the abyss of despair, then quickly snatching him back in the nick of time for redemption. It wasn't his intention, ever, to break a man's spirit.

In preparing for the Hudson, Ten Eyck taught the freshmen the anatomy of rowing. He told them this:

Many parts contribute to rowing a boat almost 60 feet long. Aside from the human factors such as spirit and courage, movements of rowing are caused by three parts of the body: backs, arms and legs.

It's very important to realize that a boat moves when its oars are out of water. Strange? Look at it another way, Ten Eyck suggested.

Boats, or shells as they're called, move between strokes of their oars. This is the "run" of the boat. A "check" in the boat is nothing more than a split second of hesitation during the boat's forward progress. As illustration, a crew rowing 34 strokes to the minute and wasting an inch at each stroke loses almost a full length of boat at the end of four miles.

Ten Eyck, next described the shell's nomenclature. You, the oarsman, he told them, sit on seats sliding along wooden tracks within nine inches of the boat's skin. Your feet are placed against stretchers and laced in shoes, positioned somewhat similar to the way you lounge in Dad's big chair back home, with heels planted firmly to the floor. This allows you to push your stretchers while driving through the stroke.

In case some of you might wonder what those projecting metal supports are used for, I'll tell you, Ten Eyck said. They are placed there on the outside of the boat for the oarlocks and are known as outriggers. They allow a boat to employ longer oars than customarily used.

At the "catch" or start of a stroke, Ten Eyck continued, the oarsman is seated in the stern end of his slide, body arched down between his knees, a position he holds when he drops the oarblade into the water. Generally, the blade is dropped vertically, but sometimes it's turned toward the shell's stern. Thus, the boat is lifted at the start of the stroke and friction reduced in the water.

Ten Eyck destroyed the misconception that an oarsman pulls the oar through the water. He doesn't. He merely pulls the boat through the water; this is done by setting the oarblade in the water and pulling, with the result that the boat glides past!

63

A recovery commences when the oarsman pulls out the blade, thereby "feathering." In order to do this, he turns his wrist so the oarblade is flat to the water when he returns it; the thin edge is perpendicular to the water, and wind resistance to the blade is reduced considerably.

"Crab catching" is an expression used to denote a blade slapping water on recovery. "Catching a crab" means the oar is out of control and is caught in the water, usually forcing the handle to strike the oarsman's stomach. Another is "knifing in," which is cutting the blade in the water with the top still turned towards the bow of the boat. This can also result in "catching a crab." One is apt to "sky" on the recovery if his hands drop too much and raise the blade.

Boat positions also came under discussion.

The ideal stroke, Ten Eyck declared, must be a patchwork of shrewdness, stubborness and brashness, with a streak of Machiavellian (to paraphrase the Florentine statesman's political doctrine: all other crews are zeroing in on your boat and cannot be trusted) paralleling these.

The stroke, simultaneously, must possess a musician's sense of rhythm and timing, drawing out, as a violinist might do, the fine tones of a crew's power and stamina. In concert with his coxswain, the stroke paces the boat, and he, alone, is answerable for the manner in which his crew races. He's the director of the movement.

The first chair violinist of this symphony of action is the coxswain. Generally small of physique, he is usually the vociferous member in the boat, the one who transmits the beat established by his stroke oar, and the one, who uses the whip-lash of the tongue often in that final forty strokes to the finish line.

Navigator as well, the coxswain must be shrewd, grabbing selfishly everything offered him such as wind, current, or tide. He occupies the only fixed position in the boat, and when he uses the rudder in steering, the more he impedes the boat's progress. A half to full length may be lost by his boat in a race if his steering runs a crooked course.

Positions next were explained by Ten Eyck.

They are numbered one from the bow aft of the boat. In other words, the bow oar is No. 1, the others being numbered consecutively down through the boat to No. 7, a position directly behind the stroke.

Number 7 oar, Ten Eyck explained, is secondary only to the stroke and is a very important position. It's his duty to transmit the stroke's pace or cadence to the others on his own starboard side.

A boat's full power is usually concentrated in the waist at oars 6, 5, 4 and 3. Forward of these waist positions in the shell are No. 2 and the bow oar. Proper leverage of the boat depends upon the latter two, and unless they know how to balance the shell, they might easily throw off the craft by causing it to roll.

Ten Eyck answered several questions of his freshmen at that meeting, then he dismissed them.

On Syracuse's third trip to the Hudson (in 1903), the crew enjoyed the luxury, to them at least, of arriving a week beforehand. An anonymous gift of money made for this purpose allowed the men to familiarize themselves with the river and the course in the days before the races.

The heat shimmered up in waves from the parched land adjoining the Hudson on race day, and the freshmen rowed stripped bare to their waists.

In the forepart of the freshman race, the Syracuse crew rowed even with mighty Cornell. Unfortunately, the stroke, Packard, caught a crab near the bridge and the boat slowed down. Down near the finish, however, Syracuse came up strong and received their first immersion under torrid pressure. The moment was propitious, Packard reasoned, and he informed the coxswain that the stroke was going up.

With the message relayed, the eight brought up their sweeps smartly, feathered and swung aft for successive strokes.

Again—

Again—

Again—

They repeated this sequence of action until their oars flashed through the air in a rhapsody of moving grace. When finished, they were spent, bone-weary, flopped over oars. They slouched down in the boat, gulping air.

When Cornell was announced winner, they stirred. When they were declared second place by half a length, they began quietly paddling towards the boathouse. On the way, they heard Wisconsin declared third, with Columbia and Penn bringing up the rear in that order of finishing.

Within the privacy of the boathouse, Ten Eyck appeared satisfied, a gleam of expectation in his eyes. At fleeting moments, smiles masked his face. Next year was 1904! Watch his freshmen, then!

The varsity event in 1903 was simply a replay of 1902, Cornell winning. After the race, Ten Eyck shook hands with his first crew on the Hudson:

            Bow—H. M. Galpin
         No. 2—Lynn Wykoff
         No. 3—Ancil Brown
         No. 4—C. H. Becker
         No. 5—Clarence Dempster
         No. 6—D. Phelps
         No. 7—Capt. Harry Elden
       Stroke—Robert Stone
    Coxswain—H. H. Curtiss

Only Dempster and Stone of this crew rowed in his 1904 varsity boat, but the glory that came to Syracuse in that regatta is already history in this story. The introduction of a different type of crew by Syracuse in 1905, nevertheless, excited the world of collegiate rowing.

CHAPTER VIII

SYRACUSE IN 1905

astonished the collegiate rowing world by forming a four-oared crew, consisting entirely of sophomores; at the same time, Ten Eyck's voice, loud and strong, protested against the tides and men of the river.

The four-oared boat involved different techniques from those employed in moving an eight-oared craft. Frankly, it required smoother and more skilled rowing by a crew. Bow oar, a case in point, asked for much greater aptitude in steering, and at the same time, required him to pull his own share of the load.

Members chosen by Ten Eyck for his first four were:

Bow—A. M. Armstrong
No. 2—O. E. Cumings
No. 3—Dwight Stone
Stroke—Darius Davis

Meanwhile, Ten Eyck complained loudly about the tide and time of the races at Poughkeepsie, arguing the folly of officials pinpointing the hours almost a year in advance. The races, he said, were rowed at ebb tide, a time when the ebb raced at its great velocity, or as rivermen described it, "at the strength of the tide."

With some justification, Ten Eyck disagreed that a man "sitting at a roll-top desk" a hundred miles away from the course could not tell a year beforehand just what tidal conditions were at a certain hour of race day.

Ordinarily, his complaint was one of those normally attributed to a coach, but the Syracuse man's argument was based on solid fact: He was a native of the Hudson River area and of the Poughkeepsie locale. By the same token, he was experienced enough to know that tide tables were sufficiently accurate only for a general guide, but none were able to predict at just what hour a race ought to begin until three days before a race, at the earliest.

He reasoned that several factors influenced these tides: hard rains, wind, number of competing crews, and the general shape and contour of the shoreline.

Crews, he argued, prepared strenuously five months for these races, and why "work a handicap on the crew that has a chance to win so that it comes in a poor last?"

Favoring instead a strong tide-water course, Ten Eyck suggested:

"It is almost never fair to all the competing crews, but since there's a time when the course is comparatively fair for all, let's select that time for the race. After the coaches agree upon an hour for the race, allow them to draw positions and thus time and tide at least might not act as handicaps."

Valid though Ten Eyck's arguments were, deafness won out. No heed was given to his suggestion.

In contrast to 1904, there were 2,000 supporters from Syracuse in 1905 at Poughkeepsie, and they joined the swell of voices that repeated and repeated:

"Beat Cornell! Beat Cornell!"

The excitement that day was furnished by the four-oared race, and as one might suspect, it was Syracuse in lane one, nearest shore, providing fireworks.

Flanked to the right of it were Columbia, Cornell, Penn and Wisconsin in that order. Syracuse trailed Cornell two lengths at the half-mile. Suddenly it moved ahead of Columbia and Penn by jumping across their lanes.

Under the bridge, Armstrong's spectacular steering helped the boat shave off a length and one-half of Cornell's lead of two lengths. Now, both were struggling for leadership.

Down to the last of the two-mile race, both fought to pull ahead of the other; back and forth, the shells moved: a century of yards from the finish, they appeared close together. The grimacing faces and the exertions of the oarsmen reflected their terrible hunger for victory, when the two boats blurred in motion across the finish line.

—B-o-o-m! B-o-o-m! B-o-o-m!

Three skyrockets. That was Cornell's lane!

No-no, wait a moment! The position of the flags hanging from the middle span of the steel archway was changed. Now—there it was. That was Syracuse!

A movement again on the archway. The flags were changed once more!

Who really did win?

If everyone at the site was confused, consider the people back home in Syracuse. The *Syracuse Herald* in time-honored tradition of getting the news out on the streets before the competition appeared with extras ten minutes after the crews finished announcing the news of Cornell's victory; and during the frenzied changes of the flags that followed at Poughkeepsie, the paper printed three more special editions trying to keep up, each one announcing a different winner.

VARSITY FOUR, IRA CHAMPIONS 1905

A. M. Amtman, O. F. Cuming, D. G. Stone, Str., D. A. Davis

Darkness settled down by the time the spectators returned to Poughkeepsie and were told that Syracuse barely nosed out Cornell!

In victory, Syracuse's first four-oared crew chipped off two seconds from Penn's record time of 15 minutes and four-fifth seconds established in 1900. Third place went to Pennsylvania, with Columbia and Wisconsin bringing up the rear.

The proud Syracuse crew accepted the Kennedy trophy, a cup donated in 1899 by Davidson Kennedy, a Pennsylvania alumnus. The Quakers won it the first year, and Cornell captured it in the ensuing regattas up to 1905.

"Our four-oared crew is a dandy," an elated Ten Eyck told everyone who listened after the exciting race.

Cornell took the remaining honors in 1905, winning the freshman race by three lengths over Syracuse, the varsity by 19 lengths over Ten Eyck's men. In the varsity race, Georgetown was third, followed in order by Columbia, Pennsylvania and the Badgers.

About the time Russia surrendered to Japan half a world away, Ten Eyck grudgingly admitted Cornell was the better crew on the river that particular day.

"Cornell has a couple of unusually strong crews," he confessed, "and while the course made some difference, they would undoubtedly have captured the races anyway."

Ten Eyck wasn't that candid again, for in the Fall, a student entered Syracuse from the family Ten Eyck; a young man, who later added additional luster to the Syracuse coach's name.

Chapter IX

THE YOUNGER EDITION

of Ten Eyck was already a national figure in rowing when he entered Syracuse in 1905. James A. Ten Eyck, Jr., two years before, at tender age of 16, won the junior single sculling championship in the New England regatta on the Charles River at Boston.

The oldest Ten Eyck son, Ned, won the famous Diamond Sculls trophy in England in 1897. Together, the men left an imprint on the rowing scene of those days, while another brother, George, spurned athletics, taking up medicine at the University and graduating in 1908.

In March of 1906, the junior varsity crew was invited to the fourth American Henley race sponsored by the American Rowing Association on Schuylkill River at Philadelphia. Syracuse accepted and the oarsmen sacrificed their Easter vacation preparing for it.

Young Jim began bringing fame to the family name, when he won the single scull race at the Philadelphia races by defeating Walter Stokes of the University Barge Club of Philadelphia. His rival edged him out the year before in the finals in Baltimore.

Rowing in the Syracuse boat at the American Henley were:

        Bow—H. J. Schiefer
        No. 2—C. B. Butz

No. 3—O. B. Heath
No. 4—H. S. Duvall
No. 5—L. C. Rice
No. 6—M. S. Whitney
No. 7—M. M. Dodge
Stroke—Darius Davis
Coxswain—T. R. Robinson

The crew trailed Penn and Harvard early in the one and one-third mile race, but at the quarter, Harvard was lost far behind Syracuse. Ahead, Pennsylvania led by half a length.

Ten Eyck's men at the mile rowed with smooth sweeps, moving big chunks of water; eventually, they drew up even with the Quakers, and from there on it was only a question of time. Syracuse won by almost a full length.

That summer at Poughkeepsie, uniformity came nearer to the IRA regatta, when officials insisted that coxswains wear "jerseys distinctly showing their university colors." Other crew members were yet to come under the restrictions, although four-oared crews were instructed to paint their colors on the oarblades.

Reserved by nature but not usually pessimistic, Ten Eyck behaved strangely at this IRA meet. He advised. everyone to place their money on crews other than his own. There was, however, one exception. He advised Syracuse rooters to place their bets on his freshmen.

With odds ranging from 4 to 1 and 2 to 1 against the freshmen, the bettors didn't hesitate to take the offers, and consequently, returned to Syracuse five grand richer. They won in this way:

Son Jim was seriously ill at the time and was placed under physician's care two weeks prior to the races. His weight dropped from 168 to 133 during the period. He insisted, however, that he be allowed to row. His father refused to decide, putting the question to the freshman crew. To a man, they voted their confidence in Jim, their stroke.

Rowing out to the starting line, the young man was hardly able to keep his head erect, and for the first part of the two-mile run, he lacked enough strength to push an oar. Under the bridge, by some miracle, he perked up. Bit by bit, little by little, the boat increased it speed until it caught, and then passed Cornell. The freshmen stayed in front to the finish.

It was a far different story, however, in the varsity race.

As the crews lined up after a rain, the crowd gasped in admiration when an iridescent rainbow arched over the bridge scintillating with the colors of all six crews entered in the race.

Stroked by Packard, Syracuse led in a downpour for a time, but Courtney's crew wasn't to be denied. They were neck and neck at the bridge, and Packard increased his stroke, but Cornell suddenly came to life and pulled away with a higher, stronger stroke. Penn flashed by Syracuse in a rapid movement near the final 40 strokes. Then suddenly, it was all over. Syracuse was third.

Cornell stamped its greatness in the four-oared race, too, nosing out Syracuse by 13 seconds. Columbia was third and then Pennsylvania.

That was the year Packard hung up his oar, and San Francisco experienced its famous earthquake and fire. Little did Ten Eyck realize that in the following year of 1907, he was to be involved in a grudge race with one of his sons.

CHAPTER X

THE GRUDGE BETWEEN

two of the Ten Eycks—the Old Man and Ned—developed after the son became coach of rowing at Wisconsin in 1907. Oldest of the three sons, Ned was hired after Andrew O'Dea, an Australian sculler, resigned following a long record of unimpressive showings at Poughkeepsie.

The first indication of disagreement came to light when Ned wrote his father:

> Most of the freshman crew are little fellows, but I am promised later that some big and husky candidates that could give you all you wanted. Watch 'em!

Hiring Ned was part of a movement to awaken the sleeping giant—Wisconsin—instituted by Dr. C. P. Hutchings, former Syracuse football and track coach. When Hutchings was hired as athletic director, he took the first step towards reviving crew by luring Ned away from a lucrative position as coach of the Philadelphia Barge Club crews.

Ned's goading letters became a constant source of irritation to his father, who worried over re-building his varsity crew, losing five of last year's varsity boat by graduation. He was patient with his son, until one day after reading one of Ned's letters, he reacted with an oath and in anger accepted a challenge to race in Wisconsin. In fact, it proved to be the excuse he needed to give his men experi-

75

THE THREE TEN EYCKS
At this time young Jim was his father's varsity stroke at Syracuse, while his brother Edward (Ned) was head rowing coach at Wisconsin.

ence before their trip to the Hudson. So, with two objectives in mind, he arranged the races with the Badgers.

Part of Ten Eyck's concern that season was the weight of his varsity crew, the oarsmen of the 1907 boat being beefier and huskier than any boated before. Their heaviness led Ten Eyck to telegraph W. H. Davey, boatbuilder of that day in Cambridge (Massachusetts), asking if it was possible to build a slightly bigger shell than customary. Davey replied promptly that it was impossible to comply with Ten Eyck's order in time for a May 20th deadline.

The men averaged 175 pounds, contrasted with Columbia's 166; Cornell's 168½; Georgetown's 165; and Penn's 162. Only Navy and Wisconsin anywhere matched his crew in size.

The crews sent to Lake Mendota for the grudge race with the Badgers were the University's first oarsmen to cross the borders of New York State, since rowing was introduced on campus in 1900.

The atmosphere in Wisconsin was one of coolness, father and son standing icily silent, eyes averted at the coin-tossing ceremony. It wasn't improved when the father in winning the toss shrewdly chose courses nearest the shore for both his eight-oared and four-oared crews. Ordinarily, this was wise, for these courses were sheltered from extremely rough water and high winds.

The father's face was wreathed in smiles, when the four-oared crew won handily by eight lengths. It darkened, however, and then lengthened during the varsity race.

Stormy conditions postponed that race until early in the evening. At the offset, with a tremendous surge, Syracuse captured the lead and grimly hung on. At half-mile, two smoke bombs wafted skyward from a chemical building, and the spectators were hardly able to see the race for the canopy of darkness; but almost instinctively they knew Syracuse was ahead.

Rowing in a flurry of 40 strokes per minute, Syracuse began to show strain of its unprecedented cadence at the mile mark. It was here that Ned's boat unexpectedly came up and rowed abreast.

For the next half mile, both clung together.

Then the early pace began to tell, and Syracuse wilted under the strain.

Oar by oar, Wisconsin inched ahead, until one-fourth mile away from the finish, it led by half a boat length. And when the Badgers went over the line, they were a good full length ahead.

Wisconsin fans were delirious with joy—shouting, hooting, screaming—from the fervor that came when a hometown victory was snatched at the last moment from ignominious defeat.

The cardinal of the son lowered orange of the father, true, but in fact, it represented a great victory for the Ten Eyck name. Touching was the sight of the father, warmly congratulating an embarrassed son, the prior coolness and misunderstanding washed away and forgotten in the exultant moment.

"A great victory," the proud father admitted without rancor, a twinkle spotting both eyes, "particularly because it's still in the family!"

Ned was aglow with pride.

Returning to Syracuse, Ten Eyck tried to unravel the mystery. He searched vainly for the missing key to the springlock of his crew—for that indescribable something in his eight oarsmen and coxswain. He wanted the answer as to why his oarsmen, who were skilled and strong and motivated to win, were unsuccessful!

To make matters worse for Ten Eyck that year on the Hudson, Ned's freshmen found the choppy river to their liking. They defeated the Syracuse freshmen by a full length. Following them were Pennsylvania, Columbia and Cornell.

Again, it was the four-oared crew that brought honor to Syracuse. The boat finished two lengths ahead of Cornell in a run-away race.

The varsity race was postponed until 7 o'clock by a driving rainstorm. As impossible as it seemed, for the day was truly dreary, there were color and excitement surrounding the races. Navy Secretary Metcalf witnessed the races from a government gunboat, while 400 of his Midshipmen cheered their Annapolis crew in its first appearance in the IRA regatta. And just before the varsity race commenced, the dying sun, as the earth spun away from it, suddenly broke out in golden streaks of color.

Syracuse experienced trouble in the race. Its boat sagged low in the water, wallowing so to speak, until Pennsylvania was half a length ahead at the two-mile mark. The Orangemen, half mile from the finish, were buffeted by waves cascading over into the narrow cavity of their shell. Sinking slowly, they abandoned ship. Eventually, they were rescued by passing boats on the river. Cornell won.

The year was, indeed, a disappointment to many people in America, as well as to Ten Eyck. A dipping stock market started the Panic of 1907. And the following year held moments of tension, too, for others. Three reputations were at stake.

CHAPTER XI

"THE OLD MAN"

as Ten Eyck became affectionately known in 1908 to his men needed a varsity victory on the Hudson that year. Yet to receive the sobriquet, "Sly Fox of the Hudson," he carried a bearing of determination that filtered down to his men and touched responsive chords. It did not take an announcement for everyone to understand that the greatest gift of all for Ten Eyck this year was a winner; four long years, he waited, and his patience was wearing thin.

Besides the Old Man's hunger for victory, son Jim desired again to experience that elation coming from stroking a boat to an IRA victory. His reputation, in fact. was at stake, too.

Champion sculler in 1904 before entering the University, and stroke oar of the 1906 freshman boat, young Jim recalled those moments of glory with great relish. Other times, however, he remembered with horror the race of 1907. His chagrin became a taste of salt in his mouth.

Vividly, he recalled the humiliation of jumping into the Hudson last year, when his shell sank beneath the waves. With sensitivity born of pride, young Jim shuddered at the memory of being ignored at Poughkeepsie, weary though he was at the time, and of feeling rejected by the crowd like an empty cartridge from a silent rifle.

Young Jim Ten Eyck! He loved the adulation of the crowd, the attention given him as result of victory; at the same time, there was something about him that always excited the minds of the spectators.

Maybe it was his flamboyancy that appealed to them, because if the truth were known, at heart, followers of rowing loved this fascination, the stimulation and the inspiration provided them by dynamic youth. To most of them, the sport and its colorful figures were the essence; loyalty for the sake of loyalty to any particular school was almost secondary.

Young Jim in time became the image of a youth-intoxicated nation, and they loved him for it.

Ten Eyck's youngest son fitted this pattern of extreme ebullition. Who cared that this was his last race on the Hudson? Or that two years later, he was the world's champion amateur swimmer? Or that within seven years, while coaching Duluth Boat Club, he saved a prominent person from drowning? Or that years afterwards, he became an executive with a New York textile company? Those were all improbables of the future.

At the same time, another Ten Eyck—Ned—was very much under pressure to save his reputation. As he was the coach of the Badgers, the eyes of Wisconsin state watched him closely. The citizens of that University wanted to see their men show the snooty Easterners a victory or two on the river.

In contrast to these underlying personal problems, the 1908 varsity crew of Syracuse was one of the most colorful in many years. Some of its vibrant colors, of course, were painted by young Jim Ten Eyck, but streaks were also daubed by Coxswain Frank Eldredge.

Brash and loud, cocky and aggressive, Eldredge was one of those youths from whence came the supreme confidence with which to move mountains. Exiguous in size, he allowed the Old Man from time to time to smoke his favorite pipe, later in life, gleefully admitting, "I had to like him to allow that!"

Earlier that season, Eldredge rode the varsity boat in victory over Harvard, Navy and Georgetown during a race on the Severn at Annapolis. Regrettably, the two latter schools were not competing in the IRA regatta in 1908, and Georgetown never returned to IRA competition.

Eldredge later donned khaki of the Army for a long career, but in 1908, he played a prominent role in the now famous berry-crate episode at Poughkeepsie, an incident involving the generosity of Cornell that eventually worked out to the Bid Red's disadvantage. The incident referred to happened forty-eight hours before the races. While there were wide discrepancies in details about it both versions were exciting.

Newspapers claimed that when Syracuse practice-rowed downstream from below the bridge, the prow of its shell smashed into a rowboat anchored out in the river. Six feet of badly splintered and torn prow resulted, with M. M. Dodge, bow oar, and M. C. Shimer, No. 2 oar, floundering in the waves.

The papers said the two men were rescued by Ten Eyck nearby in his coaching launch, and later conveyed to shore. Meanwhile, the other six men heroically paddled an erratic course with their stubbled section of a boat over to the Cornell boathouse.

Eldredge was severely excoriated by the newspapers for not seeing the rowboat in time to avoid the collision. They claimed he was conversing at the time with young Jim Ten Eyck, his stroke.

Contrary to the newspapers, however, W. Claude Fisher, No. 7 oar in that boat, explained half a century afterwards that the accident happened when the shell rammed a half-submerged berry-crate, tearing open the bow of the boat.

Aside from this, Syracuse was still in desperate need of another boat for the varsity race; yet, none was available.

Coach Ten Eyck attempted to cover up his deep disappointment by taking a philosophical viewpoint, telling his crestfallen men that it was one of those things that happened in the racing game. He advised them not to gripe.

But the winds of fortune wafted over to Syracuse. There was a Cornell friend, nearby. He was John Hoyle, boatbuilder, who with graciousness and understanding, volunteered to do the best he knew how in fixing up the bobbed nose of the shell.

All well and good, thought the crew, but was he able to finish it satisfactorily in time?

Through the remainder of the day, through the night, far into the next morning, that superb builder worked. Time off he took only for a couple of hours sleep, a hot meal and a bath; and then, Hoyle returned to his task. After dinner that following night, he summoned the Syracuse coach. and with a shrug of his shoulders notified him the boat might possibly be finished by 10 that evening.

When the hour struck, Ten Eyck's worried crew gathered at the Cornell boathouse to inspect by glare of lantern light the result of Hoyle's painstaking labors with the bandaged nose of the boat. They let out a cheer when Hoyle finally patted the repaired craft in farewell. With infinite care, they placed it carefully into the Hudson.

Into the darkness of night, Ten Eyck dispatched his crew with their repaired boat on a two-mile test run. None was to worry; both passed the acid test admirably.

Before the races, its second ruling for identifying crews was put into effect by the IRA, demanding that all crews now paint their school's primary color on the oarblades. This proved helpful, for with painted oars and coxswains decked out in jerseys with appropriate school colors, spectators were better able to follow the contestants

Ten Eyck spent a busy day at the races, carefully supervising launchings, no details escaping his eagle eyes. From time to time, he filed in and out between his men, inspecting their rigging on the boats, pausing to say a kindly word now and then to a high-strung, glassy-eyed youth, who was muttering incoherently something about forgetting his shoes and socks.

Eldredge was in fine fettle, and he was confident enough of his crew to want to demonstrate his pride. Sauntering over to the Columbia boathouse that morning, he hunted up the Lions' coxswain.

"Wanna bet, Winslow?" he asked.

'I dunno—maybe. Why?"

"I'll bet you that my crew can take yours, today—"

"Uh-huh."

"Wanna bet your jerseys?"

"Guess so—why not!"

And historically, Eldredge's brashness that day was the first formal betting of jerseys on a collegiate race. Henceforth, losing crews, in a gesture of defeat, handed over their jerseys to the winners.

Both the Hudson and the weather were harmoniously perfect for those races, and especially for the 50,000 spectators, who crowded the area. Many stood around in awe, glancing up at the Palisades, whose formation of basaltic rock towered above the earth in gigantic blocks and looked down at 3 o'clock in the afternoon upon the exertions of many young men.

Mishaps that plagued Syracuse in 1907 snubbed the Orangemen in 1908, but hung onto the other crews on the Hudson. For example, the boy in the stakeboat holding the four-oared boat of Pennsylvania accidentally pulled out the rudder pin, and the steering gear was left hanging at the beginning of the race.

Twenty strokes beyond the start of the four-oared race, Syracuse held the lead. Cornell took it away from her soon. At the bridge, the Orange boat trailed the Big Red by two lengths.

While Syracuse, Columbia, Pennsylvania and Cornell rowed down the lanes towards them, platforms with red-painted buoys placed a quarter of a mile from the bridge swayed to and fro in the water.

For some unknown reason, Cornell's boat headed straight as an arrow into one of those buoys. Upon impact, the shell began sinking! This, in turn, seemed to ignite a chain-reaction of misfortunes involving Columbia and Pennsylvania.

About the time that Cornell piled up, the Lions were rowing close to the keel of Syracuse. Suddenly, Columbia was bumped in the stern by Pennsylvania.

The collision occurred, when Penn's unhinged steering gear threw its shell over into Columbia's lane and directly into the Lion craft. The Lions stopped racing after the collision.

Unmindful of this turn of events, the four-oared boat of Ten Eyck continued to pace itself, winning by a large margin, unmolested and unchallenged. Making up that crew were:

Bow—	H. J. Schiefer
No. 2—	R. H. Bowen
No. 3—	Leon Rice
Stroke—	Timothy O'Shea

It was a far different story, however, in the freshman race, with Syracuse finishing a length and a half behind winning Cornell, but three-quarters of a length ahead of the Lions. Wisconsin was two lengths behind Columbia. Pennsylvania trailed them all.

Consequently, there was no sweep for Syracuse in 1908.

Down at the boathouse before the final race, the coach watched his varsity carrying out their oars to the float in preparation for their event. They climbed carefully into their shell and patiently awaited his parting words.

"Oh, you—Number 7. Fisher, I mean. Will you, please, remember that you've got an oar there, not a spoon!"

"Roberts—you at Number 3. For heaven sakes, don't hit bottom. Do you think you're handling a plumb line?"

"Steady men," he admonished them, lines of grimness circling his lips.

"Now—all together, remember. There—that's much better. Much better!"

The glob of sun was disappearing behind the west-side area of the Palisades, when the boats of Columbia, Penn, Cornell, Wisconsin and Syracuse swung out to their stakeboats.

The *New York Sun* afterwards commented:

Everything great in the history of boat racing on the Hudson was swept back to be merely mediocre by the wonderful race of the varsity eights this afternoon. The contests of 1901 and 1907 were tremendous until today. Now, they are merely ordinary.

1908 VARSITY FOUR CHAMPIONS
Str. T. J. Shea, L. C. Rice, R. H. Bowen, H. J. Shiefer, Jr.
Ten Eyck's boat won its race by a large margin, unchallenged. The crew took the lead at the start but lost it to Cornell. Beyond the bridge they recaptured the lead, surging ahead of Columbia, Pennsylvania and Cornell.
It was the year in which this crew recaptured the title for Syracuse for the first time since 1905.

CHAPTER XII

WITH SHIRTS RIDING

on the outcome of the race, the Syracuse varsity crew paddled briskly into the position farthest from shore. "Ready
all?"; the wait; then the pistol shot, and the Syracuse shell
leaped forward, rushing savagely and clearing the water,
splashing with those first few top-speed strokes.

Jim Rice's Lions of Columbia were hungry this year
of 1908 and on the prowl. Soon, they overtook their quarry
—Syracuse. In turn, Ned's Badgers rowing at an unheard of
42 strokes per minute raced up swiftly and passed the Lions.
Pennsylvania hung doggedly close to the pack with Cornell
far to the rear.

There was disciplined violence on the Hudson; coxswains shouting through megaphones attached to their
faces; the 40 oarsmen combining determination and
strength into a dynamic force; their beats rich with frenzied overtones.

Smoothly ran the Syracuse boat, the men experiencing
the thrill of cool, unhindered power flowing from their
pumping arms and calloused hands down to the tips of the
orange-splashed oarblades.

"Twenty at 32," directed Eldredge.

All up and down the course there were staccato barks
of the five, eager coxswains, their litany of voices urgent,

compelling, demanding; and the—sw-ish—sw-ish of the blades in the background.

Out in mid-river, the outline of the Syracuse crew and topside part of the boat blended in with the deepening shadows of twilight. Sometimes, the men dissolved into the thick carpet of darkness; reappeared and again faded.

Ned's crew was to burn itself out with the highest strokes ever witnessed in any Poughkeepsie race. It was insanity, and eventually, Wisconsin paid the price.

Before the collapse, however, Wisconsin duelled with an on-rushing Penn boat for the lead. Meanwhile, Ten Eyck's crew began increasing its stroke, the long blades and legs and arms harmonizing into a moving scene of perfect grace. There was plenty of power in that boat.

To telescope Eldredge's view from the stern end of the boat, his eyes saw this:

Dodge at bow oar appeared a mile away; faces of Duval, Roberts and Shimer in the waist section, he wasn't able to see; but he knew they were there by the pulsations of their oars. The boat slipped through the water so smoothly that the first mile was completed in four minutes and 40 seconds!

About this time, Wisconsin faded away, and the stronger of the pack came on relentlessly. Pennsylvania held its lead over Syracuse by a length.

Near the two-mile mark, a patched nose of a shell poked out in front of the bunched group; and nearer the bridge, the Orange blades pumped the slender craft to within half a length of the surprising Quakers.

Here was where the three-mile crews and the champions always parted company, and this race in 1908 was no exception to the rule.

Surprisingly, the Lions moved up, and then passed Syracuse, with Cornell sliding into third position behind Coach Ten Eyck's crew, just beyond the shadows of the bridge. Meanwhile, Wisconsin, under the bridge, fell apart.

The Badger's No. 6 oar, R. Iskisch, struck himself in the stomach with an oar handle, writhed in pain for a moment, and then collapsed. The boat left the race.

Back in the race, Columbia, Penn and Syracuse girded themselves for the final half. Each one of the trio scented the sweet meat of triumph.

Eldredge and young Jim Ten Eyck sensed it was about time to move, and the former commenced rapping on the gunwales, his high voice calling out time of stroke:

Then 12 strokes at 42!

The stroke of the boat lengthened and dipped the water in a maze of motion as the final forty strokes neared. Way down the course, the finish area was lost somewhere in the shroud of falling night. Eldredge began pounding again in dramatic movements—once more the stroke was going up.

Sweep, feather and swing aft for another stroke.

Sweep, feather and swing for another—

Sweep, feather and swing—

For ten strokes. Another ten, And another ten.

Within the area of final commitment, Syracuse raced towards the finish with the Lions glued closely to its keel!

92

VARSITY EIGHT, 1908 POUGHKEEPSIE WINNERS: Str. James A. Ten Eyck, Jr., W. C. Fisher, E. G. Champlin, E. O. Hemenway, H. S. Duvall, E. C. Roberts, M. C. Shimer, M. M. Dodge, Bow, Cox F. E. Eldredge.

The rhapsody of effort neared its climax as Eldredge and young Ten Eyck demanded and received their mates' final ounce of strength. Columbia also demanded the same of its oarsmen.

A spurt came from the men manning the Orange blades. Once more, they responded. With a final convulsion of effort, the Syracuse shell with its mended prow nudged out in front and across the line. The winner!

The crew, as well as the spectators, were drained weak from the exertions and excitement of the dramatic finish. When Cornell, Pennsylvania and the others came down to the line, their appearance was anticlimatic. Three in the Columbia boat openly wept in bitter frustration, while the men of Syracuse, chests heaving, gulped in air and rested from their successful labors.

With tears of disappointment in his eyes, the Columbia coxswain, W. S. Winslow, dove from his seat into the water, and swam over to Eldredge. Presenting his crew's jerseys, Winslow signified total submission, a gesture which was followed in the forthcoming years whenever college crews gathered after a race.

Later, Captain Dodge generously paid tribute to the Lions:

It was the hardest race I've ever rowed. Columbia made a dandy fight of it, pushed us all the way and had us working to the limit.[3]

Jim Rice of Columbia was crushed:

It's pretty hard to lose two years in succession by such narrow margins, but my men rowed a plucky race, and we will be heard from yet.[4]

Ellis Ward of Pennsylvania was disappointed:

I can't understand why we were beaten in the varsity

93

3 4The *New York Herald,* New York, June 28, 1908.

race. I was confident I had the best crew in years and felt that Penn would surely win!⁵

Courtney of Cornell said:

The crew I expected to win won. The varsity boat did much better than I expected, and I cannot say that I am entirely dissatisfied.⁶

The Old Man:

The boys rowed their best, and we are satisfied with the results. The varsity race was a gruelling contest from the start, and it required every ounce of power to beat Columbia.⁷

Ned Ten Eyck:

I would much rather have seen my crew last with all the men rowing than to have one unable to finish, for it will be taken by many that the collapse of one man was merely a good excuse for finishing so badly.⁸

While Ten Eyck assisted his men in preparing the boats for the return home, he was startled to see anchoring off the boathouse the white *Sultana,* a steam yacht owned by railway magnate E. H. Harriman. A moment later, a tender brought the owner and his two sons ashore.

Ten Eyck moved to greet Harriman, and the two men conversed for the better part of an hour. During the talk, Ten Eyck was invited to spend the remainder of the summer at Arden (N.Y.), summer home of the Harrimans, and teach the two sons to row.

Speculation about the race that day on the *Sultana* was explained by W. Averell Harriman, former Governor of New York State, and one of the two sons in the tender:

One incident in connection with the Regatta may be of interest. There was a good deal of speculation on the Sultana as to who was going to win. My father had watched the crews row, and had talked to a number of people. He wrote down the three leading crews, and he got the order exactly right. Syracuse won. . . .⁹

5-8The *New York Herald,* New York, June 28, 1908.

Mr. Harriman told of Ten Eyck spending the summer with his family:

> At that time, my brother and I were rowing at school, and my father went up to the races. Syracuse won and so he asked Mr. Ten Eyck to spend the summer with us, and we learned to scull, as well as row in pair oar. I was about 16, and my brother was 12.[10]

Ten Eyck later wrote that the summer's experience was among the finest of his life, for "Mr. Harriman was a prince of a man as well as king of finance. I was frequently amazed at the sweep of a mind which had found time to become acquainted with many of the intricate details of the sport I love.

"He knew a great deal about both the theory and the practice of rowing, and would talk to me by the hour as we sat on the balcony of his boat-house at Forest Lake." [11]

Fiction never produced a more interesting story than that which later involved Eugene C. Roberts, No. 3 oar in that 1908 championship boat.

A fine specimen of man, Roberts first rowed on the freshman crew in 1907. Son of a wealthy coal and mine owner in Buffalo, he was later told that his strenuous rowing in the 1908 race severely injured his heart. The following fall, while he prepared for law, a physician again advised him that his life span was to be abbreviated. He dropped out of college and departed for the West.

In April, 1911, he sent word to Timothy J. O'Shea, Syracuse probation officer and his best friend, that since he was only going to live a short time, he was gladly going to take his chances and "die fighting."

95

9 10Governor W. Averell Harriman, New York, N.Y., in letter to author, dated January 25, 1961.
11James A. Ten Eyck, *The Outlook*, July 9, 1924, Vol. 137, No. 10, New York, N.Y.

Roberts reportedly went to Mexico and joined the revolutionists in their fight for liberty against President Diaz.

While the varsity oarsman filled out his life in Mexico, Ten Eyck in the next three seasons faced threats to rowing at the University, threats of world war and a tornado that wiped out everything.

CHAPTER XIII

BIG NATIONS OF

Europe loudly rattled sabers during the next three years of
1909, 1910, 1911 and moved diplomats across the checker-
board of the Continent. Simultaneously, rowing at Syracuse
was busily engaged in its own game of chess, checkmating
valiantly the full forces of opposition.

The picture of athletics on Piety Hill was out of focus.
John Archbold's gift of a new gymnasium and a huge football stadium as well as the purchase of a rowing tank by
the University gave an outward appearance of munificence.
Nothing was further from the truth.

Internally, the problem of financing athletics during
these years of struggle by the institution was extremely difficult, so desperate in fact that serious consideration was
given to abandoning crew.

Nearer and nearer the deadline of extinction for crew
approached, and more remote seemed the possibility of obtaining enough funds with which to continue the sport. A
late reprieve, however, by a few friends and alumni saved
the day. Four grand was raised in 1909 to finance rowing
on Piety Hill.

Granted another lease on life, rowing faced yet another
problem. The eligibility committee of the faculty, more
severe and more vigilant than ever before, struck it a blow.

97

A number of experienced and promising men for the 1909 squad were ruled ineligible.

With the squad trimmed down to almost nothing, the nucleus of Ten Eyck's boats consisted of four varsity men, two from last year's alternate crew, and only four from the strong frosh boat.

In addition to this calamity, young Jim Ten Eyck, the stroke oar, dropped out of school.

More to Ten Eyck's marvelous coaching ability than to anything else, the squad managed to boat a varsity eight that defeated a strong Navy on the Severn River in its first race that spring.

That old bugaboo, lack of money, almost kept the crews home from the IRA races that year; but once more, public generosity made possible the trip. The donors were optimistic about Syracuse chances on the Hudson. They knew the oarsmen improved daily. As if in apparent confirmation of their beliefs in victory, they learned that the sun "set orange" on the eve of the races, portending, they thought, success. However, before many hours passed, fate shaded their sun.

Hopes for the four-oared crew were shatered early with the announcement that K. T. Klock contracted influenza. An untried sophomore, L. M. Bush, was substituted for him.

Cornell draped the Orange sun, when it raced down the course of the four-oared race, establishing a new course record of 14 minutes and two-fifth seconds. Nevertheless, Syracuse's bulldog tenacity and determination forced Cornell to the limit in posting the new record. With these two in the first group was Columbia. In turn, the Lions forced

99

First quarters for the Syracuse Crews on Onondaga Lake
Outlet. A four oared crew with coxswain rows toward the
Lake in the background. Visitors at the boathouse were few
due to the great distance from campus.

both Cornell and Syracuse to establish new marks for the race.

In many respects, the freshman race resembled the four-oared one, Courtney's men winning that one also. Syracuse was a close second after an unsuccessful superhuman effort to win near the end.

The varsity event was dominated by Cornell and Columbia.

Winless since 1895, Columbia in 1909 was favored; at the same moment, the Lions were under heavy pressure to win, for the wolves were howling for Coach Jim Rice's scalp.

The Lions made a gallant scrap of it, but in the last scant yards to the end, they horrendously saw the coveted victory slip through their hands and flow over to Cornell.

Ten Eyck's boat finished third, with Wisconsin and Penn racing across in those positions. Thus, Cornell marked up its tenth victory in a long string of 15 varsity boat races at the IRA regattas.

Nineteen ten. It was a season when only 13 men reported for the 12 open positions in the varsity and four-oared boats of Syracuse. Meantime, the Athletic Association wallowed in debt.

With $7,220 in unpaid bills staring him in the face, Samuel Cook '95, general manager of the association, appealed to Trustee John Archbold for assistance. The oil magnate agreed to pay one-half of the debt, provided the group scraped up the remainder.

In dismay, Cook was unable in time to obtain relief by borrowing or by other means in getting the amount of money required.

The Association acted drastically to economize: Row-ing was to be sacrificed the next season, although Ten Eyck was to be retained at his annual salary of $1,800.

Beset by these painful money problems, Syracuse managed in some way to race on the Hudson. With monotonous regularity, Cornell once more swept the river. Syracuse placed fourth in the varsity race, second in the four-oared; and third in the freshman event.

Relief came to the beleaguered crew supporters that fall, when Archbold paid off the debt of the Athletic Association, thereby giving rowing another lungful of life. Thankful for Archbold's timely gift, friends of crew went out and once more raised funds with which to reinforce the financial base of the sport. And in several succeeding years, crew was financed this way, mainly due to the generosity of the Syracuse public.

Another blow was dealt rowing, when in November, Lyman C. Smith, founder of the Navy, died; and his death left a huge gap in the canvass of the rowing picture on Piety Hill.

As dismal and bleak as were the rowing conditions in 1911, Ten Eyck worked hopefully with three of his fresh-man crew, Martin Hilfinger, Howard Robbins and Clifford Goes. Later, these men entered the immortality of Syracuse and national rowing. But at this time, for the most part, they were just names indented on the roster.

Governor Dix, a few days prior to the IRA regatta, signed a bill appropriating $55,000 for establishing the College of Forestry at Syracuse University; and young Jim Ten Eyck became coach of the Duluth Boat Club, an organization of enthusiastic members, whom his father coached sometimes during summer vacation.

Results at Poughkeepsie in 1911 for Syracuse remained the dismal same. Stroked by George "Cy" Thurston, the varsity finished fifth; the four-oared crew ran second to Cornell; and the freshman boat with Goes as coxwain, and Hilfinger and Robbins, finished third.

There wasn't much improvement in the fortunes of Syracuse rowing the following year of 1912, at Poughkeepsie: Varsity, fourth; four-oared, third; freshman, third. Leland Stanford that year made the first of two trips to the Hudson in those early times.

Items of interest on campus that year:

Dr. William Graham became dean of Applied Sciences; later he became the University's sixth Chancellor.

Enrollment was 3,183, third largest of any university in the nation; Columbia, with 5,669, was first.

The campus perimeter was improved by covering mud walks with cinders.

Chancellor Day, with great distress, warned students that entertainment on campus closed before 11 o'clock.

And beloved campus figure, John "Doc" Cunningham was appointed postmaster of the University's sub-station.

For the third consecutive year, Ten Eyck, the former professional sculler, defeated Jim Riley, another former professional rower, at Saratoga Springs, and demonstrated in technique what Ten Eyck, the teacher, studiously taught his young men.

As though the past defeats weren't difficult enough to try the patience of Job, rowing suffered its most serious blow of all time. A tornado on September fifteenth, 1912, whirled down Long Branch in the rowing area and smashed everything to kindling!

Lost in the rubble were the decrepit boathouse, boats,

oars, clothing, the launching dock. Total loss, not insured, was estimated at $8,000.

Cornell, in time-honored tradition of friendship, proved helpful, indeed. The Ithaca university generously offered Ten Eyck two of its eight-oared shells, as well as a pair-oared boat—no strings attached to the offer. Ten Eyck gratefully accepted.

Catastrophic as was the damage, the subsequent attacks against rowing were serious in proportion. A few rowing alumni, in a splendid demonstration of solidarity, resisted the wind of words as uttered by those endangering the bloodstream of a noble and significant part of athletics at the University.

The first attack came from the student newspaper.

Its two editors suggested that perhaps it was wise to discontinue rowing until the Syracuse Navy was put "on a sound financial basis."

The second was more subtle.

Several prominent alumni—non-supporters of crew—questioned whether the University with its strong emphasis on literary courses could compete with Columbia, Cornell, Pennsylvania and Wisconsin "whose great technical courses gained prestige."

Yet, those supporters of rowing refused to budge or surrender. They were deeply devoted and staunchly withstood the pressures placed on them. In time, the small band was credited with saving the sport from becoming merely history in the dusty volumes of the University archives.

Chancellor Day expressed more outwardly his admiration for the oarsmen in the student newspaper:

> This emphasizes the honor due Ten Eyck and the handful of students who have gone out to practice in floating

ice with storms and meager equipment and who have sacrificed the social affairs of the spring weeks and Commencement to place the name of their Alma Mater upon the highest roll of American universities.

Everything connnected with rowing seemed so futile. Confronted with loss of their boathouse and equipment, plagued by critics, and without money, the hardy oarsmen received no promises of better conditions for the future. They doggedly stuck, however, to the sport of their choice. They continued to pit muscle and mind, stamina and grit against water and the elements—things they understood and were conditioned to battle. Their example of pride and courage at a time of great challenge was a lodestar for those who came after them. Little wonder then, other people thought them a strange breed, a description of exclusiveness they learned to accept and be proud of in the forthcoming years.

Ten Eyck's continued drought of victories on the Hudson irritated him. His men soon became aware of his sensitivity to defeats; therefore, the subject was never discussed openly in training during the 1913 season. It wasn't necessarily drowned out, however, by some concern about the European war jitters. But it was there, nevertheless. It was present—sticky, ubiquitous, pervasive. One felt it. Saw it. It seemed to soak into everyone's stream of thought as if by osmosis. Spelled out, it was simply

Tension! Tension!

Contributing to the electricity in the air around the crew was Ten Eyck's demeanor: the intense peering into the tightening gloom of spring afternoons; the deep-set eyes squinting at the men on the water; the tightening corners of the mouth.

By the middle of the season, repairs and replacement were completed at the rowing cantonment and William Tousey of Syracuse momentarily brightened the picture by giving the University a new coaching launch to replace the worn-out boat.

Three men stood throwing sticks into the Hudson three days before the IRA races in June.

One was loosely-jointed. The Old Man.

His two companions were oarsmen. Cy Thurston. Marty Hilfinger.

One wondered about their mysterious actions, and why they peered so intently at their pieces of wood floating downstream. They were checking the current for patterns of flow that might give them an advantage in the races a few days hence.

Nearby, stood a stranger, unobtrusively watching the three.

Suddenly, Hilfinger glanced up and saw him. He moved forward to welcome the stranger. They met and shook hands.

Hilfinger brought him over to his companions. He was Russell—"I'm Rusty"—Callow, the No. 3 oar in Washington University's first four-oared boat sent to the Hudson.

With his infectious grin and warm manner, Hilfinger explained the rowing fraternity's custom of attending church services together in the nearby village of Highland the Sunday before the races. Callow promised to attend, too.

The pastor's sermon that Sunday appropriately enough was:

"Never Be Last."

That chance meeting on the banks of the swiftly running river forged a lasting friendship between Ten Eyck and Rusty. It enriched collegiate rowing in the forthcoming years.

Presently, a few thousand miles away, young men—college students and all—quickly assembled with guns for war. In America of 1913, a small number of young men by comparison, sun-tanned and tense, quietly gathered with wooden oars to enter a different kind of struggle for a cause on an open river in cedar boats.

CHAPTER XIV

**"BUY THE BIG PEANUTS—THEY'RE ALL
DOUBLE-JOINTED!"
"GETCHA PROGRAMS. THEY'LL TELL WHO'S RACING!"
"BUY YOUR BANNERS—BERIBBONED OARS HERE!"**
hawked the peddlers in June of 1913, the time of the
Poughkeepsie races. Beefing up the general hubbub was
the special train of the Columbia Club of New York con-
veying a noisy uniformed fife and drum corps.

In the milling crowd was an one-armed Negro playing
discordant notes with a contraption composed of a drum,
guitar and mouth organ. While he eagerly stooped to pick
up coins tossed his way, nearby, two Italians with hurdy-
gurdies and their dancing monkeys and tin cups entertained
another section of the crowd.

Festivity carpeted the scene, and although a carnival of
death was to commence shortly in Europe, the only thoughts
in the minds of the people at the regatta were the races. It
was like another Coney Island on a hot, Sunday afternoon,
and honestly, that was the only meeting Americans were
concerned about.

The area became mobbed early that morning, when
the regular trains and the specials of Commodore Vander-
bilt's New York Central released their passengers for
Poughkeepsie and Highland.

107

Color and beauty were added at 2 o'clock that afternoon. Columbia University's special train arrived with a bevy of girls flaunting the light blue and white of the Lions. People were quick to notice that many a winsome lass from the train wore a miniature lion suspended from a blue ribbon encircling her neck.

So inviting was the regatta that day that thousands were unsuccessful in obtaining seats on the packed 39-car observation train. They purchased camp chairs, instead, setting themselves up on the rocky embankments at the floor of the awesome Palisades down near the finish line. With a flourish of skyrockets, the races began.

By time of the varsity event, two Syracuse crews disappointed their huge following. They finished poorly in the four-oared and freshman races, and their supporters were glum, holding little hope for their upstate New York university in the final event.

Meanwhile, Ten Eyck bought his launch to the float at crew headquarters for purpose of picking up his varsity men and taking them up river to the Columbia boathouse where they always launched their shell.

Ten Eyck was deeply disappointed over the showings of his two other crews. Of the three he brought to the river, he expected victory from either the four-oared or freshman shells. Both failed him.

While the supporters were appalled at the results, Ten Eyck was shocked. Bereft of victory since 1908 on the Hudson, he was sidepocketed by heavy criticism. Both he and Jim Rice of Columbia needed victory at Poughkeepsie.

The varsity crewmen were dismayed, when they saw Ten Eyck. He was a picture of hopelessness. They waited for his final exhortation as they rode up the river. They stared in disbelief. He made no attempt to speak to them!

Bewildered, the crew sat there until the Columbia boathouse appeared on the horizon. They wondered what ailed him. Suddenly, and without warning, he swung around from the wheel and faced them. He struggled for a moment to speak. With a shrug of the shoulders, he turned his back on them and returned to steering. Some of the crew winced. Others, with compassion, looked away, not knowing what to say or do to relieve the embarrassment. All tried to ignore the moment.

Coming up to the Columbia float, Ten Eyck swung around and again faced them. In choked voice, he uttered six words:

"Men—you're my last hope, today!"

The fervent appeal in the voice, the gnarled hands, the age-creased face and the rough and graying hair, all sent chills chasing up and down their spines.

Quietly and with gentleness, the crew placed their shell on the face of the Hudson. Deep in thought, they silently paddled up to the starting line. With a roar, skyrockets split the sky. It was race time!

By now, Cornell was favored, and she occupied the lane nearest the open channel of the river, the coveted position. Glancing downstream from the western shore where the observation train chugged, those next in order were Syracuse, Wisconsin, Washington, Columbia and Pennsylvania.

The Huskies of Washington were making their first appearance in the East. It was their first introduction to big-time collegiate rowing. Historically, Washington rowed since the turn of the century, but mainly against club crews and not in eight-oared shells. Back in 1907, the university purchased two shells from Cornell for $800 and began thinking seriously about competition.

Without money, the Washington supporters obtained the voluntary services of their football trainer—Hiram Connibear—and although inexperienced himself, he developed his own style, a technique that became the trademark of great Washington crews of the future.

Back at the starting line at Poughkeepsie in 1913, a hush spread wide over the river. Finally, the referee gave the perfunctory rites of starting, raised his arm and fired the pistol.

—Whooosh!—

Oars swung into motion, the shells sliced the rippling water, while the skyrockets burst into the air. The observation train lurched into motion.

Nearest the shore, Ten Eyck's crew quickly caught water and began to move, Coxswain Goes calling time:

Half stroke—

Three quarter stroke—

Full stroke—

Then ten strokes at 36 to the minute—

The boat dropped, and the stroke lengthened, the power of the shell vibrating through the seasoned wood. The moment the oars left the Hudson, recovery began with a feather; and averaging 170 pounds in weight, the crew moved almost three-quarters of a ton of boat and man.

Meanwhile, Thurston stroked in the particular Ten Eyck style that was so distinctly different from any other. The technique was dubbed by rowing experts as "the get-there-stroke." Incorporating some of the characteristics of sculling, the stroke, of course, wasn't as graceful and finished as Courtney's long sweep—it's true—but it was effective, especially in smooth water.

The two favorites, Cornell and Columbia, challenged each other almost immediately, even before the first mile of the four-mile race. Syracuse remained a length behind the two, while Goes confidently assessed his opponents.

The crowd that day believed Syracuse was deliberately held back by Ten Eyck's orders, a supposition he later hotly denied. To put it bluntly, Ten Eyck admitted afterwards, his boat was in that position because "it didn't row fast enough to keep up with the pacesetters."

Nonetheless, the Big Red and the Lions set a suicidal pace. Bow to bow, they rowed on the river.

Behind them came Syracuse, Pennsylvania, the Huskies, the Badgers, the last three crews almost rowing a separate race of their own, so closely bunched were they.

Ten Eyck's crew quickly spurted forward, closing up on the leaders at the one and one-half mile mark. Behind came Washington and the Badgers, who were now coached by Harry Vail, Ned Ten Eyck's successor and the Old Man's colleague in the professional sculling days of the 1880s.

Somewhere between two and two and one-half miles— it was difficult to ascertain exactly—Syracuse abruptly pushed its way into the private struggle of Cornell and Columbia. With a burst of speed about now, the Lions gained a full length on the Big Red. Syracuse tagged along half a length behind Cornell.

As time proved, Syracuse shrewdly paced itself, from time to time, checking the others, gauging their opponents' speed, figuring the amount of strength they held in reserve, and above all, estimating correctly the rate at which the others tired.

Its move came at the three-mile point.

—Sw-ish—sw-ish—sw-ish—cut the oarblades, and Syracuse inched ahead of Cornell.

Out in front at this time, the Lions soon wearied from the earlier battle with the Big Red. Little by little, they slipped behind the Orange-oared shell. While this occurred, Hiram "Connie" Connibear anxiously watched his Huskies trying to escape their fourth-place position and exchange it for a better one. Wisconsin followed them. Pennsylvania lagged behind.

Up to this moment, the windmill of motion created by the bunched shells of Syracuse, Cornell and Columbia split into separate parts.

Rowing in a shell generously loaned them by Cornell after the tornado of the previous autumn of 1912, Syracuse oarsmen withdrew from their benefactors and departed. They quickly grabbed the lead.

A half-mile from the finish, the boat was ahead by a quarter of a length over the Big Red, nearest competitor. Behind Cornell came Columbia, followed by the two initial-W crews, with Pennsylvania's boat 19 lengths behind.

Connibear's men caught the fancy of the crowd by suddenly surging forward at great speed and closing up to less than a length behind second-place Cornell. And on its way, Washington passed the fading Lions.

In the Syracuse boat, quiet drama took place. Goes possessed keen sensibilities. Aware of Cornell's favorite trick of holding back enough for a belated surge at the end,

Goes parlayed that knowledge into his strategy for victory. With a nod from Thurston, he commenced rapping, selfishly squeezing out the final reserve power of his crew. He calculatedly prepared for the expected surge of Cornell.

—Whoomp!—sounded the oars striking the water.

—Screeech!—grated the oarlocks in the steel swivels.

—Whooosh—echoed the oars, abandoning foamy circles on the Hudson.

Strange, there was no response from Courtney's men.

Skeptical of Cornell's pose of inertia, Goes and Thurston, between them, feverishly called upon their men for additional power. Again, the shell increased its speed.

Whether Goes ever realized that Cornell was not to challenge his boat on the Hudson, his reaction is unknown. He merely pushed the crew to the limit, and the Syracuse shell was the first to cross the finish line.

Meanwhile, Cornell barely hung onto second place in the last 40 strokes, hard-pressed by Washington in the final 200 yards. Wisconsin was fourth, trailed by Columbia and Pennsylvania.

After the race, Ellis Ward of Pennsylvania, the first coach congratulating Ten Eyck back in 1904, announced his retirement after 35 years of coaching. One of the first professional scullers to coach college crews, he spent retirement in building shells and oars for his former opponents and colleagues.

And for the third time since 1904, Cornell was defeated at Poughkeepsie in a varsity race by Jim Ten Eyck, a man whom everyone now dubbed, "Sly Fox of the Hudson."

Chancellor Day was lavish in his praise that day:

114

FINISH OF THE 1913 VARSITY RACE AT POUGHKEEPSIE

I may be charged with over-enthusiasm if I say it seems to me under the circumstances, the victory of Syracuse was the greatest in the rowing history of this country. Probably no event has sent the name of our city so far around the world as the victory of her 'Varsity' crew at Poughkeepsie in a contest with the greatest university crews of the world. It was a daring venture that put these inland water crews upon the Hudson to dispute the crown with Cornell, Columbia and Pennsylvania, the three universities that had won "varsity races" in that great annual contest. Since Syracuse appeared, she has been the only university, that has broken the chain of Cornell's magnificent victories. We have had the greatest rowing competitor of the world as our neighbor. We have been treated with generous consideration, both in defeat and in victory, by her great coach, Charles E. Courtney. Were his examples followed by all connected with athletics at Cornell we should not have the spectacle of "burying the hatchet," blade up and handle in sight, but the hatchet would be buried at the bottom of Cayuga Lake and the two great universities of Central New York would be competing on most amicable and cordial terms in all college sports.[12]

The Chancellor said Syracusans weren't to forget the generous sportsmanship of Courtney in loaning the crew boats in the spring for practice that "resulted in his defeat, nor his splendid tribute to Syracuse in his philosophic and manly discussion of the varsity races after the contest. These are things quite as valuable to college ideals and manhood as victory of the oars." [13]

On November 29, Yale University disturbed Syracuse rowing.

Abandoning its unsuccessful experiment with the English style and techniques of rowing, Yale made definite overtures to Ten Eyck at a propitious time. The Old Man's contract expired.

Yale offered Ten Eyck a lucrative contract to coach its men, an offer made despite the protests of W. Averell Har-

115

---

[12] [13]The *Post-Standard*, Syracuse, N.Y., June 23, 1913.

116

1913 VARSITY IRA CHAMPIONS: Str. Geo. B. Thurston, M. F. Hilfinger, J. H. Rich, R. W. Propst, H. W. Robbins, M. H. Kuehn, W. L. Joslyn, Bow C. T. Mahan, Cox C. C. Goes.

riman, who was influential in Yale affairs and one who favored the English method of rowing.

The offer came to public attention by some of the leading newspapers. Sources of the story were confident that Ten Eyck was to accept Yale's overture.

Crew supporters in Syracuse reacted immediately. Led by Hurlbut Smith and D. Raymond Cobb, the University offered Ten Eyck another five-year contract, covering the years from 1914 to 1918, at an annual salary of $2,500, payable in twelve monthly checks.

Ten Eyck hastily signed the new contract.

That autumn of 1913, Ten Eyck suggested that fall practice for crews be instituted, contending that spring was much too short for adequate training. And if there was anything the Old Man was not to be accused of was the improper training of his oarsmen.

CHAPTER XV

TEN EYCK CREWS

were always trademarks of conditioning. Their reputation for superlative and almost inexhaustable endurance, however, didn't happen by good fortune, nor did it come about as result of picking from a large number of candidates; Ten Eyck never enjoyed the luxury of choosing from an abundance of men. Yet, conditioning was a way of life with Syracuse crews. He insisted upon it.

The Old Man harped on the old refrain of staying in physical shape, in or out of season. He, himself, stood out as a shining example of what he taught. Early in the autumn, he gathered his freshman candidates together and led them on rigorous hikes up and down one of the seven hills encircling the University. Usually togged out in a big woolen sweater and heavy walking shoes, he paced his men.

Dubbed the "get-there-stroke," the Ten Eyck rowing style was built on the man rather than vice versa. Oftentimes he was asked to define his philosophy:

"There's no secret to it nor any mystery," he revealed. "It isn't the stroke, it's the man. I try to understand men. I have had fair success. I want more. When considering a man, I consider his sand first, his physique second. There are too many shadows walking around without hearts."

As far back as 1897, Ten Eyck was first to break away from the old-fashioned concept of training on raw beef and

118

ale. In college training, he never allowed his men to eat white bread at the training table; and he advocated a diet of wheat biscuits for them. His set of rules for health found general acceptance in college rowing:

Live in the open air.
Never be lazy.
Eat only when hungry.
Don't forget how to run.
Take baths in moderately cool water.
Be temperate in everything.
Take any exercise that's interesting.

Always contending that a good crew might row any distance they were required to row, Ten Eyck said this was possible only if the crew was given sufficient time with which to practice the distance. A heavy, powerful crew, he claimed, made faster time than a light powerful crew, but the actual length of the race itself was of minor significance. Power, preparation and condition were prime factors, he said.

As for the personal equation of an oarsman, Ten Eyck said it involved the question as to the greatest single lesson learned from rowing. A young man, he argued, who knew his own strength or weakness learned to pace himself and carried the lessons learned in the boat into later life.

Once he confidentially told a close friend his own philosophy after a crushing defeat:

"When you are walloped, tell yourself, 'Tomorrow is mine!' "

In 1914, the IRA abandoned the four-oared race, replacing it with the junior varsity eight-oared contest at Poughkeepsie. Cornell took that first jayvee race, while Syracuse finished fourth. In the varsity race, Columbia presented Coach Jim Rice with his first victory on the Hudson, and its first major win in the IRA since 1895. Syracuse varsity was fourth. Its freshmen were second.

An accident the next year in the days prior to the Poughkeepsie races demonstrated clearly how the inexorable thief of time and fortune began to thin the ranks of former professional scullers, who coached collegiate oarsmen.

Those oldtimers got their start back in the 1880s when Ellis Ward, Charles Courtney, Richard Glendon and Ten Eyck, among other young men, rowed for a living. They raced up and down the continent, giving either rowing exhibitions or participating in heavily-wagered contests.

In the late Nineties, many of them, including the aforementioned four, brought their skills and knowledge to college campuses. They represented, in fact, that first wave of college rowing coaches.

But three weeks before the 1915 races, one of their number, the fabulous Courtney of Cornell, was thrown against a berth in his sleeping car by a lurch of the train on the way to Poughkeepsie. For succeeding days, he worked with his crews. On race day, however, he dispatched his oarsmen to the races, and for the first time since the accident, confessed that he needed a physician. One was obtained from Poughkeepsie. An examination later disclosed that Courtney suffered a severe skull injury, but it was thought he might be safely transported back to Ithaca after the day's races.

Lying abed in the boathouse before the varsity race, he summoned a varsity oarsman by name of O'Brien.

"Say, O'Brien," Courtney whispered. "I wanted to advise you—"

Ellis F. Ward, Penn.

Charles E. Courtney, Cornell

James A. Ten Eyck, Sr., Syracuse

121

Richard C. Glendon, Navy

James C. Rice, Columbia

"Yes, Mr. Courtney?"

"Get out in front," the coach advised him, "and stay out in front—"

"We will, Mr. Courtney. We will."

"And for gods sake, man," Courtney pleaded, his head raised off the pillow, "watch that Syracuse boat!"

The Hudson regatta in 1915, which was 20th in the IRA series, saw Syracuse and Cornell sharing honors.

Charles Whiteside, stroke of the Syracuse freshman boat, rowed a brilliant race as did his mates. Never actually extended over the two-mile course, the crew finished four lengths ahead of Cornell. The Lions of Columbia were three-quarters of a mile behind the Big Red, and three lengths ahead of Pennsylvania.

Cornell and Syracuse fought desperately for first place in the varsity race, but it took something extra for the Big Red to nose out the Orangemen. The coxswain kept reminding his crew of Courtney's illness, and it was in this grim spirit that the Courtneymen won.

Both Syracuse and Cornell stroked a high 38 beats in the early phases of the race. Somewhat tired by the early pace, the two then watched Stanford take the lead. The Indians, this year, were making a second appearance on the Hudson. At the half-mile point, Arthur Osman, Syracuse stroke, raised the beat of the oars. The resultant surge pushed his shell out ahead of Stanford, but the lead was short-lived. They merely exchanged the leadership.

Back and forth—

Back and forth—

Back and forth—

it went, until suddenly, Cornell joined the two.

SQUAD OF '15 ON THE FLOAT OF THE BOATHOUSE ON THE HUDSON

THE WHITTLEY HOUSE, HIGHLAND; TRAINING QUARTERS

By this time, Syracuse and Stanford were tired out. Helplessly, they saw Cornell take the leadership away from them and carry it to the end.

Stanford was less than half a length ahead of Ten Eyck's boat. And by a series of furious spurts, Columbia overhauled Pennsylvania in the last half mile and grabbed fourth place.

Returned to Cornell a few hours afterwards, Courtney underwent a more thorough examination that disclosed a skull fracture. He was advised to take a long period of quiet and rest.

Ellis Ward's retirement at Pennsylvania two years prior to the 1915 races and Courtney's enforced absence left only Ten Eyck and Dick Glendon of the first big four in sculling active still as coaches.

CHAPTER XVI

THREE YEARS AFTER

the Hudson River championship in 1913, the image of Ten Eyck underwent subtle changes. The Sly Fox presented an imposing figure to the collegiate rowing fraternity. One sensed it before he understood it.

The Old Man wore his dignity as another might wear a suit of clothes; not as separate apparel, but as an integral part of his body. Now sixty-five, his poise and his demeanor gave strong impressions of patriarchy.

At a time when Ten Eyck received the same salary of $2,500 as did football coach William Hollenback and track coach Thomas Keane, he resolved that his varsity crew was to win the 1916 IRA regatta.

His determination was partly based on solid fact. Prospects for the crew appeared excellent, especially in March, when several returning veterans were joined by some of the previous year's freshman crew and he greeted the following at first practice: Arthur Osman, who in 1915 won the single scull race at the American Henley at Philadelphia; Captain Walter Glass; Lloyd Sprague, bow oar; Peter Wallis, E. E. Hopkins, L. J. Worden, F. R. Williams and Charles Whiteside, as well as Coxswain George Jayne.

He tested them first on May 13 in the American Henley at Philadelphia. The varsity caused consternation in the

125

rowing world with its defeat of Harvard, Pennsylvania and Yale.

A second test for it came seven days later against Navy on the Severn River. Ten Eyck figured the race might give him a true line on his varsity. He was correct.

With Whiteside stroking 39 beats to the minute as against Navy's 42 at the mile point, Syracuse was ahead by open water. At the finish, the Ten Eyck shell was a great distance ahead of the Sailors.

While the varsity crew was decisively defeating Navy, Lew Carr's nine defeated Michigan Aggies, 3-2; Keane's tracksters were victorious over Colgate in a dual meet; and Carl Peterson '18 established a new record in the half-mile.

Simultaneously with these happenings, Harvard's varsity and freshman boats were defeating Cornell on the Charles River in Boston. Coach Courtney was absent all that season and trying to regain his health.

Captain Glass showed no hesitation in reviewing the victory over Navy, while at the same time, expressing his crew's opinion about the forthcoming Poughkeepsie races:

"Everybody is anxious to get at Cornell on June 17th!" His thoughts were shared by others, and the forecasters favored Syracuse for the IRA.

A light drizzle met the dawn of race day in 1916, but still failed to dampen the enthusiasm of the crowds pouring into the area. Automobiles carrying soggy pennants and dripping bunting threaded their way over the few paved roads.

While the stream of humanity jostled and struggled to the shores of the river, the weather cleared at 1 o'clock, a strong wind whipping up white caps on the water. Pleasure craft of all sizes and kinds lined the course, and the palatial yacht, *Noma*, owned by Vincent Astor, was anchored in the middle of the fleet down at the finish line.

Cornell led most of the way during the junior varsity race, but due to superb stroking of Syracuse's O. R. Summerville, his boat overtook the Big Red near the end and won.

Those rowing in the first Syracuse jayvee boat to win on the Hudson were:

Bow Oar—J. T. Port
No. 2—C. J. Gilmore
No. 3—W. C. Carr
No. 4—H. H. Hartwell
No. 5—W. C. Jordan
No. 6—G. D. Hoople
No. 7—L. W. Fox
Stroke—O. R. Summerville
Coxswain—K. E. Broadway

The freshman race was postponed after the junior varsity contest due to the roughness of the river. After further delay of an hour, officials took a calculated risk that the wind was to fade away and called out the varsity to the starting line.

While Columbia, Cornell, Pennsylvania and Syracuse paddled up to the stakeboats, the sun commenced to melt away behind the western outline of the Palisades. And a moment before the starting pistol, the strong wind, as if by magic, softened its tone and mellowed into a soft breeze.

Eager and tense, thirty-six of America's young men awaited the starting sign, unaware of the fact that this IRA race was the last. Afterwards, war in Europe interrupted

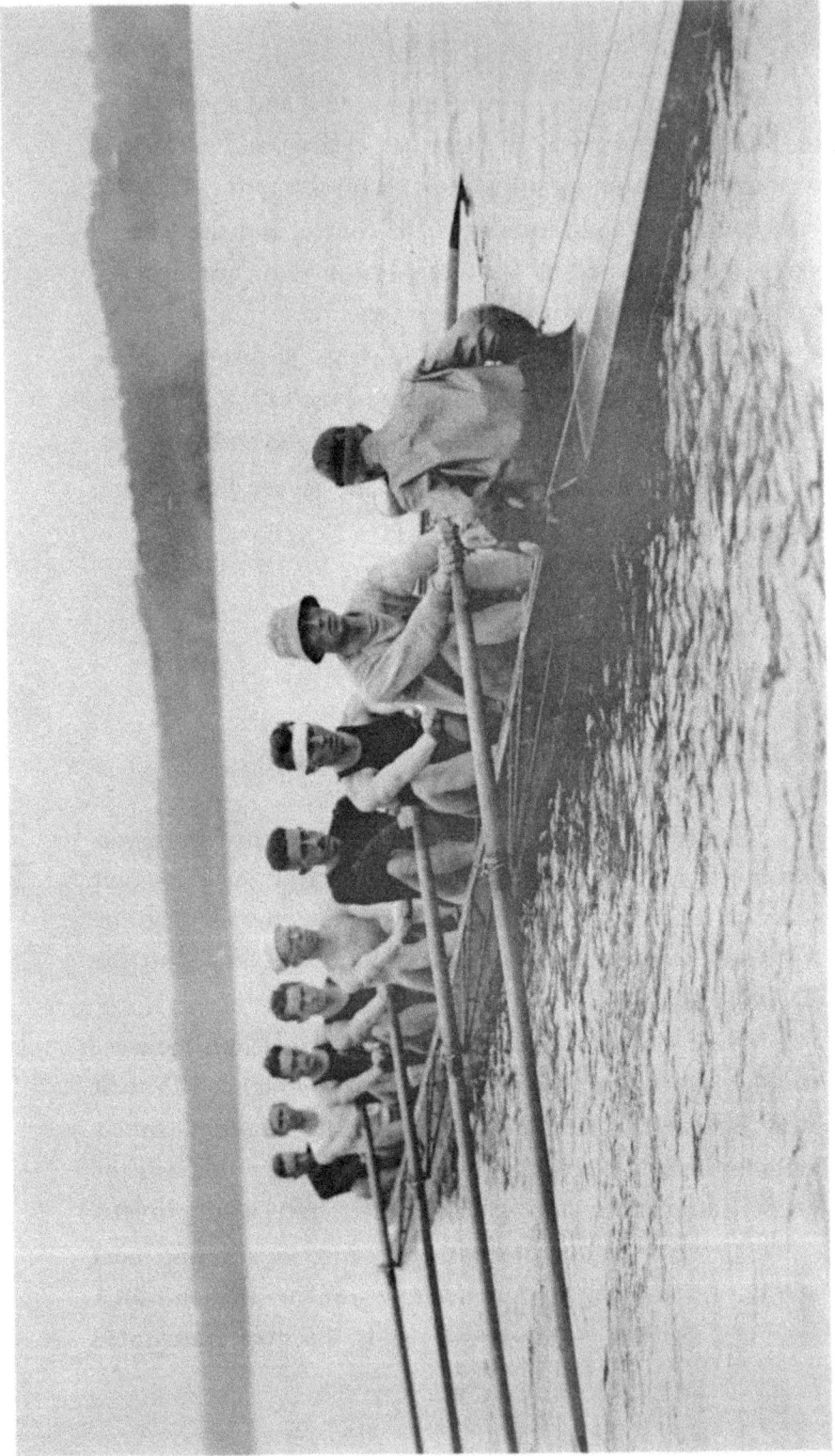

FIRST SYRACUSE JUNIOR VARSITY IRA CHAMPS

128

the IRA and rowing, and it shoved everything else off the priority list of mankind's things to be done within the next four years.

Off at the pistol, the four shells soon began to settle down for the long pull. With Syracuse and Cornell late in getting started, Columbia and Pennsylvania led. But unknown to Syracuse and Cornell, an oarsman in the Lions boat slipped a stroke at the beginning. The Lion coxswain, M. Thomas, signalled the referee for another start. Meanwhile, Syracuse, Pennsylvania and Cornell rowed downstream some five hundred yards away. They were summoned back for another start.

Aggravating though it was, the false start proved invaluable to Whiteside of Syracuse. Warned by the exceptionally rapid getaways of Pennsylvania and Columbia, he sent off his shell, at the second start, rowing a 32-stroke beat. Somewhere within the first 400 yards, Whiteside's crew forged ahead and led Cornell by a full length.

Whiteside, who years afterwards employed his acumen in coaching at Harvard, disregarded the others and lowered his own stroke now that the water was calm. Smoothly the shell ran in the forepart of the varsity race. Without warning, about this time, the wind and rain snapped out of their lethargy and acted up. The water again became turbulent.

With the rain and wind beating on them, the Syracuse and Cornell crews maintained a 26-stroke beat up to the half-mile mark. Suddenly, Courtney's men lifted their beat to 28 in a desperate attempt to go ahead of Syracuse, which led the pack at the time. Their try at this point was futile.

Under the bridge, Cornell, with a convulsion of effort, attempted once more to wrest the lead from Syracuse. Again, it was useless. With a magnificent burst of power, the Ten Eyck boat lengthened its lead and held onto it until the final 300 yards.

Here, Cornell again challenged Syracuse. And once more, Coxswain Jayne appealed for more power. His cigar-shaped craft swiftly sped downstream as water rushing on a journey to its ocean.

The canopy of night deepened when the sirens of the clustered boats around the finish line shrilled out their salutes to victorious Syracuse. Cornell was second, followed by Columbia and Pennsylvania.

Slow time of the contestants was attributed to the wind and rain which worked havoc with the crews. Columbia's oarsmen rowed ankle-deep at the finish, while others also shipped water during the final stages of the contest. But not so Syracuse.

The sly fox of the Hudson from Syracuse prepared beforehand for the elements. Ten Eyck shrewdly protected his men by installing canvas strips around the top of the shell's cavity. His crew of the four boats suffered the least from the water.

Victory came at a most opportune time for the Old Man and his crew. Before many days passed by, several of his oarsmen left and donned uniforms. The No. 3 oar of that boat, Pete Wallis, never returned to the University or to the Hudson. At war's end, he lay somewhere in Flanders Field.

Due to the storm, the freshman event was held the following day. For some unknown reason, the IRA officials changed the plans at the last moment and ordered the crews to race upstream!

VARSITY EIGHT IRA WINNER, 1916: St. C. J. Whitside, Jr., F. R. Williams, L. J. Worden, E. E. Hopkins, A. J. Osman, P. L. Wallis, W. L. Glass, L. D. Sprague, Cox, G. G. Jayne.

131

Cornell occupied lane one; Columbia, two; Pennsylvania, three; and Ten Eyck's yearlings were supposedly in an enviable position. Unfortunately, this was not the case, and a strong headwind with a strong tide hampered the Orange freshmen.

Cornell turned out to be the easy winner, finishing ahead of Syracuse by two lengths. Penn was a close third. Columbia was several lengths behind.

Gratified by his junior and varsity wins, Ten Eyck rubbed his hands together with great enthusiasm and declared:

'I'm coming back with them next year—so look out!"

Courtney, disappointed by the two varsity races, returned home and continued a long period of rest and recuperation.

Thirty days later, critics began to belabor a question of Syracuse's victory: Could Cornell have won if Courtney had been well?

The bewailing was so loud and vehement in its tone that B. A. Jessup, New York's Crescent Athletic Club authority on rowing, defended the Syracuse crew in the *Brooklyn Eagle:*

> This eight is undoubtedly the greatest of any varsity crew that had ever rowed in American waters, and is a splendid type of the finished American sweep. . . .

And still it continued, the complaining now centered on the knowledge that four students from Duluth (Minnesota), home of the professional boat club, were allowed to row in the Ten Eyck boat. Frank G. Menke in a special report to the *Daily Orange* the next autumn defended Syracuse:

The yowl raised by other colleges because Syracuse boat-ed some Duluth oarsmen in its varsity shell in June savors of sour.grapes. . . . Just why Cornell, Columbia and Pennsylvania should complain against the Duluth oarsmen is something of a mystery. The four youths against whom the kick is made are not professionals—so why should the rowing authorities make any fuss over it?

The defender argued that a number of men from Duluth entered Syracuse University. Some of Orange opponents claimed these students were influenced to choose Syracuse, Menke admitted, but he reported authoritatively, "this recruitment is done by every university in the country."

Under heavy pressure, the IRA officials took unprecedented action early in March of 1917, ruling that a man was barred from rowing on a freshman crew, who previously represented in competition any club or rowing organization other than that of a prep school. This new decision applied to both junior and varsity crews unless the candidate in question resided a year at his college.

Fortunately, the four men in question, including Captain Glass, claimed a year's residence satisfactorily and were declared eligible by the IRA.

Whether the criticism was valid or not, it appeared that Ten Eyck's son, Jim, who coached the Duluth Club, was possibly influencing young potential oarsmen to matriculate at Syracuse. There was nothing illegal in this, and criticism by other schools was ludicrous inasmuch as all of them, in turn, openly recruited oarsmen for collegiate sports. An oarsman was a good man to have around for other sports, too!

Syracuse lost an important benefactor in December of 1916, when John Archbold died following an appendectomy. Before his death, Woodrow Wilson, former head of Princeton University, was re-elected President, and Syracuse Navy Commodore, Walter E. Shaw '16, died in his home at Rome (New York).

The latest Hudson victory was added to an already imposing record of achievements by Syracuse crew. In the 14-year span of college rowing under Ten Eyck, Syracuse won 11 firsts; 12 seconds; eight thirds; four fourths; and two fifths.

It was an impressive record for a university which was yet to become an official member of the IRA. During all these years past, Syracuse and the others rowed at invitation of the IRA, which consisted only of Cornell, Columbia and

Pennsylvania.

CHAPTER XVII

THE IRA STEWARDS

early in 1917 reduced the length of the varsity race at Poughkeepsie from four to three miles; immediately, Ten Eyck protested frequently and loudly.

Sentiment for the change swelled during the previous several years among some of the universities, and it was this difference as to the length of the course which sharpened into two major factions within the IRA.

The first cleavage widened earlier, when Navy withdrew from the regatta and Wisconsin followed after the 1915 races. At the same time, Princeton refused to allow her crews to race more than two miles, whereas the Pacific Coast teams rowed the regular three miles. In a surprise move, Cornell joined Princeton in trying to change the IRA to the two-mile course, but finally compromised for the three-mile run.

Opponents of the four-mile course defended their preference by explaining that the regular run meant lengthy preparation, with their scholastic committees believing the two-mile course allowed oarsmen more time for classroom work.

Several even contended that the regular four-mile course was injurious to the health of their students. To the defense of the longer distance quickly sprang Ten Eyck.

"I can see no logical reason why the length of the courses at New London [where Yale raced Harvard], and Poughkeepsie should be changed from four miles to three miles," he argued.

"As far as injury to the oarsmen is concerned, that should not be taken into consideration as there is not the slightest danger of injury from rowing, providing the persons who indulge in the exercise are sound and in normal health at the beginning and go through a proper course of preparation."

Meanwhile, the heavy steam of criticism against Syracuse for using four Duluth men in the varsity championship boat of 1916 still boiled over. The smoke of complaint became so bad that T. H. Low '02 appointed himself an investigator of one and dug into the problem. His findings:

Three men from Duluth, yes, were in the crew. However, several other schools, including Pennsylvania, Yale, Harvard and Cornell, allowed their men to gain experience before entering regular collegiate rowing.

With Low's revelation, criticism died at last without a whimper.

Two brand new shells made by Ellis Ward were purchased by Syracuse, when rowing began in earnest in January. Captain Arthur Osman and some 93 others reported for tryouts.

While the men got into shape by working on the rowing machines, Ten Eyck was in Peekskill, attending his father's funeral. In March, Frank Barry and Pete Wallis, candidates for presidency of the campus Y.M.C.A. group, tied in voting. Thirty days later in a run-off, Wallis was elected president of the association.

Amidst all this preparation for another season of rowing, Congress declared war. Previously, President Woodrow Wilson armed merchantmen against the unrestricted warfare of German U-boats. When three homeward-bound American ships were sunk, he asked and received from Congress a declaration of war.

Seven days after the April 6 date of war, the University suspended athletics of all types. Lew Carr's baseball team, on its first tour in eight years, was recalled back to campus.

The bucolic-atmosphere of the campus changed overnight. The pace quickened. There was excitement. And 1,500 eager male students tried to join a unit of the Officers Reserve Corps on campus. Everyone's attention by this time was focused on the war.

In the midst of all this commotion, the oarsmen vainly tried to retain some degree of normalcy. They chose Frank Williams '18 as captain, but there was little interest in those first months.

Ten Eyck, himself, was without bow or rudder. There wasn't anything for him to do in the first flush of warfare excitement on campus. And he wasn't framed for idleness. He put himself to work.

He built a boat of strong oak and ash and cedar. When the New York State Barge Canal shook off her coat of ice in the 1917 spring, he obtained a permit to pass through the canal's locks and rowed away from Syracuse on his way to New York.

While American youth prepared for war, the Old Man rowed serenely down the Hudson in seven days. Two blistered hands later, he pulled out his boat onto Columbia's float in New York. It was a wonderful week for him, allow-ing him to renew old acquaintances along the route and to make new ones. In Albany, a nosey reporter spied him in his rowboat and interviewed him.

The newspaper account of Ten Eyck caused Colonel Theodore Roosevelt of San Juan Hill fame and former President to invite him to his summer home on Sagamore Hill. That meeting was described years later by Ten Eyck in an article he wrote for the *Outlook* magazine:

> He began asking me about my family and when I told him that I had four children, he said: "That's fine. How are they divided up?"
>
> "A girl and three boys," I replied.
>
> "Bully," he said. "You and I come from good old Dutch stock and I am interested in seeing it kept up."
>
> He said he had read of my rowboat trip and wanted to ask me about boats and rowing. He said he liked to row a great deal and often took Mrs. Roosevelt out with him on Oyster Bay. But he said he rarely saw other people rowing, and asked me why it was. We both agreed that gasoline had put the oars out of business. But he agreed with me, too, that rowing was the best of exercises, and deeply regretted that he had not had time to do more of it. He asked me to describe my boat, saying that he knew I wouldn't start out for a three-hundred mile row unless my boat was rigged comfortable.

With war suspending formal rowing on college campuses, Hiram "Connie" Connibear of Washington, unlike Ten Eyck, was not busy constructing boats. He retired home, idle. In September, 1917, he fell from a fruit tree on his property in Seattle breaking his neck. He died instantly. In time, the famous coach was succeeded by Edward Leader, his former Husky pupil, who was destined to become Yale's immortal coach.

Rowing was returned to the Syracuse campus as part of the Army physical training program late in the same year Connibear died. Henry Lucy was chosen Navy Commodore in March, 1918, and some 90 men, a majority of them in training on campus, worked out on rowing machines. Work was suspended, however, in March, when Ten Eyck's son, Dr. George Ten Eyck '08, died in New York City. Young Jim Ten Eyck came out from his Duluth coaching duties and filled in for his father. He spent a week working with the freshmen.

Still grieving after his son's death, Ten Eyck took his freshman crew down to the American Henley races at Annapolis on May 18, 1918. His yearlings gave him a wonderful victory, defeating both the Navy Plebes and Pennsylvania's freshmen.

It was that night after the race that Ten Eyck stunned the University and the rowing world by announcing his retirement from coaching. Fathoms deep in mourning over his son, the Old Man said he was spending the remainder of his years with sons Jim and Ned in Duluth. His contract with the University expired, he no longer seemed interested in renewing it.

The resignation caused a flurry of excitement and dismay. Dr. Day hurriedly wrote him a letter, addressing him affectionately as "My dear Jim:"

> I was surprised and distressed a few hours ago when I learned that you had resigned and were to leave us and the State. I cannot blame you for a plan that will permit you to live with your sons. And I know the discouraging outlook for college athletics for certainly the period of the war and probably for some time following. Your freshmen who did so magnificently at Annapolis Saturday will be in the drafting age before you can make Varsities of them. But I am sorry to have you go, not only because you are the greatest crew coach in America but because of your wholesome moral influence upon the students who you have coached in these fifteen years that you have been with us. . . . To teach men to row and win races and leave them

without the elements of true manliness would be a disaster to us as a University. I have always known that I could trust you with the men whether here in practice or away on your racing tours. . . . It is a matter of no small pride with us that every man of that great varsity crew with which you won at the last contest on the Hudson is now at the front battling for the salvation of the world from that last remnant of barbarism which was threatening civilization. That crew will be great soldiers because you trained them in self-control and the use of every inch of their powers at the right moment. . . If the close of the war permits us to start another crew, I want you to come back whether I am here or not, and show the boys how to start winning crews once more. . . . God bless you, my dear "Coach."

The revered Dean Frank Smalley of Liberal Arts wrote a letter to the Old Man, stating that "your absence will reduce us (in rowing) to a third-class power at once, while now we stand among the best. . . . I would favor giving you $25,000 a year rather than have you go away."

While their old coach packed, eight of the nine men in the last winning Hudson boat were participating in the war effort. Whiteside was an Army officer as was Frank Williams. Coxswain Jayne was learning to fly an Army Jenny airplane. Hopkins was a second lieutenant in charge of recruits. Wallis and Summerville were commissioned in the Army at Madison Barracks in Oswego (New York). Lloyd Sprague at first worked with the Y.M.C.A., later joined the Army. Worden was studying medicine, but expected to be commissioned shortly.

October seventh, 1918, Ten Eyck, whose first wife had died, married his second, Olivia Edna Randall, a former Syracuse University professor of Oratory and Rhetoric. The ceremony was a quiet one, taking place in Mt. Vernon, Iowa, home of Cornell College from where Dr. Day's successor was to come.

In December, Tip Goes of the 1913 crew was commissioned in the Quartermaster Corps after serving overseas in the Major Edward Van Duyn hospital unit.

Informal rowing in 1919 was pretty much in the hands of volunteers. Leon "Kid" Ellis, former varsity coxswain, Cy Thurston and Henry Curtiss '06 supervised the oarsmen.

To bring back rowing on campus, twenty-six fraternities and fourteen sororities were asked to subscribe $10 apiece for a fund. Five hundred dollars from an athletic carnival on campus were added to the fund for benefit of the oarsmen.

As the year progressed, Chancellor Day envisioned a student body of 12,000 on campus within the next few years. He wrote alumni about this, pointing out that in order to accommodate the increase, some 14 new buildings were needed. He asked alumni for financial support.

Meanwhile, agitation for Ten Eyck's return spread on campus. And if students and alumni wanted him to return, the desire was likewise shared by Ten Eyck. Actually, as time passed, he was restless to return to the scene of his many triumphs, but an iron-clad contract with the Duluth Boat Club prevented any such action or discussion of it until the end of the 1919 rowing season.

However, on March 20, he informed the University of his desire to return. He wrote a trustee, W. L. Smith of the typewriter family.

Smith replied in April:

I had a telephone call from Judge Cobb (A. Raymond '02), and he feels the boys should get together and talk over the situation. I know they all want you to return. . . . Not only do the students on the hill want you to return, but the city people as well. . . . I will probably see Judge Cobb in a few days and this matter will be taken up. I am not a member of the Athletic Governing Board, and I do not know what steps they have taken; but I certainly know what they want, and that is *you.*

The answer to Ten Eyck came loud and clear on June 19 in a letter from Walter Smith, graduate manager of athletics:

> At the board meeting on Tuesday, I was authorized to sign a contract with you on the terms outlined in our correspondence.

Meanwhile, on May 31, Captain George Busch and his mates journeyed to the American Henley on the Schuykill River at Philadelphia. Both varsity and jayvee boats finished third, but the freshmen defeated Yale, Pennsylvania and Navy on rough water.

In August of 1919, the Alumni Association of the University proudly published its first issue of the *Alumni News,* a publication which over the years became an important University publication and gained prestige.

That fall, Ten Eyck with his new wife eagerly returned to the city they loved and resumed activities and duties at the University. Nineteen-twenty was a year filled with so much promise for them.

CHAPTER XVIII

"WATCH OUT FOR

Syracuse" was the cry in 1920, when the colleges again picked up the threads of peacetime rowing after the war. The coaches and experts were of one mind, still mindful of Ten Eyck's powerful varsity and junior varsity crews of 1916.

Ten Eyck scoffed at the optimism of the rival coaches. Victories of four years past, he remembered, were nothing more than history, and no coach in collegiate rowing won races, unfortunately, based on past records.

Tip Goes assisted him with coaching duties, and he watched Ten Eyck carefully mould a crew for victory. However, to do this, the Old Man studied his men closely, beforehand. His squad was unlike any of past years.

The men were big, and they were rangy. They were youthful men in face, but more matured and poised in action. If they displayed a quiet confidence rather than the exuberance of college youths, Ten Eyck wasn't particularly disturbed. He patiently and wisely accepted their omnipresent confidence.

From the first day out on water, Ten Eyck communicated clearly his belief in their destiny; and as if to substantiate outwardly this understanding, he never substituted a man in the varsity boat during the season, a rare

143

gesture at Syracuse where there was always a dearth of good and enough oarsmen.

Early in training, he informed them of their potential —a rendezvous so to speak.

Placing himself in the coxswain's seat, Ten Eyck instructed August Rammi, his stroke, to "Let 'er run," and let her run they did; then, he ordered the shell brought over towards shore. He halted the boat beneath an overhanging weeping willow tree. Nimbly, he stepped ashore. With his eyes sweeping the upturned faces in the shell, he couched his words in soft, melodic decibles:

"Now, men—" he began, "I think we might have a great year—yes, a great year, but only if you'll do the things I ask you to do—"

His eyes searched their faces again.

"—And this includes a lot of punishment—a lot of self-denial. It means training, back-breaking practice. It means bedding early and eating what I suggest you eat."

The crew became aware of Ten Eyck's controlled excitement, his anticipation, his promise of great expectations.

"And if you're willing to do this all season—willing to pay the price—" he paused again, "we can make this boat really go. Whaccha say?"

Instantly, the crew caught his enthusiasm, and in their resultant exuberance, they cheered him standing up there on the bank.

From this pep talk onward, there was never any doubt in their minds about what they and their coach wanted. Their currents of belief ran deep, and they willingly obeyed him like the ancient Spartans; not only because they loved the lean figure, but rather that they desired victory more—

far more than any personal gain they might derive from it as individuals. This was a team!

They worked.

They sweated.

And they lived on the promises of the future.

Due to this blind devotion to a man and to an ideal, they were propelled by destiny farther over into new and unchartered victories as the season unfolded before their eyes.

On May 15, they nibbled on their first victory cake.

Navy provided the reason for that celebration on the Severn River.

Ten Eyck's varsity crew dashed off to a beautiful start, managed to hold a three-foot lead over the Sailors at the first eighth of a mile.

Navy began to come up.

Rammi raised the Syracuse beat.

Stroke for stroke, the two crews raced together until a few yards away from the finish, Syracuse with a mighty surge shot out in front by a quarter of a boat length and won.

The full importance of the victory became known later that season, when Navy Coach Glendon labelled his crew as one of the best he ever boated at Annapolis. This was, of course, later that spring; but on this particular day, he was glum with good reason.

The following week, Glendon and his sailors were given an opportunity to get revenge and smile at the American Henley at Philadelphia.

Four men in the Syracuse boat were victims of the influenza epidemic, and the Sailors defeated Ten Eyck's boat handily in their second meeting.

After the epidemic ran its course, Ten Eyck hastily called out his crew in preparation for the IRA regatta scheduled for June 19th on Cayuga Lake, Cornell's home waters, a switch from the Hudson as dictated by officials in 1917. The reason for the transfer was the inability of the railroad to provide an observation train that year on the Hudson.

The course was to be two miles!

Only crews from Columbia, Penn, Cornell and Syracuse competed, but Ten Eyck objected heatedly to reducing the course to the new distance.

A week before the event, Syracuse along with Columbia and Pennsylvania moved into Ithaca, living in Cornell's Baker Hall, an imposing edifice to nobler deeds of man.

Ten Eyck was extremely fussy about meals for his men. He prepared the menus on the Cornell campus and personally supervised preparation of their food in the kitchens. His men ate prodigiously of chops, steaks and eggs; stale bread and toast; for beverage, they sipped very weak tea. Watching over them also was Charles Porter, a huge six-foot trainer.

Two days before the races, Ten Eyck warned as they walked down to the boathouse:

"No hurrying during the try-outs."

After they rowed 'for awhile on Lake Cayuga, he directed them to ease off, saying "Turn all and point for the lighthouse. Now—all row home easy-like."

The coach was justified in his warnings. His crews were all razor-sharp and too much training might possibly push them over the hairline of conditioning. He feared staleness, particularly in his varsity boat, and he jealously guarded against it.

While Ten Eyck restrained his men, Coach Joe Wright of Pennsylvania went to the other extremes. All that spring, the Red and Blue was unable to row a full two miles in practice due to construction of the Columbia Avenue bridge over the Schuylkill River. And the Quakers attempted to make up for lack of practice while at Ithaca in the days before the races.

As the two coaches worried about their oarsmen, three Syracuse men struggled with a more personal problem.

Overweight bothered the three coxswains. William "Scooter" Jordan of the varsity, F. H. Pease of the junior varsity, and Roland Marvin, of the freshman boat, were anxious—in fact ordered by Ten Eyck—to melt off the extra poundage by road work in and around Cornell. Daily, they were seen running up to nearby Glenwood, an Ithaca suburb, resting for awhile, and then trotting back. They tried to shed off poundage and compete on race day at or below 110 pounds.

Meanwhile, preparations for the first IRA regatta on Lake Cayuga went into high gear. Alongside the eastern shore, near the finish line, carpenters sawed and hammered together a roughboard grandstand to seat 8,000 people.

The dawn of regatta day was met by perfect weather, and before nine o'clock that morning, the first of approximately 50,000 persons began filing into the area. This was the 23rd IRA regatta and the first since 1916. Locale was changed but not the traffic jam, for lines of automobiles clogged up the highways as they did in the pre-war years at Poughkeepsie.

A strong breeze came down the lake from the north and remained throughout the day until 5 o'clock, when it ruffled the green water with whitecaps, bane of all intercollegiate crews.

Sixty minutes before the races, a special train with 1,000 noisy Syracusans puffed into view, discharging its passengers in front of the planked grandstands. The Salt City visitors brought with them added colors and excitement for the festive atmosphere; some wore orange caps; others sported orange sleeve bands; and a few donned straws with orange bands. Many waved flags, some carried pennants.

A Thomas Morse airplane droned over the course, dropping out a red rosette near the finish line. When the pilot climbed into the sky, the crowd lustily cheered him. Cornellians hoped it might prove to be an omen portending victory. Meanwhile, Pathé movie men swarmed along the shore grinding up huge amounts of celluloid in capturing the activities, the color and the excitement of the crowd.

The rosette proved lucky, for the Big Red handily captured both the junior varsity and freshman races.

Although the whitecaps floated over the green water during most of the day, Cayuga Lake by 7 o'clock was quiet as a mill pond, its surface merely dimpled by a soft wind.

A lake of confidence for Cornell surrounded the spectators, and Cornell students were unable to find anyone with whom to bet. At the same time, Ten Eyck quietly indicated a degree of confidence. But Syracuse supporters did not.

Ten Eyck's confidence was shared by the varsity oarsmen, when they brought out their shell from the boathouse and gently placed the sliver of a boat into the water. Then they slipped their oars into the oarlocks with maddening absorption. Of course, tension ran high, but so did their confidence.

As a good coxswain, Scoot Jordan attempted to break the silence, jabbering about nothing of importance—until one of his mates snapped at him, "Shut up, dammit!" Slowly, they fastened their shoestrings for the pull ahead.

When crews lined up out on the lake, Columbia was nearest shore; alongside her was Syracuse; Cornell was next, followed by Pennsylvania on the outside lane nearest the middle of Cayuga.

An hour after the lake stilled, twilight commenced to creep in and the crews awaited Referee Julian Curtiss' starting—"Go!"

Employing a high 40 stroke beat, Syracuse catapaulted into an early lead. Cornell was second away, using a much lower stroke. Columbia and Penn followed, prow to prow.

Ten Eyck was concerned about Rammi, his stroke. For most of the season Rammi was troubled by a seige of boils on his body, suffering great discomfort; but today, the stroke moved his oar with a deftness and an elan belying his physical condition.

Unable to continue its torrid beat, Syracuse eventually lost its slim lead to Cornell before reaching the one-quarter mile mark. And at the one-half post, Cornell spurted to draw up slack in its lead until it led by a full boat length.

Down the beautiful Finger Lake, the crews raced. And in the deepening shadows of twilight, they appeared like canoe armadas of Cayuga Indians in Hiawatha's time.

Cornell stroked 35.

Syracuse followed.

Columbia stroked 36.

Pennsylvania followed.

The Syracuse shell was running smoothly, the catches meshing in unison, their recoveries smooth and even. And the spacing of its oars set up a series of tantilizing whirlpools aft. Rammi gently, ever so gently, increased his beat by one, and the shell continued matching its puddles clearly.

Rammi's added stroke ignited Columbia and Pennsylvania into a frenzied effort to keep up, but their boats progressed forward in a series of jumps—clear indications of poor timing.

With their boat running satisfactorily, Ten Eyck's crew commenced to shave off Cornell's lead.

CHAPTER XIX

IRRESISTIBLY FORWARD, SYRACUSE

raced in 1920 at Ithaca (N.Y.), its chocolate-colored boat gliding over wide gaps of water. In order to catch up with Cornell, Rammi was forced to increase the beat to 38 strokes a minute, then slowly he reduced it down to a steady 36. His strategy worked, as time told.

The Syracuse shell came up to within one-quarter of a length of Cornell's bow. Pasted together, the two passed the mile mark.

Cornell went up to 36 and began to move.

Columbia increased its stroke and followed Syracuse.

Pennsylvania faltered, two lengths behind the Lions.

Rammi's abrupt increase and then reduction of stroke fooled Cornell. The Big Red coxswain fell into the trap. He called on his men for a greater lead. They responded and stroked, for them, a higher beat.

By now, all four competitors stroked the identical number of beats as they neared the one and one-half mile mark.

With pressure building up, Syracuse hurried to wrest the lead from Cornell, throwing in its supply of power into those long sweeps. The men from Piety Hill commenced to creep up on Cornell.

Ten Eyck's men rowed like demons, and in a flurry of motion, they stretched out for the rendezvous promised

151

THE 1920 VARSITY: Str. August W. Rammi, Kenneth Gallagher, Alvin H. Loskamp, George P. Busch, Howard C. Hoople, Wesley S. Grimshaw, Lowell S. Nicholson, Chamberlain A. Page, Cox, Robert W. Jordan.

152

them in the spring by their coach.

Oar by oar, Syracuse sped swiftly on its way, passing Cornell.

Frantically, Cornell punished itself severely in trying to snatch back the elusive lead from the men of Orange.

Syracuse increased the beat, continued to widen the gap.

Cornell gallantly tried to equal the other boat's efforts.

All of a sudden, the Big Red broke. The strain proved to be too much!

Rammi drew out the last reserve power in the boat; and one-eighth of a mile from the end, his shell took a full length and a half lead over Cornell.

Still rowing 38, Syracuse crossed the line, followed by Cornell. Columbia was third. Five lengths behind came Pennsylvania.

To Courtney, the defeat was a heartbreaker. It was disheartening for him to see victory slip away on home water in the final moment. It was also his last race.

Courtney died on July 17, after suffering a stroke of apoplexy at his summer cottage at Farley's Point on Cayuga Lake. Behind him, he left an imposing record: Of the 59 Cornell crews he sent to the IRA, 39 were triumphant.

Back at the Syracuse quarters following victory, bedlam reigned. J. Rinn Winter of the junior varsity boat motioned for quiet, stood up on a nearby table and read a poem on which the entire crew members collaborated in writing:

Sometimes it's a delicate task
To say what we want to say
About one we love and cherish
To whom homage we wish to pay.
When the thoughts that we hold are sacred
And the memories we hold are dear

And the time has come for parting
At the end of a happy year.
For months we have been to-gether
Enjoying the comrades we've made
We've rowed in all kinds of weather
And sometimes we've rowed upgrade.
It's been hard—but through all
It's been pleasant
And at last to Cornell we came
With the greatest of all coaches
The best there is in the game.
To you we extend with reverence
The greatest toast of all
May you be with our old Alma Mater
'Til the melinial shadows fall.

Yet, the victory on Cayuga wasn't in the truest sense the crew's final destiny at all. It stretched out into other places. For example: sentiment in Syracuse arose for an entry in the Olympic try-outs at Lake Quinsigamond at Worcester, Massachusetts. This was the Olympic year of 1920 and for the first time in its history, the Games included eight-oared competition at Antwerp, Belgium. Already entered at Worcester were the Navy, the New York Athletic Club, the Union Boat Club of New York; the Century Boat Club of St. Louis; the Riverside of Boston; West Lynn, Brookline High School, Boston Interscholastic and a crew from Springfield, Massachusetts.

Called upon for financial support, the Syracuse community responded generously, contributing within 48 hours a total of $4,565 with which to send Ten Eyck's squad to the Olympic trials.

The Old Man at a farewell dinner in Hotel Onondaga promised:

"I'm going to do the best I can to make this crew a winner. We hope to prove at Worcester that we are the best crew in the world!"

Many weeks of practice loomed ahead of the crew, and to prepare for competition, Ten Eyck transported his men to Duluth, Minnesota, where he usually coached that city's boat club during summer vacation. Interestingly enough, Duluth also planned to compete at Lake Quinsigamond.

At the Syracuse train station, the crew listened to the shouts and cheers of their partisans. Someone in a burst of bravado hollered out to Rammi:

"Give 'em hell, Gus!"

Above the roar of the departing train, Rammi replied: "You bet we will!"

Coach and Mrs. Ten Eyck along with Commodore Kenneth Buckley and Graduate Manager Walter Smith waved farewell from the observation platform.

Under rigid and spartan training, the men labored for the Olympic trials until "things began happening like fireworks popping off on the Fourth of July!" [14]

With the task of training two crews a heavy burden, Ten Eyck decided to coach only the University crew, his son, Jim, Junior, tutoring the Duluth men. Consequently, an intense rivalry between the two sprang up.

Whereas, the Syracusans were previously greeted with friendliness, now they became isolated like an oasis in a desert; citizens of Duluth gave them wide berth; and there were no friendly greetings, henceforth.

The Duluth newspaper fed fuel to the fire, when it loudly proclaimed that now "it would clearly be seen whether a boat club crew was better than a college crew."

More astonishing was the declaration by the newspaper that this was the time to see who was the better coach—son or father!

155

[14]Kenneth Gallagher, Howard Hoople, in letter dated 1961.

No one with Ten Eyck's personality—highly competitive it was—shunned such a challenge, and as a result a bitter feeling developed between father and his son in the days to follow.

Ten Eyck experimented with everything he knew in an effort to improve his University crew's rowing. For starts, he made his men hold the oar not flat on the water as customary but perpendicular to it, ready to pull through—the theory being that a fraction of time might be saved.

The experiment failed, unfortunately, for the boat lost its balance, particularly in rough water.

About this time, Rammi was plagued once more with a case of boils. Someone, in compassion, told Ten Eyck that yeast might do the trick and dry up Rammi's source of irritation.

Ten Eyck dispatched Commodore Buckley to Duluth in search of the lifesaving yeast. When cakes were obtained and handed him, he directed Rammi to swallow one.

"There—that'll fix you up. Eat them!" he ordered.

Rammi nibbled at one, a frown creasing his sun-tanned countenance. In exasperation, Rammi said:

"Gosh, coach—I just can't eat it!"

"Gimme that cake," Ten Eyck angrily commanded, and sticking the cake into his mouth, he mumbled, "There —if I can do it, you can—"

The Old Man left his sentence unfinished. Jumping up, he dashed for the side of the boathouse, his mouth spewing out streams of shaving lather-like foam.

"This is the damnedest thing I ever tasted!" he finally managed to gasp, foam still covering his lips. "What the h - - - did you buy, Buckley?"

"Yeast foam, coach," was Buckley's reply.

"Yeast foam?" sputtered Ten Eyck. "Not yeast foam! Soft yeast cakes!"

Needless to say, that remedy was never tried again.

The rivalry between the hometown crew and that of the visiting collegians became so intense that a Saturday was set aside for a race between them, with proceeds going to help finance both crews for the Olympic trials.

The crews practiced while the father and son refrained from speaking to each other. They were separated by chasms of fierce pride and stubbornness.

On race day, some 15,000 citizens of Duluth were hardly able to conceal their impatience for the titanic struggle as they watched a program of water sports.

When the Syracuse crew lowered its shell into the water, the Old Man walked up and down the dock, carrying a container filled with rosin. This, he shook on the seats and rubbed on the trunk seats of his men.

"Trying to pull a something smart, aren't you?" bellowed young Jim behind his father.

The Old Man turned around, glared at his son, turned his back on him and walked off, stonily silent.

Apparently, young Jim allowed anxiety and tension to get the better of him and he blurted out his first thoughts as he watched his father using the rosin.

After this dramatic moment, a strong breeze came up and sent waves cascading into both shells. The race was postponed.

Ten Eyck after the announcement called his crew together.

"I'm going to ask you fellows something that I've never asked of a crew before," he said. "The race will be rowed Monday noon. In order to be right, we've got to row on Sunday."

The oarsmen saw the logic behind the request and willingly practiced on Sunday.

Duluth took a commanding lead at the offset of the race on Monday, but the Syracusans caught up to them later and pulled out in front by a half length. At the three-quarter flag, the Duluth Club made its bid, and in turn, Rammi raised the Orange beat.

Power flowed through the Syracuse boat, and at the mile post, Syracuse led by open water.

—Cr-a-ck!—Cr-u-n-ch!—

As quickly as you read the sounds above, the shell of Syracuse settled. The men stayed afloat with great difficulty, but long enough for their boat to cross the line ahead of Duluth!

The sudden accident in the boat was caused by the snapping of two oars on the starboard side. Gallagher at No. 7 and Grimshaw at No. 3 position only were able to move their damaged oars back and forth, matching in close rhythm the swing of the rest of the crew.

To Duluth rooters, however, the Syracuse finish was spectacular. Many refused to believe that the two oars broke. In fierce pride, they countered that Duluth was surely to win over Syracuse at the Olympic trials!

Ten Eyck missed all the excitement and the anxiety. That particular race was the only one he ever deliberately missed in his coaching career. What with difficulties with his son, Ten Eyck sat with his wife in the boathouse, wonder-

SYRACUSE VS. DULUTH, 1920 PRE-OLYMPIC TRIAL CONTEST
Note: Two starboard oars missing in Syracuse boat.

159

ing all the time about the cheers and jeers. When the oarsmen returned to the dock, he rushed out and shook their
hands, saying:

"Thanks—thanks a lot. I knew you could do it!"

The Olympic trials were a different story, however.

Just before the race, Rammi was declared ineligible
because he wasn't a citizen of the United States, and he sat
out the race.

Ten Eyck revamped his boat, placing Alvin Loskamp,
regular No. 6 oar, at Rammi's stroke position, and shifting
Harwood "Tiny" Clash from the freshman boat to No. 6
oar.

However, the loss of Rammi and the necessary shift in
personnel that followed was a change extremely difficult to
adjust to; and the Syracuse boat finished second, close to
Navy. Duluth was out of the running.

Navy later that year in the Olympics began a series of
United States eight-oared rowing victories that continued
unbroken through the years.

The varsity crew of Syracuse elected Rammi captain
for 1921, the forthcoming year that the University's first
master builder, Dr. Day, retired as Chancellor.

CHAPTER XX

THE BIG MAN

walked wearily into his office and slumped down at the desk with an audible sigh. A gray-tinted calendar tacked to the wall behind him showed *January 5, 1921,* blending in with the dark-stained woodwork and the general gloom of the room.

Chancellor Day was discouraged and with reason. Although growth in buildings and students was phenomenal, the University was saddled with debt and running financially behind in its daily operation. That morning his glance swept over the top of his desk and fell on a freshly-inked copy of the *Daily Orange* in front of him.

His eyes quickly surveyed the contents of the front page and then became riveted to lines of type indentions in a corner. As he read them, he caught his breath and his face flooded red. With an explosive snort, he lurched to his feet, all signs of weariness now forgotten. In apparent agitation he strode around the desk, hesitated, and then resumed his seat. Reaching for a pen and paper, he hurriedly began to write.

"I saw in your issue yesterday," he penned the student newspaper, "a statement that football practice was to begin this winter and continue through the spring and summer. I hope this is not true. It certainly will not have the approval of the administration of the University and I am equally sure it will not be approved by the faculties. . . . The purposes of the University still remain educational and with increasing emphasis. None too much time is left the student body to apply to the classroom and laboratories.

"No one has been more interested in providing for the physical training of our students and for our athletic sports than I have been. . . . But I am troubled by what seems to me to be a tendency upon the part of some among us connected with athletics to run wild with athletics. . . . Coach [John] Meehan should drop all thought of football practice until the time comes for his inning."

The impact of the Chancellor's thoughts on year-round football proved to be as loud as when a shoe drops to the floor overhead. Everyone listened for the other to fall.

Meehan ended the suspense immediately, when he cancelled his novel plan for football.

Four months later, a young man with a head of unruly hair stood before students in the Hall of Languages, discussing poetry. Eyes twinkling with enthusiasm, Robert Frost spoke on the topic,, "New Poetry and How Not to Miss It."

While Frost spoke on that day late in April, members of the board of governors of the Athletic Association discussed a question of importance. They wondered *whether the University should join the Intercollegiate Rowing Association!*

One member reported that Dr. Day favored membership, but another questioned whether the move was justified in light of the crew's shaky financial foundation. Perhaps crew was to be abolished shortly, he argued.

They sat there debating the question, one eye always nervously cast upon the Chancellor's office.

It was time for decision.

The position of the University's crews in the IRA as an invited guest was becoming one of profound embarrassment. Several times, Syracuse was invited to join the Association. Nevertheless, non-membership was really nothing to be ashamed of, for many others continued to row only at invitation. But Syracuse was no longer a small institution of learning. It was growing. And besides, Ten Eyck's impressive record in IRA competition since 1904 was another strong point in favor of membership.

The board voted to join.

With Columbia, Cornell and Pennsylvania, Syracuse comprised the Intercollegiate Rowing Association. Later in this same year, Navy joined. Today, the five still remain official IRA members. Others row only at invitation.

A week and three days after the poet's visit, Syracuse sent Samuel Cook, to his first IRA meeting. He was elected to the Association's governing body, the Board of Stewards.

The IRA moved back its regatta from Cayuga Lake to the Hudson in 1921, when the railroad returned its observation train to the river for the first time since the war. The length of the course was lengthened to its customary three miles. Ten Eyck, who still favored the four-mile course, objected in heated tones. His argument was aired in an article appearing in the *Yale Daily News*. He claimed a four-mile course wasn't injurious to an oarsmen's heart.

> It is the pace and not the length of the race which is the important factor. . . . It is the ability of the oarsman to rate himself, to adapt his pace and his endurance to the

distance to be covered which marks the essential quality
of oarsmanship.

This season, assisted by Tot Hoople in preparing his
crews, Ten Eyck faced major problems. While the University basked in the warmth of IRA membership, the stewards
declared Ten Eyck's freshman stroke ineligible. C. H.
Muser's intercollegiate sin was his registration at Michigan
University before transferring to Syracuse.

Besides this, two others in the freshman boat for various
reasons were disqualified. As if these setbacks weren't
enough, injuries sapped the power posture of Ten Eyck's
varsity boat.

Harlan Holcomb, No. 4 oar, was hampered by an
infected finger, and John Winter, No. 5 oar, was bothered
by a blister on his feathering hand.

Bernard Dawson, No. 7 oar in the jayvee boat, was
moved into Winter's seat, and a thick-set youth with a shock
of corn-ripe hair, who answered to the name of "Pappy"
(Lynn) Waldorf, was moved from his freshman position to
fill Dawson's vacant spot.

Waldorf later became football coach at Northwestern
and California. His transfer in 1921 from the freshman boat
left behind in that boat a substitute coxswain by name of
Roscoe Drummond, years afterwards a syndicated news
columnist of the *New York Herald Tribune*.

Seeking to obtain additional power in his varsity shell,
Ten Eyck traded strokes—Captain Rammi of the varsity for
Alvin Loskamp of the jayvees.

During those days prior to the races, he juggled his
remaining 16 men back and forth in the boats in an agoniz-
ing effort to find by some miracle the most powerful combinations.

Down at Poughkeepsie that year, two new faces appeared. One belonged to the University of California which came out East for the first time; the other was that of a huge timeboard on the bridge showing the time of the crews as they rowed beneath the spidery span.

Navy was the darkhorse of the varsity race, and its appearance in 1921 on the Hudson was the first since 1907. The Midshipmen eight, same boatload which won the Olympic race at Brussels the year before, blacked out the aspirations of the other college competitors as it sped down the course in 14 minutes and seven seconds. Following in order were California, Cornell, Penn, Syracuse and Columbia.

"It was the most perfect machine I've seen on the water," Ten Eyck commented with respect, "and during the past 50 years, I've seen a lot of boat racing."

Describing Navy as the greatest combination ever racing, Ten Eyck added:

"The Navy could easily with her five lengths lead have rowed another mile. . . . In fact, Navy could have rowed to New York City!"

The Old Man admitted his own crews accomplished all that he expected them to do.

"I have only praise for the plucky lads, who rowed for the Orange this season. We had a lot of troubles of our own.

"I'm not claiming any alibis, but I'm certainly amused by the comments of the self-styled critics of rowing, who remind me of the person described in the father's reply to his young son's inquiry as to the meaning of the word 'critic':

" 'A critic, my boy, is a fellow who can't do it himself!' "

An enthusiastic crowd of 76,000 spectators witnessed the IRA's return to the Hudson that year. Rowing the varsity race was Columbia's captain, Paul Gallico, who later become sports editor of the *New York News* and subsequently a famous novelist.

In this, its first year since Courtney's death, Cornell was handled by John Hoyle, a boatbuilder Syracusans fondly remembered. On the evening of a Poughkeepsie race many years ago, Hoyle kindly repaired a Syracuse shell that later went on to defeat Cornell.

The jayvee boat of Syracuse finished third in its race on the Hudson, and its freshmen were second to the strong Navy plebes.

But more electrifying was news back on campus a few days before the races. Sick and discouraged, Chancellor Day submitted his resignation to the board of trustees. They immediately accepted it, and with a gesture of appreciation for his service, voted him Chancellor-emeritus with his annual salary of $7,500 for the remaining years of his retirement.

Thus, Dr. Day, the first master architect of the University, left the portals of the University and the people he so dearly loved. After twenty-seven years of dedication, his name and his influence were imprinted on brick and mortar and in the minds of men.

Upon arrival in 1894, he found three colleges. He left ten. When he arrived, the student body consisted of 751 students. Now there were 5,065. He found three usable buildings and three makeshifts. He left 20.

Emerson wrote:

An institution is the lengthened shadow of one man.

And it was almost a quarter of a century later before

another—William Pearson Tolley—became the University's second architect; and it was he, who with Dr. Day, shared the image of Emerson's quotation.

Others came and went through the passing years, leaving their ideals and characters on the portals of time, but these two men shaped the Methodist-founded University, leading it to greatness and eventually to excellence.

Nineteen twenty-one was the year, when American women threw off all restraints of the past, bobbed their hair, shortened their dresses above the knees and gushed over screen idols Rudolph Valentino and Douglas Fairbanks, Senior. It was the year when Gordon Hoople, former Syracuse oarsman and now a new physician, with several others, departed for missionary duty in China.

168

1922 FRESHMAN EIGHT: Str. George Engren, Edw. Donohue, E. J. Braun, J. E. Phifer, H. B. Mac Innis. Brayton Redway, Ray H. Rogers, James Gilday, Cox, Sidney Mang.

CHAPTER XXI

NAVY WON ITS

second consecutive victory on the Hudson in 1922, when it was forced by strong Washington and Syracuse crews to shatter the time record in the three-mile varsity race. Hard-pressed by them, the Midshipmen shaved off more than half a minute to win.

Part of the exciting drama in the race occurred in the latter stages of the event, when Syracuse and its arch rival, Cornell, dueled furiously for third spot behind the Huskies. It was a duel short of sensational before Ten Eyck's oarsmen pulled out ahead by a scant four feet. It proved to be the first time in 25 IRA regattas that the Big Red finished out of the first three.

Midshipman Edward Frawley of Fulton (N.Y.) stroked that Navy powerhouse. A few years afterwards, his death, while instructing student pilots for the Navy, was responsible for bringing the Naval Academy and Syracuse University closer together.

His brother, Joseph, became an oarsman at Syracuse and in his senior year was captain of crew. During those years of varsity rowing and when visiting Annapolis, he and Ten Eyck were invited guests of the Academy at each retreat parade.

Joe's crewmate, John Laidlaw, remarked:

"I think it was a very touching scene, and one that

proved there could be a sincere and lasting feeling between our two institutions."

Navy's superiority on the Hudson despite its antipathy towards the longer courses was interesting.

Before the 1921 and 1922 races, the Naval Academy brass refused to allow its men to race more than two miles on a course, in the belief that the longer distance was harmful to its oarsmen. Yet, in these two successive years, the Midshipmen were triumphant over the best crews in the nation on the Hudson in three-mile races.

The junior varsity race at Poughkeepsie that year was a two-mile affair, sparked by Hairbreath Harry sprints of Syracuse and Columbia while they tried unsuccessfully to catch Cornell. The boatbuilder's men finished two lengths ahead of the Lions, with Syracuse another half length behind Columbia.

Ten Eyck correctly predicted Navy's victory as well as Cornell's in the jayvee race; but he wasn't prepared for a surprise handed him by his freshmen.

In the last mile, his prediction about the freshmen was shattered.

Stroked magnificently by George Engren and steered by babyfaced Sidney Mang, Syracuse surged forward and pulled even with Cornell, Columbia and Penn. Before this effort, the Syracuse boat appeared to be lashed securely to last place; but at the mile and a half position, it came vibrantly alive.

Stroking harder and faster than at anytime during the race, Syracuse crept up and passed Columbia and began nipping at the heels of leading Cornell.

Nip and tuck—nip and tuck, the two boats worked for the lead. With a sudden burst of speed, the underdog Orange freshmen shot ahead and opened up the distance between their boat and the Big Red's. They won!

Of course, Engren was supremely happy.

"There is probably no happier individual in Poughkeepsie than I am as result of our smashing victory in the freshman race—the first victory scored by a Syracuse freshman boat since 1915 when Charley Whiteside stroked his crew home in front. Not one of the critics nor Ten Eyck thought we would win; but I believed before we started that two-mile race that we were going to be out in front, and I told Coxswain Mang so!"

The stroke revealed that he was still confident when his boat was in last place near the Syracuse boathouse "about three-fourths of a mile from the start of the race."

171

Ten Eyck's statement of strategy to the freshmen for that race was simple: Watch the Cornell boat and move accordingly! When Cornell moved, Syracuse moved.

That fall, the Syracuse campus was visited by General of the Armies John "Blackjack" Pershing. And before the snows fell, new cement sidewalks were laid on campus; and electric lights were hooked up in front of each University building.

Thirty-nine years later, Mang vividly recalled amusing anecdotes of crew life under Ten Eyck:

It was a firm tradition that the freshman crew never docked until after the varsity crews because the frosh were never expected to exhaust the meager supply of warm water in the inadequate and primitive shower system. Late one afternoon, Ten Eyck sent his freshman crew down the inlet ahead of his proud varsity. The yearlings promptly docked and quickly showered. This caused the varsity men to toss Mang, the ringleader, into the cold water, but he became a hero to his crew. Ten Eyck chuckled over this boldness. The next day, Mang became the freshman coxswain.

As a freshman, Mang one day served as coxswain in one of the varsity boats. Lining up for a racing start, his boat was nearest the shore. A strong wind blew. Ten Eyck took longer than usual in giving instructions from his launch, and when he looked up, he saw Mang's shell near the shore, the starboard oars resting in the weeds along the bank. Quickly picking up his battered megaphone, Ten Eyck yelled: "Hey, Moses, come out of the bull rushes!"

On one occasion, the Old Man indulged in a bit of home-style philosophy. He claimed, as a coach, that he felt something like a rock in a stream—waves of college boys coming down the current, lingering for a short span of four years, and then flowing out into life's stream. He claimed the boys, who were trained to row a good four-mile race, were better prepared to row the race of life.

On May fifth, 1923, in the first intercollegiate race on Onondaga Lake since 1910, Syracuse defeated MIT by two lengths in front of 4,000 spectators. Sixteen days later, the crews journeyed to Annapolis where only the junior varsity boat was victorious.

At Poughkeepsie, Washington captured the first West Coast victory in a varsity race. Navy, under Old Dick Glendon's son, was a close second in that 1923 race, followed in order by Columbia, Syracuse, Cornell and Pennsylvania.

For Syracuse, unquestionably, it was the junior varsity race that caused the hair to curl and the chest to expand with pride. The boat was crowded with big raw-boned men, stroked by Casper Baltensperger.

Hubert Stratton, an attorney in time to come, was so nervous when his shell pulled up to the starting line that he "almost cried out from the tension." Although confident over his boat's chances, he felt more excited about this race

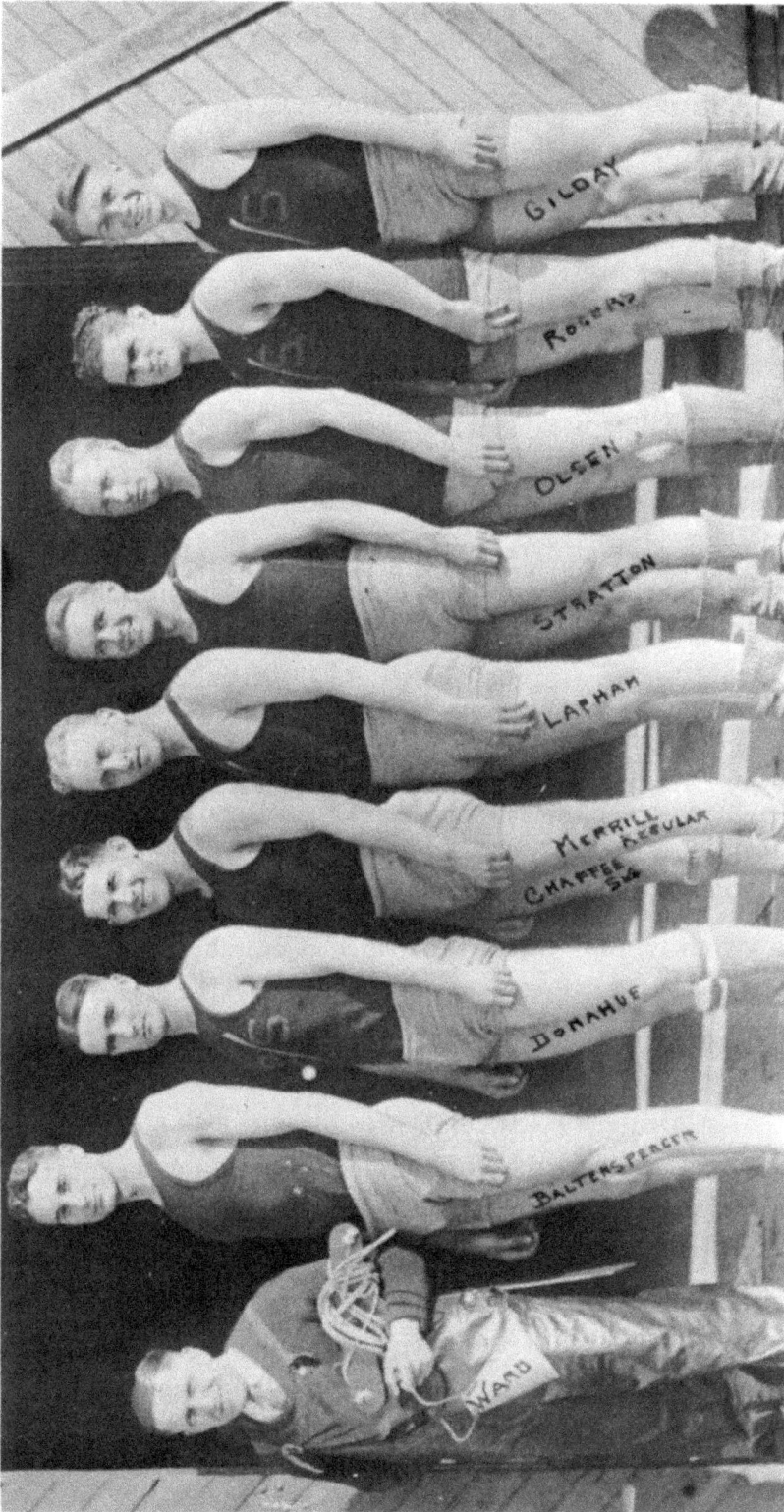

INTERCOLLEGIATE CHAMPIONSHIP J-V, 1923: Cox Thomas Ward, Str. Casper Baltensperger, Edward Donohue, Frank Chaffee (M. Chester Merrill), William Lapham, Hubert Stratton, Olaf Olsen, Raymond Rogers, James Gilday.

than in the early season race at Navy. However, at first stroke of the race, butterflies in his stomach disappeared.

Cornell drew in the inside lane, while Pennsylvania, Syracuse and Columbia filled the others. Immediately, Cornell grabbed the lead, but before stroking another ten, Syracuse took over.

At the time Baltensperger's shell disappeared behind the ferry landing, it was two-thirds of a length ahead of Columbia and rowing strongly. Cornell's stroke, Fillius, raised the beat, and his men moved the boat up to Syracuse's stern.

The slender Syracuse boat continued to fly down the river, matching its puddles and stroking in unison, the sweep of its oars in a cohesive unit of dynamic action. It led by a full length over the Lions and Cornell at the mile.

Cornell made its bid here.

Down the course they went, battling for the lead. Blade for blade—sweep for sweep, the exerting men rowed, their shells slicing the Hudson as knives sweep through butter. Tighter—tighter drew up the boats.

Slowly, the Syracuse boat inched out ahead until succeeding sweeps of its oars opened up a gap between the crafts. Ten Eyck's men flashed across the finish by a length in front.

In giving the Old Man his only victory on the river that year, the jayvee boat crumpled up four and one-fourth seconds off the course record.

Vice President Calvin Coolidge was sworn in on August 3, after President Harding died in San Francisco. And a comic-looking man with a comb-end moustache by name of Adolph Hitler was arrested after an abortive putsch in a Munich beer hall.

CHAPTER XXII

I LOVE SOMETIMES,

even now, to get into the midstream and feel the rip of the
racing tide, the rush, the swing of it. But even in those
moments of exhilaration, I'm possessed of a sense of
melancholy for the good old days that are gone. The tug-
boat, and the barges, the railways, municipal ferry and
gasoline have banished the oars and the sail. Gallant days
gone by—strenuous, wild sometimes, and even wicked, but
gallant always.

Ten Eyck wrote these lines in 1924 for the popular
magazine of the day, *The Outlook*. He sensed something
more than the passing of the "good old days." He realized,
unmistakably, that he was the last of the old professional
scullers teaching the rowing art to eager men in colleges.
In fact, he represented the last of the virgin timber of old-
time coaches, for a second crop by this time was springing
up in collegiate rowing circles.

After inking another five-year contract, Ten Eyck
early in the season was bedeviled for a time by three of his
freshman squad. All were candidates for the coxswain position: Al Travis, Edgar Shepherd and James Fredericks, who
were on equal footing after startling episodes!

Excited at starting his first practice race, Travis
smashed his shell into a buoy, breaking two oars and damag-
ing the rigging.

Misjudging distance on a windy day, Shepherd crashed
his boat into the docking wharf, necessitating expert and
extensive repairs to his shell.

In apparent self-defense, Ten Eyck dry-landed both Travis and Shepherd. Meanwhile, he figured Fredericks, his last candidate for coxswain, was the choice. Unfortunately, the third candidate, while bravely steering up the heaving Seneca River in a practice run, joined the not so exclusive circle by ramming his craft into a buoy.

Ten Eyck summoned the three.

With nerves twittering like sparrows on a telephone wire, the three steeled themselves for Ten Eyck's wrath.

Commanding them to line up, side by side, the Old Man, in turn, scowled at each.

"Shake hands, all three of you," he abruptly demanded.

"You're all in the same class, now. But for heaven sake. do better next time, or the whole d - - - Navy will be wiped out!"

If Ten Eyck feared losing his fleet, he also was aware of something else that was fading away—the art of oar making.

Obtaining oars became so acute a problem for colleges that Washington, for example, purchased oars in England. Due to scarcity of masters on this side of the Atlantic, the oars obtained by the Huskies actually made two ocean voyages, one over as raw spruce from America; the return as finished blades.

Craftsmanship in Syracuse, however, soon reduced many of those ocean trips.

Unknown to many, Bill Rose, the University crew rigger, remained one of the few masters. He worked industriously fashioning oars in a dimly lighted room over a livery stable.

Soft-spoken, Rose was just as mild in manner while shaping oars by hand with nothing more than a handplane, transforming a clumsy spruce board, with what the *Post-Standard* called, "touches as deft as those of a sculptor into a graceful 12-foot oar."

Rose supplied oars for Harvard, Penn and Syracuse crews. In 1923 when at Poughkeepsie, he asked Rusty Callow, the Husky coach, why he ordered oars from England.

"That's the only place I can buy them," said Rusty.

"No, it isn't."

"Where else?" the coach demanded.

"From me."

"From you?"

"Yes. I make them!"

"You do? Good heavens, man. Why didn't you tell me?"

"Well," replied Rose, "I just took it for granted that everyone knew I made them."

"I should say not, Bill. I've often looked at the Old Man's, but I never realized you made them. You'll get an order from me in the fall."

This year of 1924, Rose encountered problems. Where before he needed orders to keep his small business operating, he now faced a severe shortage of spruce. The good grain from the Adirondacks was becoming difficult to find, and the problem continued in the years ahead. Eventually, spruce for oars came from Alaska.

As the season progressed, the nation's sportswriters with an eye to Poughkeepsie turned their indentions of coined phrases on paper to the West, praising the Goliath of Washington. One such story came from the fertile brain of Damon Runyon:

They breed tall young men out yonder in the state of Washington. Tall men and strong—and they raise 'em to water, as is quite fitting these days. They teach 'em how to ride in narrow, spidery boats and to pull these boats through the water by the strength of their arms a little faster than the young men of the other states. Six feet, two inches is the average heights of eight young men from the land of tall men who yanked a thin-waisted boat down the Hudson River.[15]

Walter Camp, founder of football's All-America selections, surprised the rowing world by trumpeting the cause for shifting the IRA regatta from the river to the lake, and arguing that "the flat dead water of a lake is the only place where comparative records can be relied upon, but there is much more satisfaction in rowing with the current." [16]

Diminishing crowds at Poughkeepsie were of major concern in 1924, with less than 50,000 witnessing the IRA regatta.

Washington's Huskies swept the varsity race into their pockets. Harrison "Stork" Sanford rowed at No. 3 position in the Callow-coached boat. At a future date, he was coach at Cornell and brought the Big Red back to the heights established by Courtney.

Syracuse finished fifth in the big race. Navy didn't appear at Poughkeepsie because it competed in the Olympic trials later in the summer.

Nineteen twenty-four was a season, when Richard Aronson was coxswain of the Cornell jayvee crew. He became a judge in Syracuse later. It was also the year Lenin died in Russia. Nellie Taylor Ross, widow of the Wyoming governor, was elected to fill her husband's office. She was the first woman in America's history so honored.

---

[15]*The New York American,* New York, N.Y., June 17, 1924.
[16]The *Duluth Herald,* Duluth, Minn., August 13, 1924

Meanwhile, back on campus, the Y.M.C.A. cabinet elected apple-cheeked Eric Faigle as president. He became dean of the Liberal Arts College and vice president of his Alma Mater in later years.

Shortly before Faigle's election, the University's first campaign to raise money ($1 million) closed successfully. Once more on sound-footing, Syracuse peered into the future with confidence and with enthusiasm.

The IRA stewards early in January, 1925, lengthened the Hudson course to four miles. Maxwell Stevenson spearheaded the move. Former No. 6 oar with Columbia's 1901 boat, Stevenson was now the new IRA chairman.

A new face was introduced to college rowing this year, but on the other hand, old faces popped up in new places.

At Cornell, Dr. Charles Lueder succeeded John Hoyle as coach, while at Pennsylvania, James Rice, former Columbia mentor from 1907 to 1924, became Joseph Wright's successor.

Wright resigned a month before the Poughkeepsie races in 1924. Unofficially, he left due to internal troubles, caused by someone's insistence that he restore men to the varsity boat, oarsmen of Penn, whom he unseated during the course of preparation for the 1924 regatta.

Therefore, the veteran coach said that if he was deprived of the responsibility of choosing the men for his boats, he considered himself through. Pennsylvania officials understood this as an ultimatum and accepted his resignation.

Earlier in 1925, Pennsylvania was reported offering the position to Rusty Callow of Washington, but the popular and successful coach turned down the offer because his contract ran two more years on the West Coast.

During the winter and early spring, hot-stove experts of rowing pondered over statistics of the IRA regattas: Since its first year of 1895, the varsity championship was decided at four miles a total of 19 times, and four times at three miles. Average time of the four-mile winners was 19 minutes, forty-four seconds. Three-mile average was 14 minutes, eleven seconds.

Cornell established the four-mile record in 1901 at 18 minutes, 53 and one-fifth seconds. The Big Red also rowed the slowest time of 20 minutes and 42 seconds in 1910. Navy's great crew of 1922 rowed to a three-mile record of 13 minutes, 33 and three-fifth seconds. In 1924, Washington traversed the three-mile course in the slowest time of 15 minutes, two seconds.

Since the beginning of the IRA regatta, Cornell was victorious 13 out of 27 varsity races; Syracuse, five; Penn, three; Navy, Columbia and Washington, twice.

Ten Eyck that spring of 1925 re-built his boats. With Stratton lost due to physical reasons, the squad contained only two veterans of the victorious 1924 junior varsity boat. Working usually with the greenest material, Ten Eyck stamped out crews against almost unsurmountable odds.

The jayvee boat stroked by Gerald Davis proved conclusively that his patience and his teaching were not in vain. It defeated Columbia and MIT by 200 feet on May 16 on the Harlem River in New York.

Later that month, the jayvee boat defeated Pennsylvania, Harvard, Navy and Princeton at the American Henley race in Philly.

THE ENTIRE 1925 SQUAD AT THE LONG BRANCH BOATHOUSE.

181

At Poughkeepsie, Navy upheld the prestige of the eastern colleges by handing Callow his first varsity defeat on the Hudson in three years. Stroking the Huskies was Alvin Ulbrickson, later a coach at his Alma Mater.

Syracuse finished sixth in the varsity event, but its junior shell came in fourth behind Washington, Cornell, and Pennsylvania. Columbia was last.

It was the freshmen of Syracuse, however, who impressed the crowd. They swept past Pennsylvania, Columbia, Cornell and Wisconsin in a photo finish for victory.

With this Poughkeepsie showing, great things were expected of oarsmen from the freshman boat in the next year, but rowing at Syracuse became threatened with extinction.

CHAPTER XXIII

A NEW CHRYSLER

touring car cost $1,075, and tuition at the University was
$250 a year in 1926. Against the backdrop of these prices,
rowing required $25,000 annually, an expense the Athletic
Governing Board continued to find unbearable, particularly since the sport was not self-supporting.

As in the past when the sport was threatened, alumni
strongly protested, and on June 11, at traditional class re-
unions, friends of rowing studied the problems.

They were told by a representative of the Board that
financial support for crew came largely from gate receipts
of football. Rowing, said he, was to be given proper facilities, financial support, and an injection of enthusiasm, not
necessarily in that order, or crew was to be abolished on
Piety Hill.

Support for rowing came from William Young Boyd,
former track star, who came back from Panama for his 25th
class reunion. He stressed its importance in the educational
picture and in the preparation of young men for future life.

Stimulated by Boyd's understanding, the rowing
alumni appointed a committee headed by Tip Goes, consisting of J. P. Stimson, Dr. G. M. Price, Douglas Van Duser,
and Student Commodore Wesley Planck and Crew Captain
Raymond Gordon. They were requested to prepare a report, either recommending that crew be abolished or sug-

gesting new ways to give it new life.

After a two-day study, the packed committee, of course, urged that rowing be continued, suggesting several ways of obtaining financial support.

Besides the report of the committee, Goes sparked their enthusiasm further with plans for an adequate boathouse for Ten Eyck and his young men. Cost of the structure was figured at $40,000.

A helping hand was given by alumni that year in an effort to revive rowing interest on campus. Part of this enthusiasm was directed toward one of the most unusual reunion scenes that May ever seen at Ten Eyck's headquarters. The Kum Bak crew pictured on the opposite page celebrated the return of several prominent ex-crewmen at the time of the annual class day races.

Beset by financial problems, student apathy and a shortage of oarsmen, supporters of the sport satisfied themselves with what little solace they found in the stature and wizardry of the coach.

There was no doubt but what the Old Man himself was the cohesive force that kept rowing alive in the days of gloom. And one of his cherished techniques was to draw out more than a man's natural ability by using shrewd psychology:

"Well, Jim," he might say, "you've seen this other bow oarsman. You're as big as he is; you can stay as long and pull as hard, can't you?"

"You bet I can, coach," was the usual reply.

On the water that May, Ten Eyck employed shrewdness and pulled off a typical Houdini at Annapolis, when

THE 1926 "KUM BAK CREW"
Leon Ellis, Hubert Stratton, Ken Gallagher, Howard Hoople, Ross Hoople, Gordon
Hoople, Robert Hoople, Harry Rainbow, Philip Gorman.

he changed his heavier and more powerful jayvee crew for the varsity crew.

The transformed jayvee crew handily defeated Navy in the varsity race, but the varsity crew rowing as the jayvee boat failed to keep its part of the bargain and lost to the Midshipmen over the mile and three-quarters course on the Severn River.

At Poughkeepsie, it was a far different story, nevertheless.

For a fleeting moment, Washington's crew was as close to defeat by Navy as the pulse of a single heartbeat, the Huskies finally slipping over the line a scant fifteen feet ahead of the pressing Midshipmen in the varsity event. Syracuse was third.

And in the junior race, Callow's men caught up to the Quakers of Pennsylvania in the first half mile and held onto a substantial lead until the finish. Behind Pennsylvania in order were California, Syracuse, Cornell and Columbia.

The monotony of Washington's victories was shattered in the freshman race when Columbia, coached by Navy Dick Glendon's son, swept over the line ahead of California and Syracuse, Pennsylvania and Cornell. Thus, for the first time in 29 IRA regattas, a Cornell boat finished in last place.

During 1927, the Orange frosh crew was much stronger than the varsity boat, and a string of yearling victories over the varsity in practice created morale problems. The frosh were cocky; the varsity men were depressed.

The extent of the tribulations was vividly remembered by Clayton Frink, stroke oar, in a letter, April fourteenth, 1961:

> I was taken to Annapolis for the Navy race on May 21 as a port substitute. On the Friday morning before the

boat and asked me to stroke the crew. We beat the frosh in a race in practice for the first time. The Coach put me in again as stroke in the afternoon, and again, we beat the frosh—badly this time. That night, the Old Man asked the varsity crew members, with O'Connor and me absent, to vote on who would stroke them against the Navy the following day. They voted for Okie (O'Connor), which was natural since he had trained with them all season. The Navy won by about seven lengths and the Coach gave me a permanent assignment as stroke of the varsity crew. We went to Philadelphia and practiced for the race on the Schuylkill. In that race, there were no stakeboats. Each boat had to work up to the starting line and wait for the gun. "Skin" Tolley said, "Touch it up, bow and two," and while their oars were in the water, the gun went off! I stuck in the first stroke and was up against a brick wall! None of us had sense enough to call for a new start, so I finally got them swinging. We lost two seconds at the start and finished two seconds behind the winner.

Frink related how he assumed Ten Eyck was to take him out of the varsity boat, but the Old Man talked with him, explaining he understood how the misfortune occurred.

"He even wrote me a letter asking me to flunk a course and come back and row another year. My senior year was only my third year of rowing. This did my heart good, coming from him, even though I couldn't do it."

Poughkeepsie, 1927, the river current maneuvered the boats.

The varsity crew practiced false starts over and over again while awaiting the regatta. They jumped slides, broke shoelaces and prepared for all eventualities and mishaps until the men were letter perfect.

The whole boat yelled for a new start after two strokes. The oarsmen weren't going to suffer another "Philadelphia" start.

SYRACUSE CREW HEADQUARTERS WERE MOVED TO THE HILL-AIR HOUSE
IN HIGHLAND

TRANSPORTATION TO AND FROM THE BOATHOUSE

THE BOATHOUSE ALONG THE TRACKS

And in the big race, Syracuse called for a new start after receiving a poor one. Finally, the crew was away on a good start and rowed superbly.

In lane one, the men experienced the customary vagary offered to the occupant of that lane on the Hudson. The tide started its irresistible pull near shore, where Syracuse rowed, and at the same time, the water swirled out like the rush of a mad bull in lane eight occupied by Columbia.

Restrained by the tide, the crew still managed in some unexplainable way to keep near Cornell. Their boats were so close together that when the Syracuse oars were in the river during the last half mile, the bow was ahead of Cornell by two feet; but when the red-tipped oars of Cornell dipped the water, its boat was ahead by two feet.

See-saw, see-saw went the lead—back and forth down to the finish line.

Cornell won fifth place by twelve inches!

This proved to be the IRA varsity race in which Columbia's rampaging Lions resurged back to national glory for the first time since 1914. They beat out both West Coast crews as well as Navy; and behind Syracuse in last place came Pennsylvania.

For Syracuse, the freshman crew caused all the excitement. It led for one and one-half miles of the two-mile race, but Navy commenced sprinting and won by one and a quarter length. After Syracuse came Columbia, Cornell, Penn, California and Wisconsin.

For the first time in history of rowing at Syracuse, a frosh crew returned the next year of 1928 virtually intact for its sophomore year. Then, before Ten Eyck counted his blessings, ineligibility tapped several men on the shoulder and broke up the spunky frosh-crew and the rest of his squad.

With just enough men remaining to boat three crews, Ten Eyck took them to a meet at Cornell. They were defeated; and on May 19 in East Chester Bay in New York, a meet with Columbia ended ignominiously, when boats from both universities became lost in a fog and paddled furtively around for two hours.

Amid this despair, Frederick Plumb, vice president of the Merchants National Bank & Trust Company of Syracuse, in his position as president of the Athletic Governing Board, described rowing's precarious position at Syracuse in a letter dated June 9 and sent to Captain Joseph Frawley at Poughkeepsie:

> . . . I retire on Tuesday next after four years of service on this Board. I can truthfully say to you that since my election I have done everything possible that I could for the maintenance of the Navy (Syracuse crew) in the face of severe opposition all the time. This last year with the help of Mr. T. C. Cherry, chairman of the Finance Committee, and other members of the Board, in order to prevent people connected with the University from demanding the suspension of the Navy activities because of its cost, we succeeded after a long time, in having eight different branches of sports abandoned so that the expense from these sports could be saved and that the Navy might continue to exist. The student body fought this and we were obliged to re-establish four of these sports much against my wishes . . . I absolutely believe that no branch of sport in Syracuse has been of as much benefit to the University as our Navy. It is a branch of sport that has the cleanest athletic record and the finest of traditions. It has helped more than anything else we have in the University to make it known around the World. If the Navy should be abandoned for any reason, Syracuse would go backward and would not recover its standing for a generation. There is at the present time, a real danger facing the Navy outside of money it costs to run it . . . the great lack of interest in the study body at the present time towards Navy affairs . . .

It therefore becomes necessary for you young men, who are giving so much to give still more and innoculate the student body with the same spirit of loyalty that you possess. . . .

In his letter, Plumb added that he thought it might be necessary for the oarsmen to organize some type of association and begin with the next entering class in the fall.

"See that they become Navy-minded as Syracuse men have been in the past," he urged, "some organization that will breathe a spirit of blood and iron into the student body which so many of our intercollegiate neckers lack at the present time."

In the Poughkeepsie races: Syracuse crews finished:

Varsity—6th

Junior Varsity—3rd

Freshman—3rd

California's Golden Bears copped the varsity race on the Hudson, with Cornell finishing fourth. Columbia was second.

The following year of 1929, Columbia's rampaging Lions again won the varsity race at Poughkeepsie on a stormy day, during which MIT, Syracuse, California and Cornell were swamped by the heaving river. Finishing, however, were Washington, Penn, Navy and Wisconsin.

The freshmen of Syracuse saved the day for Piety Hill. Coached by Charles Whiteside, they alone tasted the sweetness of victory by a good margin. In that shell were Francis Speiker, Sterling Ashcroft, Prentice Abrams, Webster Keefe, Al Bloomquist, George Kratina, Edward Easter, Milton Weiler and Ernest Brower, coxswain.

On March 4, Herbert Hoover was sworn in as 31st President. On October 29, the stock market crashed, and the great Depression spread across the nation.

192

IRA FRESHMAN CHAMPIONS, 1929
Spieker, Ashcroft, Abrams, Keefe, Blomquist, Kratina, Easter, Weiler, Brower.

IRA FROSH CHAMPS, 1930
Lombardi, McKean, Johnson, Buff, Meacham, McCully, Vandewater, Gower, Cady.

CHAPTER XXIV

THE FRESHMEN SAVED

the day once more for Ten Eyck at Poughkeepsie in 1930. Their victory also partially salvaged a season made dismal by Syracuse losses to Cornell on Cayuga Lake and to Navy on the Severn.

In their race, the first-year men occupied the sixth lane in mid-Hudson, while spectators talked excitedly about them as being a crew composed of heavyweights and skinny welterweights. A star football tackle, Thomas Lombardi, stroked their boat.

Syracuse supporters were dismayed at the beginning of the race, when Pennsylvania set the pace. The Orangemen appeared content to sit back and row placidly. When Columbia passed the Quakers, the spectators' faces lengthened. But after the three boats passed the railroad bridge, their chins lifted. And with good reason.

Quickly committed by Lombardi to a much higher stroke, Syracuse swung its blades in cadenced measure. Their boat moved. Shortly afterwards, they pushed ahead of Pennsylvania. Then, they went on the prowl in search of the Lions.

Sliding forward by precise movements, the boat caught and then passed the Lions at a spot half a mile from the finish. Free and now unchallenged, Syracuse widened its gap before the end.

After recovery, the spirited crew paddled up river, reveling in its victory. Big Lombardi, for example, sitting in the narrow coxswain seat lopped over, while small Cady, the coxswain, was lost in the stroke position as he imitated Lombardi's rowing movements. Sharing the triumphal return with them were Byron Gower, bow; Don Van de Water, Don McCully, Ed Meacham, Ernie Buff, Bob Johnson and Herb McKean.

The freshman victory was auspicious. It perpetuated a frosh record of never finishing worse than third in the past 28 years of IRA competition. And their triumph, seventh in the series, allowed them to retain the Stewards Trophy for the second consecutive year.

The varsity was second to Cornell, which in victory, won a main event for the first time in 15 years. Rowing in the Washington boat that finished sixth was Loren Schoel, a youth of 20, who stood six feet three inches tall in his stocking feet. He rowed No. 5 oar that day. A quarter of a century afterwards, he was Syracuse crew coach.

Ernest Buff, No. 5 oar in the 1930 freshman boat, wrote his mother early in 1931. The information he penned probably amazed her:

> Dear Maw: At last I've got me a position of a lotta prominence on this here man's campus. I'm stroking the crew now, and I'm getting paid twenty dollars a week for it. Oh, I suppose I shouldn't be accepting money for it, but you know, the bucks come in handy . . .

Little did Mrs. Buff know, but her son wasn't paid for rowing at Syracuse University. He was compensated for giving his fellow oarsmen their rub-downs, while attempting to erase muscle aches and pains!

If Mrs. Buff was amazed about her son's activities, no less surprised was the Old Man and the supporters of rowing in the country about the Syracuse crews. The surprise occurred early in the season at Annapolis in races with the Midshipmen.

With tension high, the crews of Syracuse were exasperated by delay of the races when a nervous Navy Plebe accidentally shoved his foot through the bottom of his shell during launching. One Syracusan exclaimed:

"How in the H___ do they expect to row when they don't even know how to get into a boat!"

That outburst luckily helped to break the tension in the Syracuse squad.

Its effects were noticeable in the freshman race when Syracuse broke away from a pressing Navy shell after the first 100 yards. At the mile mark, Syracuse widened the distance and won by two lengths.

Designated as the junior varsity boat at 1 o'clock that afternoon by Ten Eyck, Lombardi and his sophomore mates won their race by four lengths.

Of equal strength and ability, the crew stroked by Milton Weiler and composed of almost the same men who lost to Navy in the 1930 race won the varsity race handily by one and one-half lengths.

Clean sweep for Syracuse! For Navy, it was the first triple defeat in history.

Equally amazed with Ten Eyck were the experts on the Severn that day. They were impressed by the finesse of the Ten Eyck crews in the Henley distance of one mile and five-sixteenths. Syracuse was the underdog inasmuch as the men were experienced only in three and four-mile grinds rather than the shorter sprint distance.

Jubilantly, Ten Eyck said:

THE TRAINING BARGE FAMILIAR TO FROSH IN THE SPRING.

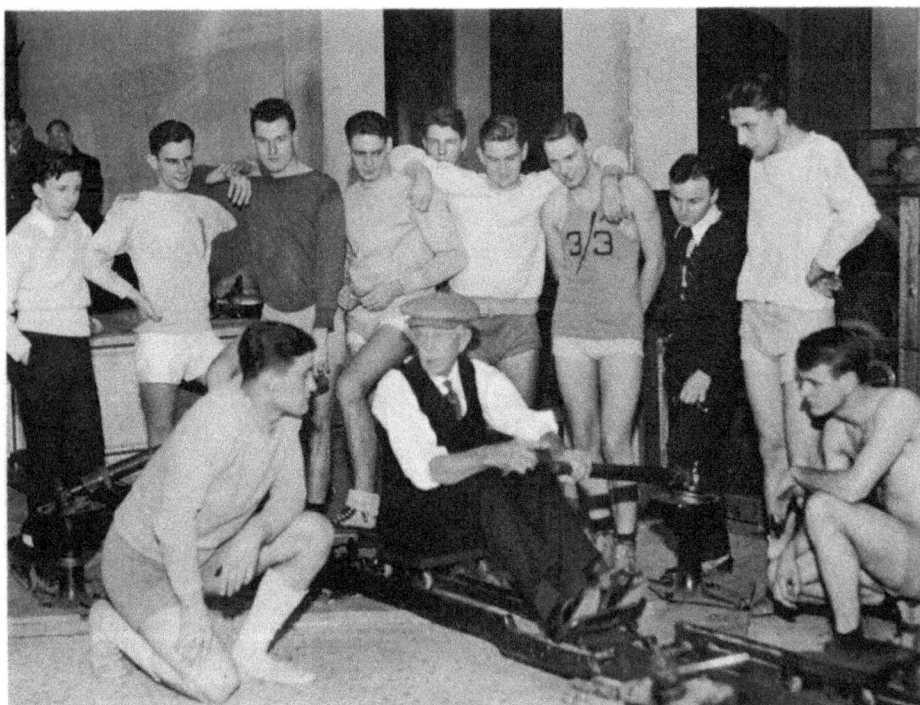

When weather prevented conditioning in the shells, Coach Ten Eyck at eighty showed how to do it on the machines.

"Each crew put up its best rowing. They rose to the occasion in wonderful fashion and exceeded my fondest hopes. I didn't think, truthfully, that it was possible to win all three races, and I'm awfully proud of all the boys!"

Commented Navy coach Dick Glendon, who went to Navy in 1904:

"Jim Ten Eyck is certainly to be congratulated for turning out three crews like the ones Syracuse put on the river, today. I knew the Old Man would have something by the time Poughkeepsie blew around, but I didn't think he'd have them ready to turn in a performance like the one today!"

Three days later and back on Onondaga Lake, Weiler collapsed in practice. Returned to the boathouse, he revealed that he was suffering from lumbago. Frantically, Ten Eyck began to juggle his two boats for the quadrangular meet at Cornell.

Flushed with the victory over Navy, the crews eagerly awaited the races at Ithaca. Ten Eyck, however, feared overconfidence. He enlisted the help of his wife, Edna, and she wrote a letter to Edward Meacham, No. 2 oar:

> Dear "Meacham": That's what the Coach always calls you and I don't know your first name—but I hope after the races—to call you a real College Hero! One who comes into a difficult position and wins out! I know you and your crew will row a good race and I've got confidence in you all to believe it will be victory. Just keep doing the things the Coach tells you to do—and the things you all know how to do and we'll make it unanimous again—just as you all did at Annapolis two weeks ago. *What has been done can always be done again.* So here's for Victory with a capital V. All good wishes for you and the crew.

The meet with Cornell, Harvard and MIT was called off, however, by stormy weather on Cayuga Lake. The Orange crews returned to Piety Hill.

Final examinations late in May disrupted Ten Eyck's preparations for Poughkeepsie, with the oarsmen generally reporting for practice late in the evening. Often, the crews rowed two-mile distances under moonlight.

Once more, Ten Eyck held races between his two heavyweight crews in order to determine which one was to race in the varsity race. Finally, he chose the Weiler-stroked boat over Lombardi's.

Another step in better identifying crews on the Hudson was introduced by the IRA in 1931. Besides painted blades and coxswain's colored jerseys, each crew was required now to carry a small flag of its college perched on the bow of the shell. The flags served a purpose the day of the regatta.

The sun crept furtively up into the sky after dawn and hid behind dull, gray clouds, making it almost impossible to identify the shells out in the river. After the freshman race during which Syracuse finished third, the clouds opened up and rain fell. Then later, as if in apology, the clouds lifted fingers to their lips and the wind fell away, calming the stormy Hudson for the junior varsity race.

Columbia served early notice that she considered herself landlady of the course, and if any outsider attempted to displace her, that crew must contend with her. This was apparent as she led the pack down the river in the first two miles. However, entering the third and final mile, the Lions met their challenger and rather than protest vigorously, they tired and vacated their ownership.

Meeting and passing the fading Lions were Syracuse and California. Syracuse rode the crest of the ebb tide in midstream. Sometimes, she rowed at 30. Sometimes 32. Up and down changed her beat. The tide helped her, somewhat, but Syracuse was unable to shake off the Golden Bears. Only half a length separated them most of the time.

Lombardi raised the beat and Herb McKean at No. 7 oar transmitted the message down starboard to Byron Gower at bow. They passed the docile Lions. Meanwhile, California clung tenaciously, somewhat like ants at a picnic, glued to the other boat, refusing to remain behind Syracuse.

All of a sudden, Cornell came calling. With an extraordinary stroke of 39 beats, she began in the last mile to overhaul the leaders.

Fortunately, untapped power remained in the Ten Eyck shell. And Ten Eyck's sculling stroke, with its easy catch and bladewhipping follow-through in the hands of a talented crew—and this crew was talented—proved too much for the Golden Bears.

California began fading—little by little—its prow receding opposite, first with Syracuse's No. 3, and then No. 4 positions, and 5 and so on. Soon, the tight race evaporated, and Syracuse moved out in front by open water. The boat's finish was anticlimatic.

Quite unexpectedly in the varsity race, Navy became ruler of intercollegiate seas in less than twenty minutes. To win in the downpour, the Midshipmen edged out Cornell, the heavy favorite, and then thwarted a stirring bid made by Washington. Navy's victory without question saved Coach Dick Glendon from loss of his job due to a losing spring season.

Ten Eyck's crew was fifth, followed by Pennsylvania, Columbia, Wisconsin and MIT. Ahead of these crews in fourth place were the Golden Bears of California.

Rowing fans remembered that particular year because of the dramatic Syracuse jayvee victory. Others recalled it as the time Knute Rockne of Notre Dame football died in an airplane crash. Few noticed that it was also the period when Japan invaded Manchuria.

Before the start of the 1932 season, Ten Eyck agitated once more for a change in starting time of the Poughkeepsie races. His complaint for the moment, however, fell on plugged ears. On January nineteenth, 1932, the IRA stewards did meet in New York for the expressed purpose of studying the problem of inequality of racing lanes on the Hudson. A strategy Ten Eyck pulled in the 1931 races sparked the inquiry. Charles Parker reported in the *New York World-Telegram:*

> The Board of Stewards . . . went into annual session today, and there was a hint that certain changes in the conduct of the event might materialize before the adjournment. Whether the latter was an outgrowth of the happening of last year, when Syracuse representatives, after delaying the start of the freshman event, forced the varsity race to a later hour by further tardiness in appearing for the junior varsity event, is not known. . . . Back of it all, of course, are the varying conditions on a tidewater river. When the tide begins to ebb its downriver low is first noticeable on the waters near the shore. Gradually, the same tidal speed moves out until for thirty minutes there is approximately even flow throughout the full width. . . . Obviously, if the race is started in advance of that time, the crews nearest the shore have the advantage, while if the main event is delayed beyond that brief half hour period, there is greater speed in the middle river and the outside crews profit thereby. It was because the Syracuse varsity had drawn the outside lane in the main event that many felt . . . that there was a motive behind the tardy reporting of the Orange freshman and jayvee combinations. . . . Syracuse offered alibis. In the freshman race the Orange crew missed connections with the stakeboat and had to swing around and pick it up again. That did

not explain the original tardiness in reporting, nor did it account for the extensive circular excursion made in going 200 or 300 yards down the river, swinging round, coming back the 200 or 300 yards . . . and then proceeding very casually to their places on the starting line. In the junior varsity event, the alibi was a broken oarlock and the necessity of returning to the boat house for a new one. . . . But, whatever the substance of the alibis, the varsity event was long delayed and Syracuse thus provided with the swift water. . . .

Result of the meeting? The starting times of the 1932 Hudson races were scheduled an hour later than in former years.

Chapter XXV

TEN EYCK BEGAN

his 29th year at the University in 1932 confined to a hospital bed. In February, he contracted pneumonia and was absent from his coaching duties until late March. Meantime, Ned substituted for his father in handling the crews.

The son sent the oarsmen out to the Seneca River for the first time early in March, while the area still remained in the icy grip of winter. Paddling a barge, the shivering crews went up the river on a zig-zag course, dodging floating chunks of ice. In time, the Old Man returned, and Ned remained to handle the freshman squad. Both faced a delightful problem.

Three varsity crews of almost equal ability and two strong freshman crews competed daily for designation as "first crews." It was the first occasion on Piety Hill that quantity as well as quality of material presented itself to Ten Eyck.

"We aren't straightened out by any means," he confessed joyfully to Robert Kelley of the *New York Times.* "We don't know yet which is which. I'm frank to admit we have the men."

With a gleam in his eyes, Ten Eyck added:

"We believe they row pretty well, and we have hopes of good crews. In the meantime, we're simply rowing along getting into shape."

Getting into physical condition was the least of the problems facing Ten Eyck. His happiness was partly predicated on the presence of three veteran strokes—Lombardi, George Kratina and Weiler. Any one of the three in former years might easily be stroke oar in the varsity boat, but this spring their equal ability caused keen competition and rivalry among them for the position. Supporting the strokes were oarsmen of big and rangy physiques, majority of them standing six feet or more in height.

Little wonder then that father and son smiled smugly in anticipation of the season's opener against Navy. Even though their men were held back in training due to weather, they exhibited a sort a quick step in their strides as they prepared the men.

"Sit up—put your shoulders on. Pull 'er all the way through," the Old Man advised them. He repeated as litany: "Pull together. One man can lose a race, but no one man alone can win it!"

To those not pulling an oar, he cautioned:

"Now is the time to sit up and row—when you're tired!"

On May 7, came the moment of truth for both Ten Eycks. The crews met Navy at Annapolis in the season's opener for both schools. For Syracuse, the meet offered an opportunity to measure up to Ten Eyck's confidence in them; but to Navy, the races offered an opportunity to avenge their debacle of defeats in 1931.

Thus was posed the scene of one irresistible force colliding with an object of immovable resistance. Both crews rowed their hearts out.

THE FRESHMAN-PLEBE RACE. Stroked by Bart O'Hearn, Syracuse grabbed the lead at the get-away and hugged it to the finish line for a boat-length victory.

JUNIOR VARSITY RACE. Stroked by Kratina, the shell trailed Navy all the way down the course until 300 yards from the finish. Then in a blot and blur of motion, it displayed awesome power and caught up to the Midshipmen. For a moment, the two shells posed as one. Inch by inch, one nose poked out in front of the other. It was Syracuse! And over the finish line, it was Syracuse by the margin of one man, or an eighth of a length.

VARSITY RACE. Least exciting of the races, this one was won handily by the Lombardi-stroked crew. Promptly grabbing the lead, the boat stayed out from arm's reach throughout the mile and five-sixteenths course. Victory was by one and three-quarters length.

Syracuse swept the strong Navy off the Severn for the second consecutive year. The Midshipmen were in a state of shock.

The sweet flavor of success continued for University oars. On Onondaga Lake before 20,000 excited spectators, the varsity and junior varsity crews soundly defeated Cornell crews.

Basking in the afterglow of five consecutive victories, the crews were responsible for the increased interest of Central New York fans in crew racing. Many residents went to Boston the following week for the Syracuse contest with Cornell, Harvard and MIT.

Regrettably, Ten Eyck was unable to enter all three of his crews. Insufficient funds kept home the jayvee and freshman boats.

Ten Eyck's varsity—which one? asked the fans—was heavy favorite of the scribes even before the Old Man chose his final crew. Selecting the eight rowers and coxswain wasn't easy for him. He employed the only formula which gave true evaluation of a crew: racing the men daily.

Twenty-four hours before departure for Boston, the Old Man raced two boats: one stroked by Lombardi; the other by DeFois Siegfried. Finally, he chose Lombardi's boat.

Under the warming sun that afternoon of May 28, on the Charles River, Syracuse became a strong contender for the Olympic trials the following July.

Victory for Ten Eyck's boat was narrow, but it proved conclusively that the University was qualified for greatness on the American rowing scene. By eking out a close victory over the Big Red of Cornell, the crew established a new record for the three-quarters of a mile course on the Charles River. The time was eight minutes, 48 and two-fifths seconds—more than 20 seconds better than the previous time. The record stood unbroken for the next 27 years!

On June one, 1932, the sprinting season for colleges closed. The final eastern records looked like this:

	Won	Lost
1—Syracuse	3	0
2—Yale	5	0
3—Cornell	2	2
4—Penn	7	2
5—Harvard	2	3
6—Navy	3	3
7—Columbia	2	3
8—Princeton	1	4
9—MIT	0	5

The excitement which carpeted the Poughkeepsie races was part of anticipating the Olympic trials scheduled the following month at Lake Quinsigamond, Worcester, Massachusetts. Crews, coaches, college officials and fans knew that a solid victory in the varsity or junior varsity race on the Hudson for a crew was tantamount to strong participation in the sprints. The Olympics, of course, offered a college the opportunity to represent the nation in world-wide competition.

Despite the fervor of fans for the races, the Depression kept the crowd smaller than customary. Poughkeepsie itself was deserted, the usual flags and bunting missing from the streets. Only the noisy assembly of people at regatta headquarters at the Nelson House resembled anything like former days. Noticeable in the crowd were football coaches, including Lou Little of Columbia and Major Ralph Sasse of Army.

That year the weather smiled on the races. The Hudson was smooth, and a blue sky provided an appropriate canvas for a warm sun. To accommodate the spectators, the IRA moved the lanes out into the middle of the river.

—Cr-a-c-k!—spoke the pistol, and the oars of seven freshman boats dipped the water for the first race. Navy's Midshipmen sped into the lead and stayed in front for more than half a mile before Ten Eyck's boat came abreast and challenged them.

The Syracuse oarsmen, with ease to their swing but with power in the long, steady strokes, raced farther and farther ahead. That concert of power manipulated by maestro Bart O'Hearn at stroke and echoed in cadence by Coxswain George Kirkwood drove their boat over the line a good length ahead of Navy.

After Navy came Cornell, California, Penn, Columbia and MIT.

IRA FRESHMAN EIGHT OF 1932.
Webster, Mulholland, Hildebrand, Edgerton, Rader, Stark, Matasavage,
O'Hearn, Kirkwood.

A GREAT VARSITY CREW IN 1932, UNDEFEATED EXCEPT IN THE IRA
Lombardi, McKean, Kratina, Buff, Gramlich, Abrams, Ashcroft, Donaldson, Trnavsky.

Ten Eyck in a last minute shuffle installed Siegfried at stroke and Kratina at No. 6 oar for the jayvee race, and as in affirmation, the boat swung into the lead. With beautiful rhythmic sweep of the oars, the crew was a stranger to the other company on the course for two of the three miles. Then, unwanted California came calling.

Upping its stroke to 36 beats per minute, the Bears gradually shaved off the Syracuse lead until with each sweep of the oars, they drew nearer . . . and nearer . . . and nearer.

The unexpected surge of the California boat wasn't lost to Coxswain Murray McKaig, who restrained himself from sounding the alarm to Siegfried until the West Coast visitors were only one-half length behind. Then he sounded the call. The stroke of the boat increased.

Up to this point, the crew never put its stroke over 33, but now it was gradually put up to 36. Uninterrupted in its smooth motion by the increased beat, the shell moved forward, and its manpower put a tremendous run on it.

One-half minute from the finish, the jayvee crew, its beat by this time a powerful 37, shook off the intruders. The gap between Syracuse and California boats was one-half length at the finish. Behind the Bears came Navy, Cornell, Columbia and MIT.

By the time of the varsity race, pinkish tinges of sky were beginning to deepen into darkness. And the crowd on the observation train spied Ten Eyck in his launch discussing strategy with Coxswain Trnavsky near the west shore, They let out a cheer for the frost-haired coach, and he acknowledged the tribute with a gracious smile and a hearty wave.

Few times before in the long history of the IRA regatta

on the Hudson were crews from one college winners of all three races in a single day. Twice that day, Syracuse crews won, and the possibility beckoned for Ten Eyck's greatest triumph in his long life.

Unfortunately, the other two victories didn't act as a cathartic for the varsity crew. California's Bears draped Syracuse with the pool-room gloom of defeat.

Employing a much shortened stroke, the Bears unceremoniously grabbed away the lead from the Lombardi-stroked boat almost at the start and over the course lengthened it to absurdity. Only Cornell near the finish gave any evidence of comparable ability, when it rushed up to reduce California's lead. But the Bears won by two and one-half boat lengths. After them and Cornell came Washington, Navy, Syracuse, Columbia, Penn and MIT.

Thus, California moved over into Worcester for the Olympic sprints followed later by Syracuse.

Before Ten Eyck's crew entered, however, money was needed and the Syracuse community generously gave $3,500 with which to make participation possible.

Misfortune struck Syracuse a cruel blow at the trials as it did in 1920. Sterling Ashcroft, captain and No. 2 oar, was disqualified for the race due to naturalization difficulties.

Ashcroft was a Canadian, and although a resident of the United States for ten years, he was technically ineligible because his father in taking out blanket citizenship papers for his family failed to follow through.

That other blow to Syracuse hopes in the Olympic trials occurred in 1920 when Gus Rammi, the varsity stroke, was lost also because of a technicality of citizenship.

Despite this, Ten Eyck's boat rowed a gallant race at Worcester before being narrowly defeated by the Pennsylvania Athletic Club. The Penn A. C., in turn, lost to California by one measurable foot; from this race, the Bears went on to win the world's championship by defeating Italy in the Olympics.

Before the year 1932 closed, Franklin D. Roosevelt was elected President. In the fight world, Jack Sharkey of Boston walloped Max Schmeling of Germany for the championship. And Ned Ten Eyck became coach of crew at Rutgers University.

Nineteen thirty-three. Depression.

Unsettled economic conditions in America bit deeply into rowing as into other walks of life. The Poughkeepsie regatta was postponed. Ripe for the ax, too, was rowing at the University. But energetic alumni resuscitated the sport by novel means:

A dance was held to raise funds for rowing.

A committee of Tip Goes, Roy Martineau, Edward Thompson, Hubert Stratton, Kenneth Gallagher, Dr. Gordon and Howard Hoople, Frederick Plumb and F. Gordon Smith revived the University Navy Ball in Hotel Onondaga. Proceeds from the waltzes and fox-trots retained the sport at a time when other campus activities were curtailed.

Ten Eyck without the Poughkeepsie regatta as the season's objective felt cheated of a golden opportunity.

Both his varsity and jayvee crews again this year were good—so good, in fact, that Ten Eyck himself wasn't absolutely certain which one to call the varsity or junior varsity.

A race with Cornell on the Lake found Lombardi's boat designated "varsity" while Siegfried's was junior varsity. Nonetheless, both won.

Over at Ithaca, a second race was held, and Ten Eyck switched them. Yet, both boats won.

While 7,500 spectators watched University crews triumph at Cornell, a former grid star and coach at Syracuse and New York University introduced rowing at Manhattan College in New York.

Chick Meehan, now the Jaspers' athletic director and football coach, aided by Harvard and the New York Athletic Club which contributed used shells, obtained an old barge anchored in Sherman Creek on the Harlem River. Engaging a volunteer coach, Meehan put Manhattan for the first time on the water.

It was the year of despair. Hitler became German Chancellor. Roosevelt closed the banks. And the Twenty-first Amendment abolishing Prohibition was passed.

Only the forthcoming years of rowing at Syracuse provided excitement and relief for many from the drab curtain of the Depression.

Chapter XXVI

"THE MAINSPRING OF

my crew is gone," Ten Eyck lamented in April of 1934, when informed that his varsity stroke, DeFois Siegfried of Rochester (N.Y.) was ineligible. With Siegfried's departure due to academic failure, Ten Eyck's hopes for a successful season appeared impossible.

His plans received another setback when Russell "Swede" Swanson, the logical oarsman to succeed Siegfried at stroke, became bothered by an infected hand that refused to respond quickly enough to treatment. He saw only limited service at the position.

In a sense, these misfortunes probably were responsible for the topsy-turvey season that followed. Against arch rival Cornell on Onondaga Lake, only the junior varsity captured a victory flag. But in return races on Cayuga Lake, the varsity finished in the winning circle. Ten Eyck's comfort over this triumph was short lived. Navy threw water on his momentary happiness.

At Annapolis, an accident to No. 6 oar thwarted the varsity's hopes for a third consecutive win over the Midshipmen. Edward "Red" Gramlich caught a crab at the start and snapped off an oar.

Summoned back for another start, the crew sped into the lead, and retained it for the first half-mile, but unfortunately, the oarsmen never fully recovered their poise from the disconcerting accident and they lost.

Ten Eyck took some comfort from his jayvee and freshman crews which continued the Syracuse victory skein over the Sailors before Poughkeepsie.

On the eve of the IRA regatta, a cookie-shaped moon beamed down on river and men. Trained to razor sharpness by two weeks of preparation, the University oarsmen lolled about in a quiet, somber mood.

The Old Man rocked in an old green chair on the porch of the Syracuse headquarters. The conversation was unhurried, and he enjoyed talking to these men, who by this time were toasted a deep bronze by wind and sun and hours on the Hudson. He was in the middle of an old, old story, when an inquisitive reporter broke up the conversation.

"Coach, what is the physical condition of your crew?" he inquired.

Before answering, the coach rapped on the arm of his chair in exaggerated movement as if to ward off any misfortune which might come to his men as result of his reply.

"We've got three good crews—" he declared, "and the boys are all fit and ready."

The reporter guffawed loudly. Even he knew that answer was the stock reply of all coaches at Poughkeepsie! He wanted to know more details.

Then, he became aware of the thick silence.

Only he, himself, laughed, he realized.

In confusion, the scribe tried to resume the conversation.

"Coach—I mean what are your chances for—"

Silence.

"I—I—I mean—" he stammered in embarrassment, "How do your men stack up against the others?"

Silence.

"Well—" he tried to recover, "Mr. Ten Eyck—Mr. Ten Eyck—sir—!"

The Old Man ignored him by resuming his story. And with bowed head, the reporter shuffled off down the walk and into the shadows.

Ten Eyck's reluctance to talk about his men's chances on the Hudson probably wasn't due to the reporter's personality. More likely it was due to a combination of reasons:

A span of 18 years passed since a Syracuse varsity led the IRA pack down the course running from Krum Elbow to the finish line opposite Vassar College.

Many experts, gamblers, alumni and friends, thought 1934 was the year to end the drought.

Syracuse was heavily favored.

Washington and California were only remote possibilities.

Talk of such confidence before his oarsmen, the Old Man knew, might cause difficulties of over-confidence in the races.

But as time was to tell, Ten Eyck needed not to worry. The California Bears spoiled his reason for caution. They won the varsity race. Syracuse finished sixth, trailing behind California, Washington, Navy, Cornell and Pennsylvania. followed only by Columbia.

Viewed by some 75,000 spectators, the jayvees thrilled the Syracuse supporters that day on the Hudson.

In the final 200 yards to the finish, Navy closed up open water and rowed evenly with Syracuse. Both rowed valiantly.

Navy clung to Syracuse like a panther at the flank of an antelope.

The distance to the finish line shortened.

Still, Navy kept coming.

Syracuse responded beyond its normal endurance.

In desperation, Navy gave its supreme effort.

The two pea-pod-shaped boats swept over the line as a single silhouette of men and wood.

Hoarse by this time, the fans eagerly awaited the final verdict.

Who did win the race?

The race officials huddled. Finally, they announced their decision:

Syracuse was victorious!

And the margin of the Syracuse triumph was less than half a length.

Washington joined its other West Coast entry in the regatta events and spoiled Ten Eyck's chances in the freshman race. The young Huskies grabbed an early lead and won by four and one-quarter lengths over Syracuse. Following them were Cornell, Pennsylvania, Columbia and Rutgers.

Times were difficult in 1934. The Syracuse crews journeyed to Poughkeepsie only by money raised from a dance held again in Hotel Onondaga that May. What of the future? wondered rowing supporters. With the nation wallowing in the depths of Depression and despair, how was rowing in the colleges to survive?

That intercollegiate rowing did survive is a tribute to the dedication and devotion of college administrators as well as of the coaches, the oarsmen and the spectators. Grimly they held on to the sport at a time when everything else was disappearing.

Meanwhile, rowing coaches under the leadership of Ten Eyck formed a group of their own in New York two days after New Year's Day of 1935. They called themselves the Rowing Coaches Organization of America, with Ten Eyck as permanent chairman and serving as vice president for the first year. Callow, now coaching at Pennsylvania, was voted president. Charles "Buck" Walsh, successor to Dick Glendon at Navy, was chosen secretary-treasurer. Coach Edward Leader of Yale, Father Sill of Kent and Frank Mueller of the Pennsylvania Athletic Club were directors for the group whose purpose was to advance and improve rowing in clubs, schools and colleges by "suggestion and advice to the proper authorities."

Father Sill was instrumental in the group inviting both Oxford and Cambridge crews to the Hudson that year for the IRA's 40th anniversary. Due to financial troubles, however, the English schools declined the invitation.

That spring at Syracuse, Ten Eyck greeted a small squad. Graduation, academic failures, heavy study loads, drop-outs and personal problems reduced what he figured might be a strong University Navy. In characteristic style, he worked to improve upon what was available to him.

Previous to a meet with Cornell, Harvard and MIT on the Charles, he juggled his crews, trying to utilize the best talents in the squad. At the final moment, he removed most of his previously designated varsity boat and substituted another with Swede Swanson as stroke oar.

Ten Eyck's switch was copied at the same time by a former pupil. Charles Whiteside of Harvard also reversed his two varsity crews. This meant that the President's son, Franklin D. Roosevelt, Jr., rowed in the jayvee boat against a Syracuse junior varsity stroked by Captain Bart O'Hearn.

Without precedence at Harvard, the action was qualified by Whiteside:

The varsity eight lost to Princeton several days prior to this race, and was out-raced all the week in practice by the jayvees.

To this point, nothing is said about the habit of some coaches, particularly Ten Eyck, in switching crews just minutes before an important race. And to some mentors, it never seemed, somehow, to be "cricket."

In time, the habit became a point of acrimony among many coaches.

Although not illegal, switching quite often was necessary for coaches not blessed by many numbers of oarsmen, and it meant sometimes an opportunity of providing the best competition against the powerhouses of collegiate rowing.

On the Charles, Swanson set a high stroke of 42 beats a minute after his boat got away to a splendid start. The crew lengthened its lead to a full length at the quarter-mile and from there on, majestically led the others over the victory line.

"That wouldn't be a nice thing for me to do," Ten Eyck admitted when questioned by Boston reporters as to the reason why his boat won by such a wide margin.

217

"But I had my best crew together," he hastened to explain. "It was rigged right. And I'd call it a good crew, considering I only had sixteen men to choose from!"

Turning to a figure nearby, Ten Eyck put his hand on one of his former oarsmen of 1913 and exclaimed:

"When Howard Robbins rowed under me, I knew more about him then he knew about himself. But I don't know so much about him now. He's got away from me."

Bubbling with enthusiasm over the victory, Ten Eyck finally admitted his reason for switching the crews:

"We had more than our share of bad luck before the race."

Francis Crowley left college three days before the race to attend his brother's funeral in Binghamton (N.Y.), rejoining his mates on the eve of the Boston race.

Howard Blocher, No. 3 oar, was summoned home from Boston by his father's illness and subsequent death.

And Lawrence Wells, freshman stroke oar, was called home when his mother died in an automobile accident. His misfortune caused Ten Eyck to withdraw the boat from the race.

While in Boston, the veteran Syracuse coach proudly announced that the single scull his son, Ned, rowed to the world championship in 1897 in England was scheduled for display in Smithsonian Institute in Washington, D.C.

"About time, too," the proud father declared.

At Poughkeepsie, California took the varsity race for the third year in a row. Syracuse finished fifth and its jayvee boat was fourth. Ten Eyck's frosh was fifth and last.

A few days prior to these Poughkeepsie races, a green Rutgers crew under Ned Ten Eyck stroked its way to an impressive victory over Pennsylvania, Wisconsin, Manhattan, Rollins College (Florida), and Marietta (Ohio), in the Mid-America regatta on the Ohio River at Mariettta. Rutgers finished its season undefeated.

Prophetically, Ned declared to the newspapers that the IRA regatta might someday be shifted.

"It's not impossible for Marietta to wean away the national intercollegiate races from the famed Poughkeepsie on the Hudson.

"This course," he added, "has Poughkeepsie backed off the map. It has everything that any crew could desire, something which cannot be said about Poughkeepsie."

After Poughkeepsie, Syracuse took the long trek to California for the National Intercollegiate Sprint Regatta at Long Beach Marine Stadium. Others competing with Syracuse were Pennsylvania, Wisconsin, Washington, California and the University of California at Los Angeles (UCLA).

Two years previously, in the first such regatta, Washington nosed out Yale by four feet in a race that also included Harvard and Cornell.

Rowing for Syracuse and Ten Eyck were Russell Swanson, Vincent Matasavage, Francis Crowley, Edward Otis, James Hildebrand, James Nunan, Sterling Bettinger, Robert Collins and Ralph Weston, coxswain. Mark Conan and Percival Jackson were spare oarsmen, who traveled with Commodore William O'Brien and Dr. Leslie Bryan.

It was quite a battle on water!

219

220

THE 1935 SYRACUSE CREW ENTERED IN THE NATIONAL COLLEGIATE WESTERN SPRINT REGATTA.

In the regulation distance of the Olympics—2000 meters—California's Bears continued on their winning ways. They established a new course record in a blanket finish with Syracuse and Washington.

Victory for the Bears came in the last few yards to the finish. They just managed to stave off admirable challenges of the Orange and the Huskies. Rusty Callow's Pennsylvania Quakers finished a length behind the third-place Ten Eyck boat.

Chancellor Wesley Flint, former president of Cornell College in Iowa, who in 1922, succeeded Dr. Day, sent a laudatory letter to each of the Syracuse oarsmen:

> Heartiest congratulations to you and your fellow oarsmen for the magnificent way in which you represented the University on the West Coast. It was mighty fast company especially for a light crew . . . I am gratified also to learn of the excellent impression you made in the west as men as well as oarsmen. Thank you.

Two months afterwards, Congress passed the Social Security Act; much later, Will Rogers, noted humorist, was killed in a plane accident with globe trotter Wiley Post.

On December 15, back in Syracuse, Ten Eyck became an honorary Rotarian. F. Gordon Smith, University secretary, was club president, and he introduced the coach.

Knife-thin, the Old Man stood up and spoke.

In a light vein, Ten Eyck talked about some of his experiences over the years. Then, he disclosed his last ambition in life (quoted from his own typewritten notes) :

"When I get through coaching, I'm going to write a book. I can't do it as long as I hold a coaching job, for before I break into print, I have got to send my vocabulary to the dry cleaners.

"But I'm gathering data for this literary work which I think I will call: 'Reputations and Realities, or How to See Yourself as Others See You.' I get a new story for the book every little while."

His latest story, he told them.

"Frank Hugo, our trainer, picked one up last summer at Poughkeepsie. He was talking to one of the maids in the kitchen at the Elms [where Syracuse stayed]. He said to her, 'What do you think of these college oarsmen?'

" 'Well,' she replied, 'I don't think they are so hot. I thought they would all be very handsome and very tall; why they've got some big fellows to be sure, but there are several little runts not more than four or five feet tall. I thought they would all be dressed up in striped jerseys and Hart, Schaffner and Marx clothes.

" 'They mostly wear dirty white cotton pants. And I heard so much about this wonderful coach of theirs. He don't look to me as if he could row very hard on an oar. I tell you, I don't believe that old fellow could row a mile, let alone four.'

"So, gentlemen," said Ten Eyck with a broad grin, "there is the College Coach as seen by the eye of a house-maid!"

Of course, the Rotarians laughed and enjoyed the Old Man's humor. An episode, however, early in 1936, caused Ten Eyck to lose some of his humor, temporarily at least, and presented him with a discouraging experience.

CHAPTER XXVII

THE SPRING THAW

early in 1936 caused Ten Eyck to lose his humor and his patience. Melted snows boosted the level of Onondaga Lake by five inches and isolated the ramshackle boathouse. Ten Eyck and his rigger, Charles Keller, and some of the oarsmen removed the nine shells and equipment valued at $12,000; with great difficulty, they carried them a quarter of a mile to a summer "fish fry" stand perched on a higher level. Training for the oarsmen was delayed by the slowly receding water.

These conditions were responsible for the famous tiff between Ten Eyck and his boss, Dr. Leslie Bryan, director of athletics.

Late April, the University physician, Dr. Paul Lowry, announced that the oarsmen weren't in any condition for competitive rowing. Since a race was scheduled with Yale and MIT in New England on the 25th, the Old Man asked Bryan to cancel it. This, Bryan refused to do. The crew was already committed to race, he declared.

Upon hearing Bryan's refusal, Ten Eyck angrily pulled out a worn briar pipe from his pocket and filled it from a Prince Albert can. Speaking between draws on the pipe, he retorted, "Never in my thirty-three"—puff, puff, puff— "years of coaching on the Hill"—puff, puff—"have we been faced by conditions as they are at present"—puff, puff, puff—

"We—we are laboring under tremendous difficulties"—puff, puff. That night, he fired off letters to the parents of his oarsmen.

> If my son were a member of either of these crews (varsity and junior varsity), I should not let him row in this race under these present conditions. I should appreciate an answer to this letter at the earliest possible date.

One of the fathers, James Crowley of Binghamton, promptly answered Ten Eyck:

> I believe that a race held at such an early date would not only be injurious to the health of the oarsmen, but may result in a very poor showing for the crew. It gives me great pleasure at this opportunity to extend you my sincere appreciation for the excellent work you have done in the past on behalf of Francis and the other oarsmen of this team.

In the next few days, Bryan was bombarded by letters from parents, received protests from alumni and read editorials in the local newspapers. He finally withdrew the crews from the race.

Delay in training was only part of the reason for Ten Eyck's irritation. He was now 85, and still waiting for an adequate boathouse. Thirty-two years ago, he recalled receiving a telegram on the Hudson from the Athletic Association promising that showers were to be installed. Still, his men continued using buckets..

Despite his concern over the inadequacies of facilities, he managed to lighten the spirits of his squad. He did this by equipping them with a belly-laugh.

Since logs and debris were in the flooded area of the outlet and Seneca River, Ten Eyck refused to allow his men to travel far. He told them:

"You are the fastest crews turning around I ever saw, but that's because you've had more practice at it than any crews that ever rowed. About all I do is to tell you to turn around. We'll start rowing in length, someday."

Eventually, the crews rowed at length and hastened to catch up with their belated training. And in May, Ten Eyck went to New York.

A testimonial dinner was given him by the New York Alumni Club under direction of Joseph Nelson. J. Robert Rubin was toastmaster and arrangements were in charge of Dr. Leon Cornwall, G. Edwin Brown, W. C. Fisher, H. D. Stephens, H. W. Faus, and Dr. Ray Nelson.

Tributes were paid the Old Man by Maxwell Stevenson, IRA chairman; Referee Julian Curtiss of Yale; Chick Meehan and by the captains of three Hudson winners—Robert Stone '04, Mayhew Dodge '08, and George Busch '20.

Ten Eyck spoke briefly on the advantages of college rowing. He concluded:

"I wouldn't be surprised if when I go there (the other side of the river) , the old ferryman on the river Styx handed over the job to me."

Resuming his seat, Ten Eyck settled down to listen to 87-year-old John "Doc" Cunningham, beloved campus figure, relate humorous anecdotes of early University life.

Unexpectedly, the frail figure with snow-white hair leaned over and placed his right hand on Ten Eyck's shoulder. In a voice that faltered, he said:

"Jim—you're the best friend I have at Syracuse. God bless you!"

Awestruck at the tribute paid him, Ten Eyck sat immobile for a moment, his face a blank. Then his eyes watered up, and he abruptly buried his face in his gnarled hands.

A hushed silence enveloped the room in the Hotel New Yorker.

In contrast, accolades at Poughkeepsie in 1936 for the Orange were non-existent. Washington swept the river. Syracuse finished seventh in the varsity race; fifth and last in the jayvee event; and fifth in the freshman contest.

Syracuse crews were moved this year from the Elms House at Highland because the lodging place installed a bar. They took up residence in Hotel DiPrima, located a mile north of the village on the Kingston Road.

Ten Eyck, while sitting on the porch, answered a *New York American* reporter's question if he ever regretted not coaching at Harvard.

Sticking a pipe in his mouth, he answered:

"Well, I'll tell you a story that will answer your question. Back in the middle nineties, a group of Harvard oarsmen formed a four-oared crew for the summer races. They asked me to come down to Worcester to coach them for a week. Of course, I told them that I couldn't help them much in a week's time, but was willing to try—"

Ten Eyck puffed a moment on his pipe before continuing.

"After a couple of days the bow oar was absent," he recalled. "I was asked to stroke the crew so others could get a workout. I gave them a real workout! Yessiree—when we stopped, their tongues were hanging out.

"They decided they'd had enough rowing for the year. I was satisfied because they didn't have a good shell, and they weren't too good, anyway. It wouldn't have done my coaching reputation any good if they had carried on. That's the closest," he continued, "I ever came to coaching at Harvard."

Ten Eyck journeyed to Princeton, New Jersey, in July and watched the Washington Huskies defeat Pennsylvania, California and New York Athletic Club crews for the right to represent the United States in the Olympic Games at Berlin the following month. That November, Chancellor Flint resigned.

Trustees at their annual meeting received Dr. Flint's decision to leave the University and accept a position as Methodist Bishop. They chose one of their faculty members, Vice Chancellor William Pratt Graham, to succeed him. The kindly scholar was the first layman and alumnus chosen for the University position.

News of great significance was announced by the retiring Chancellor. A new building to house the entire social sciences was slated for construction the following July. It became the Maxwell School of Citizenship and Public Affairs.

And a second building, this one for the medical college, Dr. Flint reported, was to be constructed at the same time. Made possible by a federal loan of $825,000 which was to be paid back in 1966, the structure eventually became a part of the State University of New York known as the Upstate Medical School.

Changes in the faces of collegiate rowing began occurring in the winter of 1937-1938:

Harrison "Stork" Sanford, former Washington oarsman, left his private business in Seattle to become coach of crew at Cornell.

227

Ralph Hunn, 1931 Wisconsin coxswain, succeeded George Murphy as coach at his Alma Mater.

And Pennsylvania, one of the three original members of the Intercollegiate Rowing Association, withdrew from the regatta after 60 years! It claimed its crews were unable to train for four-mile races; and that the four-mile course gave western crews an advantage.

Thunderstruck, Ten Eyck in his role as permanent chairman of the coaching group, moved with alacrity. He petitioned the IRA stewards to change the varsity length back to three miles. In other words, he willingly sacrificed his own wishes for a longer course for the sake of unity and keeping Pennsylvania in the IRA!

His friend, Rusty Callow, wrote him:

> Dear Coach . . . In my opinion, Penn will never again
> race four miles. Ninety per cent of their alumni are glad we
> have quit Poughkeepsie. . . .

But depart she did, and Pennsylvania remained absent from the IRA regatta until 1947 when the course was returned to three miles in length.

Although a miracle didn't happen to bring Pennsylvania back to the Hudson, one did occur to Ten Eyck. After a long wait of 34 years, Ten Eyck was given his boathouse!

How the Old Man at 87 years finally received the facility is quite a story in itself. And although many assisted in obtaining the boathouse, it was really the determined and drudging work of Tip Goes and Ten Eyck who made the dream a reality.

As far as early history revealed, interest was supplied in 1926, when the Athletic Board appointed Goes to study the problem. Later, the Board approved a plan to obtain funds from the rowing alumni. Some money was raised, but simply not enough. In 1928, Chancellor Flint became sympathetic to the cause and ordered another study. The subsequent report indicated no money was available after expenses for rowing were paid—in fact, the sport caused a $20,000 yearly deficit in the athletic budget.

Still, Goes and Ten Eyck persisted in striving for their dream; and then, the former coxswain accompanied by George Bond began a whirlwind tour of the country, speaking to anyone interested enough to listen and wringing many hands. They raised $10,000 as result of their campaign.

Goes moved quickly by conducting an important deal in 1937.

In one hand, he held money; in the other, a title to a decrepit shack of a boathouse with a parcel of land on the west side of the outlet. The Onondaga County Board of Supervisors desired that land with which to complete a lakeshore park near Liverpool.

Goes offered to exchange the University property for a 99-year lease on an east side parcel of land for a boathouse. The county board approved of the trade. However, he still needed money with which to build the boathouse.

The Federal government promised him money, if New York State provided some funds. And Frederick Plumb, Eric Will, Jacob Gramlich, Sr., and Cy Thurston applied the pressure. New York State eventually appropriated the necessary funds.

That spring as Orange shells nosed out to the Lake, they passed the remains of the ancient eyesore:

Broken boards. Split timbers. Bent pipes. Debris.

To remove the landmark that winter, wreckers simply cut the guy ropes that held the building together and carted off usable lumber as the shack slowly settled to the ground.

In May of 1937, the two-story brick building costing $35,000 was finished and dedicated. About 100 of his former sweepswingers watched Jim Ten Eyck receive the keys to the James A. Ten Eyck Memorial Boathouse.

Happily, the indefatigable Goes was not finished. He urged the appointment of Ned Ten Eyck as assistant to Old Jim. Besides this, he recommended:

(1) an increase of at least 100 per cent in size of freshman and varsity crews.
(2) establishment of a regular program of autumn rowing.
(3) expansion of the crew schedule.
(4) organizing a Syracuse Boat Club patterned after Princeton's.

In time, Goes' recommendations were adopted, but not before the posture of rowing at the University suffered greatly.

The spring races of 1937 were disastrous to the crews, but the varsity and junior varsity men salvaged something by winning at Cornell in the annual Spring Day races. At Poughkeepsie, the varsity gave an excellent account of itself, when it raced prow to prow down the Hudson before Washington won out. The Huskies that year for the second consecutive time swept the river. And it was a time in rowing history when the man who stood all those years on the bridge near Poughkeepsie firing off aerial bombs was severely burned.

Michael Bogo, Poughkeepsie tavern keeper, was seriously burned, when he tried to herald the victory of Washington's junior varsity. One fuse of an aerial bomb ignited before he escaped. His face and left hand were seared.

THE NEW LOOK—A REAL CREW HEADQUARTERS
(Memorial to James A. Ten Eyck)

Father and son, Ned, coach together in 1937, stand with Howard Robbins at the
boathouse dedication.

VARSITY OARSMEN, 1937

Bettinger, Belko, Foster, Otis, Stuhlman, McNeil, Horrocks, Kerr, Weston.

Shortly after a race the next fall on the River with Toronto, the crew and University lost its beloved campus figure. "Doc" Cunningham died.

New Chancellor Graham in his eulogy said:

"John Cunningham never claimed Syracuse as his university. But it was his university by right of the service he rendered it; by right of the love which he had for it; and by right of the pride which he took in it."

On a plaque in the Hall of Languages appropriate tribute describes Cunningham:

Always on his way somewhere to do something for somebody.

Time and events in 1937-1938 went racing through the historical camera of Syracuse rowing, intercollegiate rowing, and of men in rowing.

The squad elected Edward Otis of Wakefield, Massachusetts, and M. Leslie Foster of Jamaica, Long Island, as co-captains of crew for 1938, and Ten Eyck on December 16, received appointment to the advisory committee on sports for the 1939 World's Fair from Commissioner Grover Whalen.

President Roosevelt was serving his second term, Aviatrix Amelia Earhart was lost on a flight in the Pacific, and Ten Eyck became ill.

The coach fought two bouts with pneumonia and found it difficult to recuperate in the wintry blasts of Syracuse. And while war clouds began to gather over Europe, he left early season training to Ned and journeyed south. Attempting to shake off a lingering chest cold, he once again gazed upon the same white beaches of Miami that he saw in the 1880s when he was a professional sculler.

He let it be known in Florida that he confidently expected to be coaching until he was a century old. But needless to say, his time was running out. His final rendezvous was drawing near.

Apparently one of his sieges with pneumonia severely strained his heart. He suffered a coronary in January and was rushed to Jackson Memorial Hospital. Tenderly placed in an oxygen tent, Ten Eyck later appeared to recover. In a gesture of defiance, he informed his sons not to hurry to his bedside—he was fine! Ned was back in Syracuse and Jim, Jr. was coach of the freshman crew at Princeton.

Bill Corum, sportswriter and later radio sports announcer, the previous year wrote:

> Some spring, Jim won't be going down to Poughkeepsie
> any more and that spring it will be a poorer place.

That spring of 1938 at Poughkeepsie and Syracuse was a poorer place, for suddenly in the early morning of February 11, Ten Eyck weakened without apparent reason; and

at 6:20 o'clock, he quietly slipped away.

For the first time since 1903, the lean man in the blue reefer coat and green cap was missing from the ice-draped Onondaga Lake and the choppy Hudson River.

Tributes flowed into the University from all corners of the world, from all walks of life, and in all forms, while the world of sports bowed its head in reverence.

Memorial services were held in Hendricks Chapel on campus on a cold February afternoon. Afterwards, Ten Eyck's body, by prior agreement, was cremated and the ashes strewn later that spring in the twilight of an evening on his beloved Hudson.

CHAPTER XXVIII

THE COLORFUL LEAVES

burst out in bold relief against the dying gloom of night. Heavy frost was everywhere around Tompkins Cove near Krum Elbow that morning. And from the rustic homestead came the wail of new life. This was the setting of the birth of the new born babe. Nearby was the river Hudson that some-day, soon, shaped the destiny of the son whose father was a riverman as was his father before him. It was this child, who upon reaching maturity, became a legend on the campus of Syracuse University. Thus was born James A. Ten Eyck in the fresh, invigorating dawn of the tenth month of 1851.

The young boy and his mother were close, but she died when he was ten. Wanderlust replaced her in his life, and soon, young Jim left the one-room schoolhouse and began to make his own way.

Recalling his father often boasted that a Ten Eyck never lost a race, Jim and a chum scraped together $2.50 and challenged two grown fishermen on a two and one-half mile course. They seized a heavy fishingboat equipped with straight ash oars and rowed. The older, wiser men employing "jockeying" tactics won handily, but friendly spectators in sympathy took up a collection for the boys and made up their lost wager.

Through the years, Jim remained on the water, and in a race at Ossining (New York), he showed his mettle. A

friend paired him up with a native of the community, saying, "I know a boy (Ten Eyck) who can beat your kid; and
I'll wager a five-spot on him!"

"Does the boy belong in this town?" the friend was
asked.

"Nope—he doesn't belong here, but he is here."

When the other boy saw Jim, then a stripling about as
wide as a necktie and weighing less than a hundred pounds
soaking wet, he scoffed, taking the challenge:

"You're on, kid!"

The race was rowed, and of course, Jim flashed across
in his scull a big winner. He received nine dollars for his
efforts; but more important, his prowess with the oars came
to the attention of Josh Ward, one of America's earliest
professionals. Josh, who was brother of Pennsylvania's later
coach, Ellis, invited Jim to Cornwall (New York), on the
Hudson River to train with him for a few weeks. Then
later, Jim became a professional, and the schoolhouse for-
ever lost a malcontent.

The next few years, Ten Eyck spent rowing, fishing,
ferrying and sailing boats. The Hudson was his, and he loved
it. His first important race as a professional was against Billy
Scharffe of Pittsburg (Pennsylvania). His opponent at a
later date became champion sculler of America. Their race
was staged in Philadelphia, and Jim Ten Eyck won. In those
days, teams of professional oarsmen, like the baseball teams
of today, toured the country, appearing on every rowing
course from Frisco to Halifax and from Miami to Duluth,
even invading England and Australia.

The races in which they participated were usually pro-
moted by industrial corporations, railroads and particularly

by summer hotels which used the spectacular rowing contests as advertisements for their facilities.

Outstanding among the professionals with Ten Eyck were such men as Charles Courtney, Richard Glendon, George Lee, Albert Hamm, Peter Conley, Edward Hanlan, Wallace Ross, John Teemer, George Hosmer, Jake Gaudaur, Henry "Dad" Vail, Warren Smith, Fred Plaisted, Peter Priddy, John McKay, Gilbert, Josh, Ellis and Dan Ward, and Jim Riley.

During the years 1875, 1876 and 1877, Ten Eyck succumbed to the lure of settling down and becoming a harbor policeman in New York. But the life proved monotonous at best, and he gratefully returned to professional rowing.

Ten Eyck grew adept in moving his frail-appearing boat; in 1886, a crew consisting of himself, Edward Hanlan, John Teemer and Albert Hamm in their straight four-oared shell defeated the best of England.

While in the land of Shakespeare and Tennyson, Ten Eyck in single scull events won three other races on the historic Thames.

The tonic wine of adulation came to Ten Eyck and to the other professionals, too. They became household names in America. Their names and faces adorned cigar-boxes and cigarette packages. And the smallest boys of the day followed them with the same interest and awe and admiration that years later their sons and grandsons bestowed on Christy Matheson, Babe Ruth, Dizzy Dean, Mickey Mantle and Ted Williams.

Once, Ten Eyck rowed in another four-oared crew which swept everyone else aside on its way to win the American championship at Duluth. After those races, he rowed single scull more and more, and in the late 1880s, won the single scull championship of New England, an area widely known for its giant oarsmen of that day.

As the years passed, Ten Eyck became more involved in the coaching phase of rowing. His first crew was the Newark (New Jersey) Boat Club. Later he guided the famed Wauchusett Boat Club of Worcester (Massachusetts) and then the Worcester Boat Club.

While coaching at Worcester, Ten Eyck taught his son, Ned, his first lesson in rowing, and a few years afterwards, as his coach, with fatherly pride watched Ned win the Diamond Sculls at the English Henley on the Thames. Ned established a new record in that race.

He coached the first Navy crews on water in 1899 and 1900 and then served the Arundel Boat Club of Baltimore (Maryland). Shortly afterwards he was summoned to Syracuse.

However, from time to time, Ten Eyck swung an oar to keep in rowing shape. When he was nearer fifty than forty and at Syracuse, a New York City oarsman issued a challenge to any oarsman in America to a match race from New York to Albany for one grand. Ten Eyck accepted the challenge. He won, but his hands were so blistered from the 150-mile trip that he was hardly able to handle the prize of crisp bills. His time was 24 hours and twenty-four minutes.

One of many of his prized letters of admiration that he kept through the years came from Jerome D. Barnum, a Cornell alumnus and at the time a resident of Syracuse:

> Ever since hearing the news on Saturday that Syracuse won two splendid victories at Poughkeepsie, I, as a Cornell man, have wanted to salute you. I have liked you ever since the first day I met you. I have realized that your person-

ality, and your splendid sportsmanship were bound to give Syracuse winning crews. Of course, as a true Cornellian, I am anxious that victory should first come to our men, but as a citizen of Syracuse and as a resident of University Hill, my heart beats strongly every day for the ideals and achievements of the men who bear the Orange. Winning or losing is of little account with me, and in the end, with the men of any college, it is the fun that you have out of participating in the athletic events either as spectators or teammates that counts. It is because you are such a splendid, wholehearted good fellow that I know that Syracuse men on the water will always win as long as you are at the helm. Win, I say, because they will obtain while under your instruction the seed of fine character that will make them good citizens in their after days in the business world.

And after Ten Eyck went back home, back to Poughkeepsie, back to the Hudson, Rusty Callow composed this poem as an eulogy of praise:

Men of yore, launch your shell on the golden shore.
Here comes the coxswain, Captain and coach of the crew.
He'll pick his crew from a chosen few,
Courtney, Connibear, Johnny Shultz and Gaudaur, Ward, Hanlan, Cook, Young, "Rich" Glendon and "Dad" Vail.
Yes, "the Old man" has come to the end of a trail.
Swing wide the portals of the boathouse door.
Make way, here comes your new stroke oar,
And you'll give him ten good ones when he comes,
Ten for Coach Jim, that lovable old son of a gun.

PART III

Maintaining the Pace

CHAPTER XXIX

OARSMEN OF SYRACUSE

were under the megaphone of someone else for the first time in thirty-five years in 1938, but still under a Ten Eyck. Ned, former coach at Wisconsin and Rutgers, assumed the coaching job left vacant by his father's death. Thick-set and in his 60th year of life, Ned was a mild-mannered man.

He was bedeviled, too, as was his father before him, by a late thaw in his first spring as coach of the crews. The ice-frosted Onondaga retarded conditioning of his numerically few oarsmen, and this in turn, hampered his picking a varsity crew.

In order to obtain a better line on them, when weather allowed, he sent three boats out on a trial run; he gave the freshmen a lead of twenty seconds, and then sent his two varsity crews sweeping down the water after them. One of the boats stroked by Gerald Bradley, last year's varsity stroke, demonstrated more savvy and know-how than the other crew in that particular test.

Bradley's boat, in the mile and three-quarter run, rowed over thirty strokes to the minute all the way, caught the winded freshmen at the mile point and stood off a determined threat from the other boat. His crew won by a full length over the one stroked by Bruce Whitehead, No. 2 oar with last year's freshman boat who later became a clergyman.

If his crews were to present representative showings

that season, Ned knew the squad was unable to sustain many injuries or academic troubles. But he was comforted by the thought that the two varsity boats were almost on a par, while the freshmen presented future possibilities of strength.

Robert F. Kelley, *New York Times* rowing expert, visited the new boathouse that spring and came away impressed by what he saw. Later, he wrote:

> Bradley is light, weighing only 168, and he skies a bit at the catch, shoots his slide away and when pressed, is inclined to shorten the stroke in his excitement. But he keeps the oarsmen working behind him and they are a racy looking lot.

All that spring, the men practiced and listened patiently as Ned taught many for the first time the art of rowing. From time to time, he experimented with various combinations of men, but it was no secret that it required a close understanding with willingness and cohesive effort to "jell" the crews that year.

Ned received an opportunity on May 14, to see how far his men were coming in attaining proficiency.

In a quadrangular regatta with Cornell, Harvard and MIT, the crews rowed into a headwind and rough water on the Charles River in Boston. The varsity race was exciting—compressing the thrills, the gallant efforts and the fine arts of the sport into one congealed struggle, but at the finish, the Syracuse boat finished third. The freshmen finished third also, but the junior varsity crew with Bruce Whitehead at stroke brought Ned's first victory as Orange coach.

The shell grabbed a marginal lead at the offset, and by the time the bridge spanning the river was reached, it held a full length of open water ahead of Harvard. Behind them

241

at this moment, the Cantabs were locked in a grim struggle with Cornell.

Although Cornell surged ahead and passed Harvard a short distance beyond the bridge, the Big Red was unable to shake off the Cantabs. In the last quarter mile, Harvard caught and then passed the Big Red and gained on the Ten Eyck boat near the finish.

With Whitehead in that boat were Robert Emery, bow; John Horrocks; Gomer McNeil; Phil Irvine; Wilbur Stuhlman; Richard Gaudern; and Paul Hart, coxswain.

The rowing coaches a few days before the Poughkeepsie regatta honored the memory of Ned's father by refusing to elect a president of their Intercollegiate Rowing Coaches' Association.

"We'll leave Jim Ten Eyck as our permanent president," Navy's Buck Walsh said, and the group paid a moment's silence of respect.

With Old Ten Eyck's departure, the first wave of college coaches from the ranks of the professional scullers was gone. Now, for the most part, the ranks were filled by former college oarsmen, most of whom came from the great Washington crews of recent years. For example, watching the IRA races that day in June were former Huskies, all famous coaches in their own rights: Thomas Bolles and Harvey Love of Harvard; Edward Leader of Yale; and Charles Logg of Rutgers.

Many spectators on the observation train at the Hudson regatta watched at one time during the afternoon a boy peering through telescopic sights at the races. If by chance the lad remained transfixed to the lens during the varsity race, he witnessed a race worthy of retelling someday to his grandchildren; for it was the fastest, if not the wettest, race in the long history of the event.

Rain and gloomy weather kept away the normal crowd from the races; even President Roosevelt passed up the invitation due to the inclement conditions; and the observation train instead of its customary 18 hauled a dozen half-filled cars.

The crews literally burned up the water, according to those who saw the race. Navy in a whirlwind finish shattered the all-time record, rowing down the four-mile course in eighteen minutes and 19 seconds to eclipse Washington's mark of 1937 by fifteen seconds! Syracuse finished seventh and last.

Navy's victory was heralded throughout the eastern campuses, for it broke the long victory grip of Western crews at the Poughkeepsie regatta. But at the same time, victory meant much to Buck Walsh, the Navy coach, who was ill and confined to the hospital.

Sweet was the triumph for the Midshipmen inasmuch as they led the pack for the previous two years, only to see victory snatched from them by the Huskies in the last few hundred yards.

"I told them," Walsh confided to friends, "to keep ahead of Washington and California crews; and they did almost all the race!"

Washington took the three-mile junior varsity event. Syracuse was fourth. And in the yearling affair, California won, with Ned's men placing a strong third.

Shortly after Poughkeepsie, "Wrong-way" Corrigan flew from Brooklyn to Dublin in a light airplane, claiming he meant all the time to fly to Los Angeles. And on a more somber note, English Prime Minister Neville Chamberlain raced to Munich for a meeting with the German dictator.

Back in Syracuse supervising the care of the shells during the winter months was an erect, brown-eyed man with a sly grin. He was Charles Keller, and since 1923, when the Old Man took him to Poughkeepsie with him, he cared for the precious boats of crews. In fact, he was one of the few men on the University staff who served as year-around custodian of equipment.

Aside from Ned, the grey-haired rigger represented the last remaining link between the Old Man and his filial successor.

Charlie's job consisted of babying the five shells that represented a $10,000 investment. But when the shells went on a trip, it was his task to dismantle them, pack them into tailor-made trucks or trains and then assemble them upon arrival at the destination. He is remembered for handling his chores as if delicately balancing valuable chinaware in a lady's dining room closet.

The seats, the slides, shoes and out-rigging were assembled by him as they were when taken apart. Each man's out-rigging and other equipment were set to specified positions. Nimble fingers, a deft mind and a certain touch were all required to return them back to the preferred positions after dis-assembly.

That spring while James Decker, director of publicity, ground out press releases on the prowess of Orange crews, pyramiding statistics and facts for the nation's mass media, the oarsmen impatiently pawed the frozen ground and looked forlornly out at the iced Lake. Spring of 1939 once more forgot the calendar and was tardy in Syracuse.

SYRACUSE RIGGER, CHARLIE KELLER

Winter tank work at the Gym. The tank was the first of its kind in the country, built in 1908.

The extent of their delay in physical conditioning was very much in evidence on May 13 at Derby, Connecticut. Yale swept over the placid Housatonic, scooping up all three races from Syracuse and MIT. The Eli boats were far ahead.

A somewhat freak accident in the varsity event almost became a legend in the off-season hot-stove circle. It happened when Yale moved smoothly along at a steady 34 beats, came from behind to pass Syracuse and the MIT Engineers. It led by a deck length.

"Aiyeeeee!" shattered the air suddenly. Shouting was the No. 4 man for Syracuse, sophomore Bill Hall, who struck the side of the shell and then was plunged wildly into the frigid water.

Hall's mates back-paddled to pick him up, believing that the five foot-11 inch oarsman was unconscious. By now, he was at least 20 yards behind his crew. However, he was ignominiously fished out later by Ned's launch and hurriedly wrapped in blankets.

The 300 spectators who saw the incident from shore gasped when they saw Hall's oar strike a coarse marker, the impact of the blade against his stomach catapaulting him into the water.

With three starboard swingers and four portsiders, the crippled Ten Eyck boat staged a gallant uphill effort, but MIT crossed the finish line by a length and a quarter ahead.

The warm weather of June brought Ned's crew into trim physical peak, and they defeated Wisconsin over a three-mile course on the Lake by two lengths.

At Cornell it was a far different story, and the crews

gave good accounts of themselves, but the Big Red and Harvard took the honors.

It was a time in history when a second generation of Syracuse oarsmen came to Piety Hill. George Hilfinger, son of Martin, No. 7 oar in the "miracle crew" of 1913, was varsity stroke and one of four sons of former oarsmen on the roster:

Robert and Edward Rice were sophomores, sons of Leon Rice of the first championship crew of 1904, and brothers of Frank Rice, recently graduated.

William Hall, Jr., who experienced the misfortune in the Yale race, was son of the man stroking the last Syracuse four-oared shell in 1913 at Poughkeepsie.

On the other hand, Howard Hadley of the same Syracuse squad was son of a man who rowed for Cornell's Courtney back 30 years ago.

Faint stirrings of revived interest in rowing came to the surface on April 12, when students formed the University Rowing Club with Samuel Cook as its sponsor. Purpose of the group was to "promote and support interest in the sport of rowing among the undergraduates and alumni of Syracuse University."

First on the agenda was the election of officers. Chosen were: President, John Warren; vice president, John More; secretary, Frank Stuhlman; and treasurer, John Horrocks. Each officer was a varsity crew member.

Although support increased for the sport, Ned's varsity slowly shaped up in practice. In the IRA, the crew finished fifth.

While the East expected to continue its mastery over the Hudson, Coach Ebright's California giants from the

248

JUNIOR VARSITY CHAMPIONS, IRA, 1939

Str. Gerald Bradley, Howard Hadley, Bruce Whitehead, Robert Emery, John Nixon, Arthur Wilcox, John Horrocks, Bernard Tainter, Cox Paul Hart.

Upstream time trial; two great bridges over the course.

Fancy showers in the boathouse, cold river water in tank drops through holes in its bottom.

WASH ROOM

SCENES OF THE HUDSON

249

Hotel Di Prima, last quarters in Highland.

Boathouse and launching float.

land of the redwoods decided otherwise. They shattered Navy's 1938 time record in winning.

The Syracuse frosh finished fourth in its event, but the junior varsity pulled the upset of the day, scoring a sensational victory after Washington caught a crab on the portside, one-half mile from the finish.

If this was construed to be a cheap victory for Syracuse, nothing was further from the truth. It was a break, yes, but it was likewise a good one only if Ned's crew seized it and rowed their hearts out. They did.

Stroked by Bradley, the boat caught the Huskies at the two-mile mark and then lost them when the crew began to splash badly and shipped water in their craft.

Washington momentarily was halted by the crab, and Syracuse with a steady and even pace of 38 beats to the minute passed the Huskies. Victory was by the width of a whisk feather, or by four-fifths of a second.

Returning up the river after recovery, the crowd on the obsevation train saw something to cheer lustily about. Paul Hart, the Orange coxswain while waving to the cheering spectators lost his balance and fell into the Hudson, and Bradley, stroke oar, dragged him back into the shell.

Two months after Poughkeepsie, Germany invaded Poland for the beginning of another World War; that October, President Roosevelt was informed by Albert Einstein and other scientists about the possibilities of developing something they called an atomic bomb.

CHAPTER XXX

ROWING AT SYRACUSE

established no distinguished records in 1940 and 1941, although Ned's small squads were noted for tenacity and spirit in their races. In the background, however, silently watching and waiting were those who sincerely believed the athletic program on Piety Hill was served best if rowing was abandoned.

Rumors circulated early in 1940 that rowing was to be dropped, and the student newspaper, the *Daily Orange,* courageously supported crew. To substantiate the reasons for its belief, the paper conducted an opinion poll. It interviewed 100 undergraduate men chosen from the four university classes in an effort to discover if students were apathetic and indifferent to rowing. A majority of students approved of rowing and strongly opposed any plans for dropping the sport.

As if spurred on to prove themselves worthy of this confidence, the three crews gave Cornell and Harvard close races that May twenty-fifth, 1940, on Cayuga Lake in a driving rainstorm. Of course, they lost, but not before displaying heart-warming evidences of courage and determination.

On the Hudson that June, Syracuse fooled the experts by finishing third in the varsity race. The oarsmen were picked to finish sixth. They gave good account of themselves by battling for the lead with Cornell and Washington until near the finish, the Huskies pulled away from everyone in the last two furlongs and won on the wind-lashed Hudson.

Previous to the varsity race, all junior varsity crews swamped in the wild waters. Hence, the event was postponed to follow the varsity race. Later in the day, all jayvee crews raced down the course in good order, but darkness overtook these oarsmen before they reached the bridge. There in the black of evening, coxswains crossed lanes until at the finish no one was certain who won. It was not until the following morning that Washington was named the winner.

The following year at Poughkeepsie, Syracuse once more was out-manned and out-rowed, but the plucky varsity crew offered nothing more than heart and grit against the manpower and ability of its opponents. Finishing fourth, the crew came from far behind the pack to make a fight of it. Ahead of them were Washington, California and Cornell.

Refereeing those 1941 IRA races was Howard Robbins, one of Jim Ten Eyck's favorites in the 1913 championship crew. An attorney in Boston, he became an active referee in the New England area as well as at Poughkeepsie.

Ned began worrying about the next season early in the fall, but Pearl Harbor burst into flames on December seventh, 1941, and interrupted collegiate rowing. Prospective oarsmen and those veterans of the shells were called upon to journey into other waters than those confined to America's rivers and lakes.

When the young men left their civilian pursuits, it was an era of Buck Rogers comics, the nickel hot dog and pay phone toll. When they returned to home and to campus in

1946, it was a new age—the time of the atom. New words such as fission, neutron and reactor appeared in the newspapers and on the radio for the first time. It was also an era of great adjustment, of confusion and of hesitancy. Already guiding the University at this time was its second master architect—Dr. William Pearson Tolley, '22—who came to his Alma Mater from the presidency of Allegheny College in 1942, upon retirement of Dr. William Pratt Graham. He directed the institution in a dramatic time of growth and of turbulent post-war problems.

Dr. Tolley as Chancellor personified the dedicated, driving and dynamic image of administrator-educator whose courage and vision were needed in an age of upheaval in higher education in America. Under him, Syracuse once more began to move.

Not unmindful of this resurging spirit on campus was Ned Ten Eyck, who returned to coach crew. Now in the twilight years at 68, he faced mandatory retirement within two years.

Ned tried gallantly to get into the swing of the new period, but he faced an enormous task of taking inexperienced men—few of them ever rowed before coming to the campus—and shaping them to a cause in a very materialistic time. Although most of them stood over six feet tall, the freshmen were as green as the sod that surrounded the buildings.

Hans "Whitey" Driessnack stroked the frosh boat, a crew that relied upon brute strength and beef rather than on good form and timing. Ned's short layback stroke, somewhat different from his father's, served the yearlings best.

Largest in that boat was Joseph Grzibowski, the No. 5

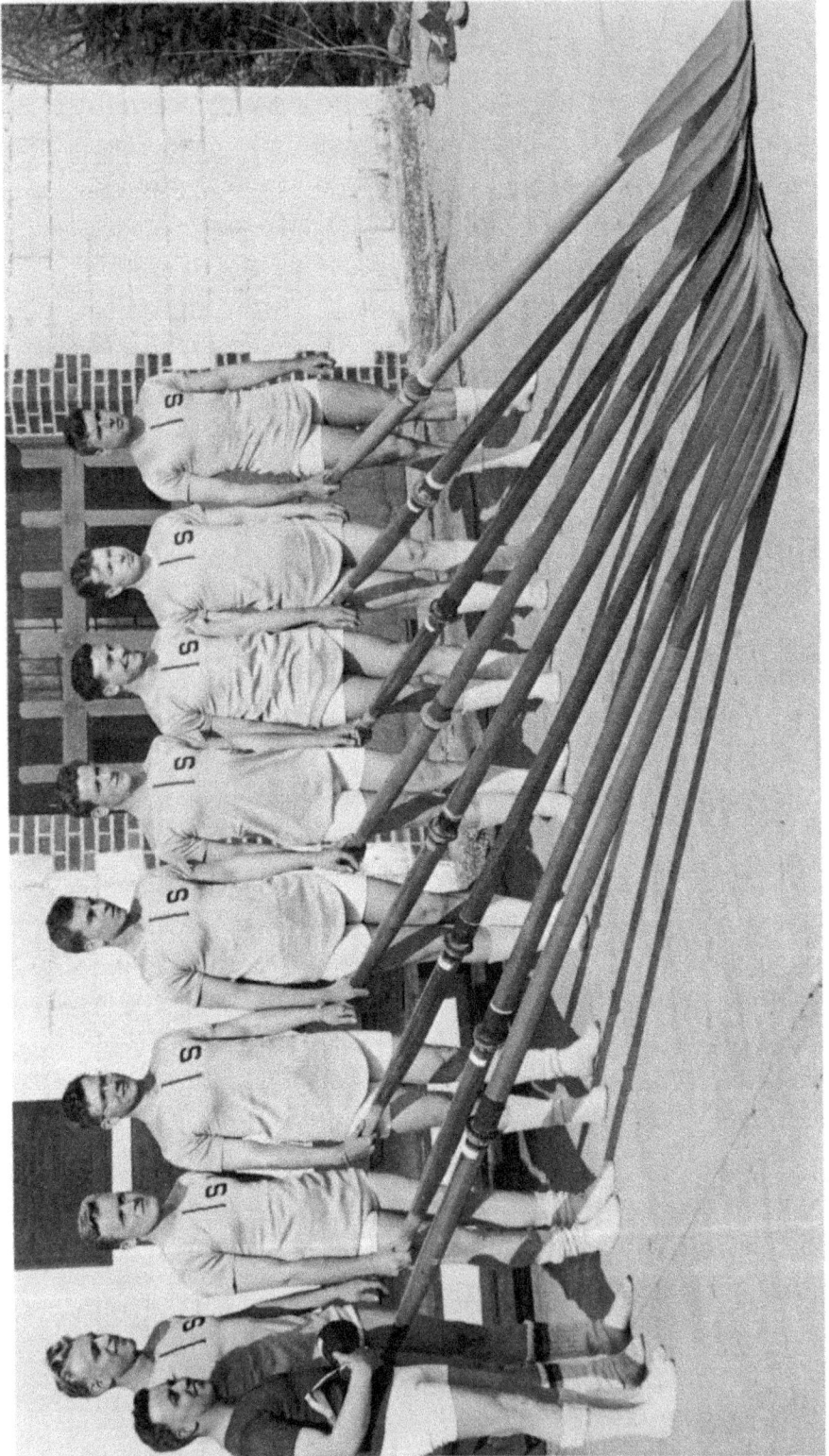

254

1947 FRESHMAN CREW

oar, who was over 76 inches tall and who carried 206 pounds of solid weight. A popular story about him demonstrated his feat of athletic prowess.

It seems that while standing around at a track meet one day in Archbold Stadium, Joe picked up a javelin for the first time in his life, and hefted it. Later, in some unexplainable manner, he was entered in the event and when he hurled the metal spear a good distance in the contest, he was awarded second place. And football lost a star tackle the following autumn when he devoted all his interests and energies to rowing.

This freshman powerhouse crew won all its races that season of 1947:

Won by five lengths over Buffalo's West Side Rowing Club in the University's first post-war victory on the water.

Won by one-half length in New York over Columbia and Rutgers after trailing early in the race.

Won by one and one-quarters lengths over Cornell at Ithaca.

Won by four and one-half lengths over Cornell on the Lake.

Shortly afterwards, the frosh were designated the University's official entry in the ten-college invitational meet of 2,000 meters at Seattle, Washington, scheduled for June 28. Such designation was unique in rowing history, but the freshmen were chosen because they demonstrated their superiority repeatedly in races with the varsity and junior varsity boats.

When they went to Poughkeepsie for resumption of the Hudson races, they were sharp and eager for victory.

They came upon a far different scene from those of former IRA regattas. Things were changed. Missing were the excitement and tension of those pre-war races. Poughkeepsie itself resembled a ghost town of the old west; the pennants of competing colleges adorned Main Street, but the townspeople appeared unconcerned.

Excitement still shrouded the Old Nelson House, home and meeting place of the crews and their followers. But it wasn't generated by supporters of rowing; rather by a convention of New York Exchange Clubs.

Missing from the Poughkeepsie scene, too, was the old railroad observation train that hauled spectators alongside the races for so many years. Dismantled for wartime use, the ancient train wasn't re-assembled by the New York Central for another regatta.

256

Motorists were irked. They were forced to park their autos in the now abandoned ferryboat house at Highland at exhorbitant prices. Besides this irritant, spectators stood on the banks of the river, kept informed partially by ship-to-shore radio, at best a second-hand observation. Most of the racing was out of their sight, and even reporters were unable to present the customary timely and accurate minute-by-minute coverage.

On the brighter side, however, Pennsylvania returned to the IRA fold after an absence of ten years. One of the three original founders of the IRA, the Quakers returned to Poughkeepsie in 1947 when the length of the varsity race was shortened from four to three miles. The longer length was the major reason for Pennsylvania leaving the Hudson in 1937.

Navy and Cornell upheld the honor of the eastern

crews with their titanic struggle for the lead in the heavy-weight event. Both battled nose to nose down the line where Stork Sanford's Big Red crew lost out by inches to the Sailors. And Syracuse surprised everyone by tying for seventh.

For Syracuse fans, however, the freshmen caused chests to swell with pride. They led for the first mile in a pack of seven contestants during the two-mile race. Nevertheless, Washington came up and passed them at the railroad bridge, forcing the frosh to be satisfied with second place.

In Seattle (Washington meet), the Syracuse freshman crew finished fourth behind Harvard. The Cantabs from Boston won in a spectacular finish on Lake Washington. Yale trailed by a length. Washington was third. Finishing in the next five after Syracuse were Cornell, California, Wisconsin, Princeton and MIT. Pennsylvania, Columbia and University of California at Los Angeles finished in a dead heat for eighth place.

Rowing for Syracuse in that national event were:

Bow—Vincent Fernandez
No. 2—William Wilson
No. 3—Floyd McCormick
No. 4—E. E. Kelly
No. 5—Joseph Grzibowski
No. 6—H. W. Hinkley
No. 7—Eugene Perry
Stroke—Hans Driessnack
Coxswain—Albert Curson

Early the next year of 1948, Ned's younger brother, Jim Ten Eyck, Jr., stroke of the championship 1908 crew, died. A decade earlier, he was freshman coach at Princeton. Since then, he was affiliated with a textile firm in New York.

Anxiety covered campus that spring. For some unknown reason, the freshman crew of the previous year that became eligible for the varsity boat failed to jell. With all their power, their strength and experience, they still lacked something. Ned was dismayed.

By the time of another Poughkeepsie he switched Grzibowski from his regular position at No. 5 oar to No. 7, replacing him with Don Hurry from the junior varsity boat.

On race day, Syracuse's varsity placed alongside California. Echoing in his men's ears were Ned's instructions to stay with the favored Bears regardless of any extenuating circumstances.

"Ready, all? . . . Row!" bellowed Referee Robbins, and Syracuse shot off to a smooth start, settling down to a 32 beat. Running smoothly and with power, the shell stayed even with California until a mile from the finish.

Suddenly, the rigging of stroke Jack Castle snapped off. From his coxswain seat, John Palmer megaphoned:

"Never mind, Jack—keep rowing!"

But in the ensuing burst of effort, it became quite evident that Castle wasn't contributing any power to the boat; in fact, his dead weight hampered the run of the sleek shell.

"Can you jump?" inquired Palmer.

"Yeah," replied the unemployed stroke. "Hey, fellas, shall I jump?"

"Get out pal—take another boat—try hitchhiking," rejoined his mates almost in unison.

Castle threw out his oar to starboard and dove into the water.

"Good luck, gang!" he shouted when he broke surface.

Tension was relieved somewhat by Donald Reichart at No. 7 oar when he wise-cracked:

"At last—I'm the STROKE!"

Once more the reduced crew grimly set out to catch up with the pack. Without thought of quitting, they rowed magnificently, but the distance separating them from the others was too much. They finished ninth, a few feet behind the Wisconsin Badgers.

The Poughkeepsie Regatta Trophy was presented for the first time that year. Donated by the city's firm of Luckey, Platt and Company, the bronze figure of an oarsman was to be awarded yearly to the school gathering the most points in the regatta. Navy as winner in 1948 was the first to receive it.

If possible, rowing at Syracuse struck even lower bedrock in 1949 than in the two previous years. Few freshmen reported for practice, only a few veterans bothering to report. Ned was serving his final season. He was tired. He was sick. And he fervently hoped for a Poughkeepsie triumph to close out his career.

The odds were stacked against Ned for a successful season. The posture of crew was weak and one of inexperience. Two of the 1948 freshman boat were lost even before the season began:

Jim Hart, stroke of the shell, was killed in an auto accident in Nebraska the previous summer.

Vincent Fernandez, bow oar, of whom so much was expected for 1949, left school due to a rare kidney disease. Two years later, the ailment caused his death.

One of those veterans in the 1949 boat was Don Thayer. And if crew was to be drab for the others, a prank he and others played on Cornell brightened up the season somewhat for him. It began when Cornell students painted a big red "C" on the ramp of the Jim Ten Eyck boathouse.

In retaliation, Thayer and his companions rode to Ithaca. After dusk, they hid in the bushes until the Cornell watchman departed from the rowing area. Then, they climbed over the fence surrounding the docking area on Cayuga Lake. While Thayer busily sketched out a huge "S" with accompanying crossed oars in chalk, two companions filled in the area with orange paint. Fifteen minutes later, the project completed, they retired to an Ithaca pub and toasted their successful foray.

Nineteen forty-nine was the year General Dwight Eisenhower became president of Columbia University, and also a time when Syracuse embarked upon its first development campaign for $15 million. Blueprinted for construction under the program were a new men's gymnasium to replace the old Archbold gymnasium that burned in the winter of 1946; a woman's building; dormitories; and a facility for training teachers in working with the handicapped.

At Poughkeepsie, the varsity crew finished ninth. Swinging No. 7 oar in the race was Eugene Perry, later freshman coach at his Alma Mater.

After the regatta, Ned hung up his megaphone and his oilskins for the life of retirement. He was tendered a testimonial dinner before saying farewell to the campus and community, and then he moved to Florida.

The mid-point of the Twentieth Century introduced new faces, new waters for the regatta and new records by crews of the collegiate world. For example, Syracuse chose as successor to Ned a former Washington oarsman. And for the first time in forty-seven years, a Ten Eyck wasn't on hand to direct the crews.

Gosta "Gus" Eriksen, a graduate of the Husky school in 1939, succeeded Ned Ten Eyck. He was freshman coach at his Alma Mater in 1948 and 1949, and his yearling crews never lost a race in competition with 40 opponents over the two seasons. With him, Eriksen brought to Syracuse another Husky alumnus, Victor Michalson, as Freshman coach.

When Eriksen arrived on campus, ten of the 14 college crews entered in the 1950 regatta were served by the following former Washington oarsmen, most of them former pupils of Rusty Callow now at Pennsylvania: Ky Ebright, California; Charles Logg, Rutgers; James McMillin, Massachusetts Institute of Technology; Walter Raney, Columbia; Sanford, Cornell; Delos Schoch, Princeton; Norman Sonju, Wisconsin; and Alvin Ulbrickson, Washington.

Allison Danzig, veteran crew writer of the *New York Times* wrote for the official 1949 IRA souvenir program a penetrating analysis of the Washington influence:

> The vogue for Washington coaches is comparable to the demand for Notre Dame graduates in football in the late Twenties and Thirties. Notre Dame during the regime of Knute Rockne, as well as now, stood for the best in football, and Washington has enjoyed comparable prestige in rowing. So it is only natural that colleges looking for a rowing coach have turned to Seattle where Hiram Connibear started something really big.

It was folly not to admit that upon Eriksen's arrival on campus, the emphasis was shifted definitely to football at Syracuse. Men, who otherwise might row, were discovered forsaking the sport for the glory of the gridiron. And consequently, funds for rowing were pared down to the bone.

Despite this condition, Eriksen and Michalson brought

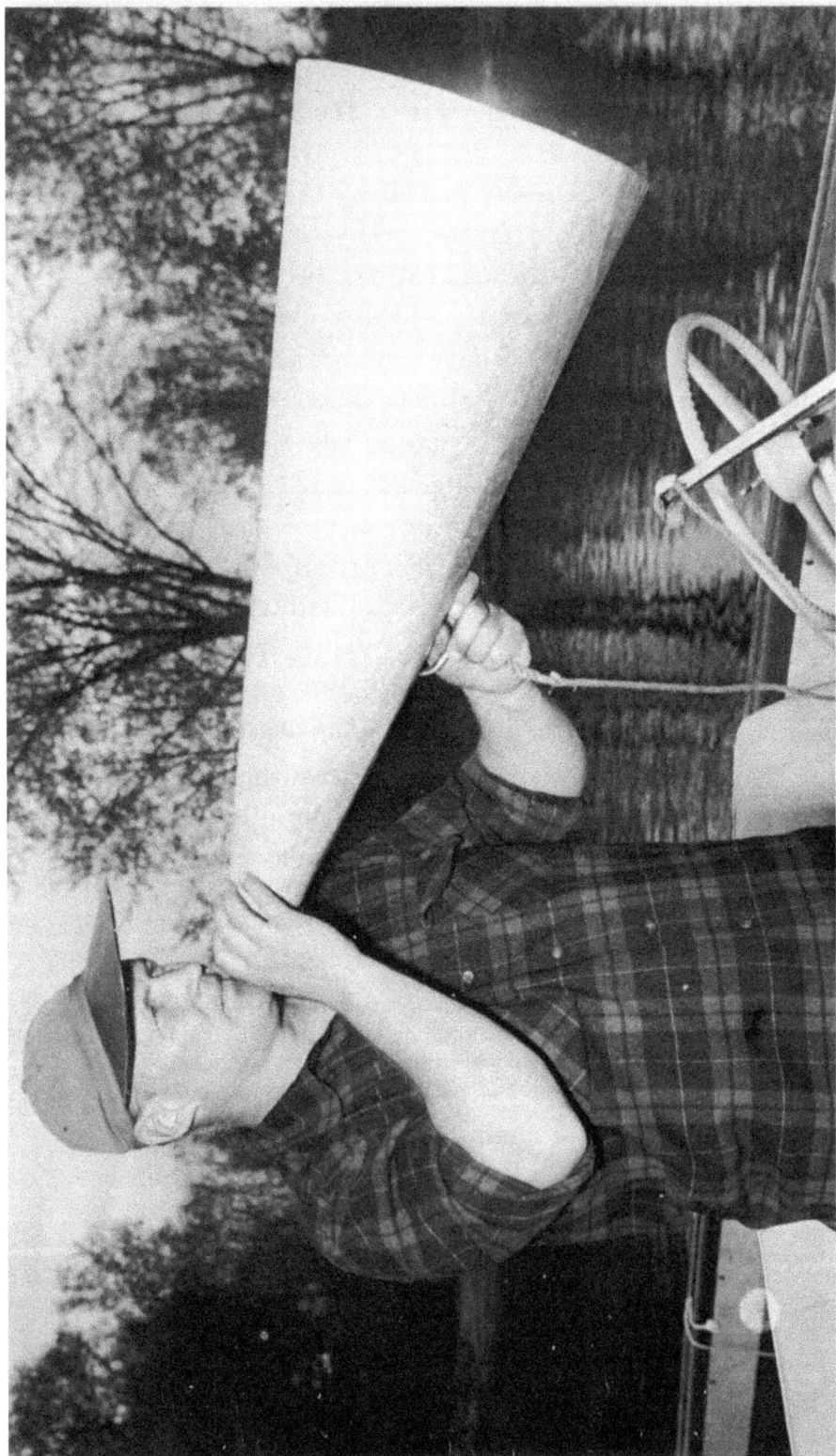

262

COACH GOSTA (GUS) ERIKSEN

with them a new spirit and a knowledge of dedication to the art of rowing. Their enthusiasm was contagious and rubbed off on many of their oarsmen. For example, so imbued with the new spirit was Don Thayer, the sign painter at Cornell, and a senior, that he began a starvation diet in order to meet demands of the coxswain position. He became coxie of the junior varsity boat.

One of the first changes made by Eriksen at Syracuse was the style of stroking the boat. He introduced the long reach and long layback technique of western crews. This was in contrast to Ned's short layback style.

A perfectionist even to the smallest detail, Eriksen equipped coxswains with stop-watches strapped to their knees and facing the stroke oars. Strokes, in this way, were constantly aware of their time.

On a windy day, the coxswains carried tin bailers with them for the purpose of dumping out the water that sloshed inboard. Eriksen said this lightened the boat.

In some respects Eriksen was no different from other coaches. He contrived signals for increasing the stroke. And prior to a race, he always took his coxswains out in a launch on a preview run of the course, picking out landmarks for guideposts for employing the signals.

While Eriksen trained his first crews at Syracuse, IRA officials and authorities began making arrangements for the transfer of the regatta from Poughkeepsie to a new site in Ohio.

CHAPTER XXXI

INCH BY INCH

with the eddying motion made by her motor, the pleasure
boat backed away from the wharf and clumsily turned her
bow to the open river and to Poughkeepsie, downstream.
It was a few hours after the final event of the IRA regatta
in 1949, and the officials in the boat looked backwards at
the scene. It was to be the last time this boat, as official
launch, was to churn the waters of the Hudson. The IRA
later decided to leave the historic area near Highland.

Henceforth, the races were held on other waters. The glory
and the glamor of rowing that was exclusively Poughkeepsie's was hers no more.

Several factors were responsible for the IRA's later
decision to move:

Poor support by the city of Poughkeepsie.

General apathy of the townspeople.

Dwindling crowds.

And the railroad's decision not to provide once more
an observation train for the races.

Before deciding to shift the regatta, the officials stood
on the wharf of the Columbia boathouse, where the crews
used to launch their shells for the races. Before them lay the
gear and traces of the years' races and of a half-century's
habitation:

Silent boathouses.

Abandoned docks.

Overturned K-ration boxes.

Collapsed chairs.

Empty bunk beds.
surrounded by litter of young men—torn papercups, twisted candybar wrappers, forgotten letters, an empty sock or two, a moth-eaten sweatshirt and the frayed end of a tiller rope.

Mostly, the site of racing crews resembled something lost; a spirit, it seemed, or an age; but certainly a picture of the quietness of a cemetery.

Time and men passed Poughkeepsie. But actually, rowing in passing her by was adjusting to a new age of change with new faces. And therefore did depart the historic IRA regatta from the place from where she was born in 1895, nourished in the 1900s, and ripened in the 1920s. With her went the memories and the records of achievements, all part of the heritage that belonged to young rowing men.

There was so much history poured into the diary of college rowing from the face of this water! Upon this river in 1895 was held the first regatta, with Cornell, Columbia and Pennsylvania as participants. Originally scheduled for a Friday, a wake from a passing tug smashed Penn's shell against a float, and the race was postponed to the following Monday. With a display of sportsmanship, both Cornell and Columbia refused to row without the Quakers.

On the re-scheduled date, Pennsylvania was swamped in rough water halfway through the race, leaving Cornell and Columbia to fight it out. In this race, Columbia was rowed to victory by its captain, Hamilton Fish, who, three years afterwards, was killed in a charge up San Juan Hill in Cuba with Teddy Roosevelt's Rough Riders.

Courtney, the scourge of Syracuse crews in later years, piloted his Big Red to victories on the Hudson in the succeeding races of 1896 and 1897. However, the Spanish-American War interrupted the regatta in 1898 on the Hudson. It was shifted for that year to Saratoga Lake. Competing on the three-mile course was Wisconsin, the first crew from outside the East to enter up to that time. Pennsylvania won the race as she was to do the next two years, but unfortunately in the following half century, she failed to win a varsity contest in the IRA.

Up to and including the 1949 regatta, but excluding the years of two wars, Cornell garnered 14 varsity races; Washington, eight; California and Navy, six; Syracuse, five; Columbia, four; Pennsylvania, three. Wisconsin was scoreless in those many years she raced.

The IRA regatta was held on the Hudson course each year except in 1898 and in 1920. However, even with all this history and fame, the crews of the IRA couldn't claim the beginning of college crew racing. That belonged to Harvard and·Yale. It was started something like this.

Desiring to promote the recreational facilities of Lake Winnipesaukee, New Hampshire, a superintendent of the Boston, Concord and Montreal Railroad suggested a race between Yale and Harvard in 1851.

Not officially sanctioned by the officials of the two schools, the first race was held between the private rowing clubs. Harvard won that first collegiate race.

Those first boats forty-four years before the first IRA regatta consisted of eights with coxswains; later, they were sixes, steered by the bow oars. Successful though that first race was, Yale and Harvard didn't race again until 1855, because the administrators and faculties of both schools disapproved.

Five years after the surrender at Appomattox, three events of importance occurred between the two universities:

One of the three famous breaks in Yale-Harvard relations happened.

A Yale crew introduced, for the first time by a college crew, the sliding seat.

And New London was inspected and considered as a possible race site.

Up to this time of 1870, races between the two were held on circular courses. This year, it was decided to dispense with the turning races for those with a straightaway course, and New London was checked for such a course, but at that time, nothing came of it. It was to be several years before the race was transferred to New London. The circular course this year of 1870 caused the famous break between the two.

The race was held at Worcester (Massachusetts), over a one and one-half mile course to a stakeboat, around the craft and return to the starting line. The boats were sixes.

In the race, Yale accidentally slammed into Harvard at the first turn, tearing away the wooden bar which held the rudder wires. Steering was useless, and the referee disqualified the Elis and awarded the race to the Cantabs. In this race Yale used crude greased sliding seats made by sculler Walter Brown.

Consequently, there was no race in 1871. Robert Kelley, in his *American Rowing*, explained:

> . . . merely some correspondence as crisp as the notes
> exchanged by diplomats of estranged countries. . . .

During this exchange of notes, Yale challenged Harvard for a race on a straightaway course. Harvard agreed, but in turn, suggested a general regatta with other contestants. Yale disagreed, saying she wanted to race Harvard, alone. Harvard answered promptly: she wanted to meet others, too. In another note, Harvard specified that if the Elis still insisted on a separate race, she must agree to a circular race, the same type of contest in which Yale was defeated in 1870. They didn't race.

It wasn't until 1876 that the two began exclusive engagements. That year, Yale resigned from the general college rowing association—Rowing Association of American Colleges—and she was followed the next year by Harvard. In 1878, they moved to New London for their races. Major reason for the shift was the straightaway course and the introduction of the first railroad observation train for spectators in America.

Rough tactics in football in 1896 caused another open break between the two schools. Then Yale went to the British Henley, leaving Harvard without competition. The Cantabs accepted an invitation to race at Poughkeepsie in the IRA against Cornell, Columbia and Pennsylvania. She finished second behind Cornell.

Following that race, Cornell signed a two-year agreement to meet Harvard, but in 1897, Yale and Harvard patched up their differences and neither one desired to race in the general Poughkeepsie regatta. They did agree, however, to meet with Cornell on the Hudson a week before the general events.

Cornell defeated both schools in that race. Although the Big Red urged Yale and Harvard to join the IRA regatta, the two refused and returned to racing at New London. Consequently, the opportunity for a single intercollegiate regatta on American waters was lost.

In the following years, Yale was unable to win consistently on the water, and in 1912, she returned to the graduate system of coaching. The next years, William Averell Harriman assisted in coaching. Unable to make the varsity because of his light weight, Harriman was widely known for his remarkable smooth style of rowing. He was an excellent coach.

Nine years afterwards, the New Haven (Connecticut) school called upon a former pupil of Washington's immortal Connibear to lead her to triumph on the water. He was Edward Leader. Under his leadership until 1931, Yale was beaten by Harvard only twice—in 1927 and 1931.

Meanwhile, Harvard writhed in despair over the long string of defeats to Yale. In 1930, she took action, hiring a former pupil of Jim Ten Eyck's. Charles J. Whiteside, one-time stroke oar at Syracuse, went to the Charles River. The following year, his Harvard crew defeated Yale for its second victory over Yale since 1921.

The long history of college rowing is formidable. Whereas, Yale and Harvard instituted formal college rowing in 1851, other schools weren't far behind. In 1859, Brown and Trinity joined the two pioneers in a race. The following year, freshman and sophomore races were added to the varsity event among the four. But college rowing was interrupted by the Civil War.

Representatives of Harvard, Brown, Amherst and

Bowdoin in 1871 formed the Rowing Association of American Colleges. They held the first straightaway race between more than two schools. Massachusetts Agricultural College, now Massachusetts State, defeated Harvard and Brown over a three-mile course. The next year, Amherst defeated Harvard, Massachusetts, Bowdoin, Williams and Yale. The association grew to 11 members by 1873, consisting of Yale, Harvard, Dartmouth, Amherst, Columbia, Bowdoin, Massachusetts, Cornell, Trinity, Wesleyan and Williams. Yale won.

On Saratoga Lake in 1894, Columbia was triumphant, and the following year, Cornell won over a pack consisting of Columbia, Harvard, Dartmouth, Wesleyan, Yale, Amherst, Brown, Williams, Bowdoin, Hamilton, Union and Princeton.

As mentioned previously, the distinct cleavage in American college rowing that resulted in two separate regattas—Yale-Harvard and the IRA—came about in 1895 when Yale and Harvard turned to eight-oared shells. Yale withdrew from the association and Harvard followed the next year.

Shifts to the eight-oared shells and the subsequent expensive cost of rowing caused many schools in the 1880s to abandon the sport. Besides, football and baseball, less expensive to support, were just then coming into popularity.

College rowing in those early times was confined largely to the eastern schools, but Washington and California in the late 1890s boldly introduced rowing on their campuses.

At Washington, enthusiastic students organized their first crew in 1899. And in 1900, at the time Syracuse formally entered collegiate rowing, the Huskies raised money with which to purchase two rowing barges. They held class races until 1903, when the first intercollegiate regatta on the West Coast was held on Lake Washington between the Huskies and Golden Bears. Washington won.

The sport on the coast grew by leaps and bounds, and the Golden Bears defeated Leland Stanford University in 1904, the year Syracuse won for the first time on the Hudson. Four years later, the West Coast crews received an invitation to race at Poughkeepsie, but a shortage of money made the journey impossible.

Washington, two years later, went out to Wisconsin for a race with the Badgers, and in 1913, came East to the Hudson, where she finished third to Syracuse and Cornell.

And so, after fifty-five years, the historical Intercollegiate Rowing Association moved its regatta to the Ohio River at Marietta in 1950. Here on the waters over which George Washington once rowed as a surveyor almost two centuries before, college crews met.

Eriksen devoted time and effort of his crews before the regatta to maneuvering a dogleg on the course a mile from the starting line. He taught his crews how to employ the best angle in the dogleg. Then he waited for the race, his optimism high.

The 20,000 inhabitants of Marietta were wild with enthusiasm over the approaching races, but on the eve of the events, heavy rains descended upon the site of the 48th IRA regatta, and the Ohio became a raging flood. On the following morning, uprooted trees and debris were catapulted along the boiling torrent, making the course dangerous for the slim shells.

The starting times of the races were pushed ahead an

THE ENTIRE VARSITY SQUAD IN 1950

THE ENTIRE FROSH SQUAD IN 1950

hour as result of the chaotic conditions, and the length of the course was shortened from three to two miles. The starting line was established below the dogleg where the river broadened somewhat and was less turbulent.

Crews lining up for starts experienced nightmares. The swiftly running current forced them repeatedly to miss their stakeboats and narrowly escape collisions with each other.

Eriksen's junior varsity boat finished sixth in a field of nine, but his varsity crew stayed glued to Wisconsin in third place for the forepart of the race. Then the river threw the boat and the men quickly into a maelstrom.

The Syracuse shell hesitated for a moment in the middle of its run, suspended in air, the oars churning the water as if on a treadmill. For less than an eyewink, the shell's forward progress ceased. Suddenly, the boat was shot ahead as if released from a slingshot. Meanwhile, the others passed Syracuse, and the Orangemen finished tenth out of 12 boats.

Scratching his head that night, stocky Eriksen attempted to explain the phenomenon that bear-hugged his varsity boat. He reasoned that while rowing in an inside lane next to shore, apparently the shell ran into a strong singular reverse current. Listeners merely shook their heads in commiseration.

Washington swept the regatta. In the varsity contest, the Huskies were followed in order by California, Wisconsin, Stanford, MIT, Columbia, Cornell, Pennsylvania, Princeton, Syracuse, Rutgers and Navy. Movies were used however, to show that Wisconsin finished third instead of fifth. In turn this meant some of the other final placings were changed the next day.

The following fall, Rusty Callow, by this time dean of

American rowing coaches, left Pennsylvania after 23 years and succeeded the late Buck Walsh at Navy. Joe Burke, Yale's freshman coach succeeded Callow at Penn. Burke, an oarsman for the Quakers in 1932-1934, won the Diamond Sculls in England in 1938 and 1939.

A few weeks after the 1950 IRA regatta, the Korean War broke out, and General Douglas MacArthur was appointed UN Commander by President Harry Truman.

While the international picture in 1951 remained unsettled by events in Korea, Coach Eriksen's varsity crew gave signs of new vigor and spirit.

On April 28, the varsity upset heavily-favored Cornell in a race on storm-tossed Onondaga Lake. Stroked by Harold Weibezahl, the crew with power and precision in its long layback stroke took the lead at the start and never relinquished it. The margin of victory was three-quarters of a length. Boston University finished three lengths behind Cornell, while Dartmouth came in another two lengths to the rear.

Hope for success ran high in Syracuse quarters that year of 1951 at Marietta. At a time when the University student body was about 12,000 and tuition raised by $50 to $600 annually, rains once more bedeviled the Ohio.

Similar to 1950, the swollen waters and floating debris again created confusion and consternation among the crews in the IRA events. And the elements chilled whatever hope Syracusans held for their varsity crew. The boat limply finished eighth in a group of 12, after a stormy race.

That was the year Wisconsin won its first varsity race in IRA competition. Coached by Norman Sonju, former Montana gold miner, the Badgers upset favored Washington in the race shortened from three to two miles because of the flooded waters. The Huskies were second, followed by Princeton, California, Pennsylvania, MIT, Stanford, Syracuse, Cornell, Columbia, Navy and Boston U.

California took first place in the junior varsity race, but not before proud Navy lost its rudder in the swirling water. Replacing the rudder in mid-stream, the Sailors became involved in a comedy of errors. Their shell swerved sharply to the right, sheared off Princeton's rudder and then went underwater. Meanwhile, crippled Princeton finished seventh, but its coxswain, Carl Lyle, was the regatta's hero by steering his damaged shell with his hands.

In the freshman race, the Navy Plebes struck a buoy at the starting line and capsized.

Angered and frustrated by dangerous conditions of the Ohio for two consecutive years, the coaches and officials pressured the IRA board of stewards to transfer the 1952 regatta. So, for the second time since 1949, the IRA packed up its gear, and departed for the placid waters of Onondaga Lake in Syracuse. It was the home of Hiawatha, the legendary Iroquois Indian.

CHAPTER XXXII

HIAWATHA WAS A

name long associated with Onondaga Lake; and it evoked thoughts of Longfellow's famous poem in the minds of some of the college men in June of 1952, while they prepared to war on the calm waters.

Here on the eastern shore of the Lake, according to Indian legend, Hiawatha faced the assembled chiefs of five tribes and urged them to unify. To demonstrate strength through unity, he held an arrow in his outstretched hand. With effortless motion, he snapped it across his knee. Then he grabbed five arrows bound together with deer thongs. In vain, he tried to break them. The chiefs understood and, consequently, formed the great and powerful Iroquois Confederacy.

Now in June of 1952, another group of strong men prepared for a meeting. Instead of the birch bark canoes of Indians, cedar shells measuring 62 feet long, 24 inches wide, 15 inches deep and one-eighth of an inch thick, transported here from across the country, were placed in the water for races. Now, instead of Indian families bidding their warriors good-bye, families and friends wished the rowers good hunting in their forthcoming IRA races.

Months before the June gathering, preparations for the regatta were carefully guided by a new organization in Syracuse—the Syracuse Regatta Association. Spearheading

276

EXECUTIVE   COMMITTEE   OF   THE   SYRACUSE   REGATTA   ASSOCIATION

Committee members pictured above were among the first or-
ganizers of the Association. It was to the credit of this organization that the IRA Regatta came to Syracuse and remained
here. Left to right standing: Stephen Rogers, James D. Taylor
Jr., T. Frank Dolan, Jr., George A. Scobell, A. Thomas Schade.
Seated: James P. Stimson, James F. Gilday, Bernard M. Dawson, Joseph F. Owens, Sr.

this group's enthusiasm were Bernard Dawson and James Gilday, assisted by Crandall Melvin, Eric Will, Dr. Gordon Hoople, Joseph Owens, Earle Machold, James Taylor, James Stimson, George Scobell, Robert Roney, Anthony Henninger, Thomas Schade and others.

Prodigious effort was required for the arrival of the big intercollegiate event. The park area, the lake course, the boathouse area with its housing for the IRA and crews, all were put in order by the Onondaga County park and highway departments. And since that time, these county units enthusiastically throw themselves annually into the herculean task of preparing for the IRA races.

Some 25,000 spectators gathered that day in the same area where the chiefs of long ago met, unaware that forty-two years previously, Charles Courtney of Cornell urged that the regatta be shifted to lake water, and thirty-two years after Jim Ten Eyck declared that Onondaga Lake was best suited for the races.

Even the boathouse area sported a new face. Four new quonset boathouses constructed for the regatta spruced up the area. Together, they held 30 shells of regatta competitors and were named after four Syracuse strokes whose crews won on the Hudson: Edward Packard '04; Jim Ten Eyck, Jr. '08; George Thurston '13; and Charles Whiteside '16.

There working in the center of all the bustle and activity were two men long connected with Syracuse rowing. Charley Keller, the rigger, and Dr. Frank Hugo, the trainer, were busily engaged in using nimble brains and fingers in their tasks. Their combined years of service to the University were 60!

Bill Reddy, *Post-Standard* sports editor, held an interesting interview before the races with Edwin Booth, a former resident of Poughkeepsie whose mother sewed the flags for Columbia, Cornell and Pennsylvania for that first regatta in 1895. Now a Syracuse resident, Booth said that his father was "Local Poughkeepsie manager" of the regatta on the Hudson for 17 years. He admitted that he witnessed that first regatta.

"We used to hang big markers from the bridge to show the lanes to the coxswains. The markers had huge numbers on them. For the first race, the numbers were '1, '2, and '3. And I was the one who painted those numbers," Booth said proudly.

Already, the IRA regulations required the oarsmen to wear jerseys with their school colors. This provided the spectators with better identification of their favorites, as well as assisting the race judges.

Eriksen stood in the background of all this activity, preoccupied and worried about his inexperienced crews. Despite good form, his oarsmen were light. He knew this and it bothered him, for the men faced veterans from other colleges.

As time proved, Eriksen's crews as well as others never stood a chance. While Navy's boathouseman, John Sembley, humorously rubbed a rabbit's foot over Rusty Callow's face before the races, the Midshipmen demonstrated something much more important and necessary than luck:

Superb rowing ability.

Navy swept the Lake that year.

With its three triumphs, Navy atoned for its humiliating experiences of 1951 on the swollen waters of the Ohio River. In victory, Navy became the first Eastern crew in

Jim Ten Eyck
MEMORIAL TROPHY
SYRACUSE REGATTA ASSOCIATION

THE JAMES A. TEN EYCK MEMORIAL TROPHY (second design) presented each year by the Syracuse Regatta Association to the college accumulating the greatest number of points in the events. A hand carved wood plaque.

many years to win all three races (freshman, junior varsity, varsity) of the Intercollegiate Rowing Association. Her Midshipmen won the Challenge Cup as well as the newly-introduced Jim Ten Eyck Plaque presented to IRA by the Syracuse Regatta Association. The school accumulating the largest number of points in the day's races received the hand-carved wood award.

In order to win, Navy's varsity rowed machine-like over the three-mile course in 15 minutes, eight and one-tenth seconds, ahead by two and one-half lengths over Princeton. Cornell was third, followed by Wisconsin, California, Columbia, Washington, Stanford, Pennsylvania, MIT and Syracuse.

The Midshipmen in those races held on Onondaga Lake, for the first time, joined the select circle with Washington which completed the "sweep" cycle of "Eights" four times in IRA competition. Syracuse in 1904 swept the Hudson at a time when there was no junior varsity race.

Tears welled up in Rusty Callow's eyes as he stepped forward to receive the Ten Eyck Plaque. He heard Ralph Furey of Columbia, IRA chairman, praise his crews and his coaching. Accepting the award, he attempted to explain his deep emotions:

> It is a great pleasure to accept this Ten Eyck award. I think old Jim would appreciate my winning. Jim was an old friend of mine, a great teacher and once a Navy coach.[17]

Tip Goes, regatta refereee, was enthusiastic about the results and the Lake where he once served as coxswain of th 1913 Syracuse crew:

---

[17]The *Syracuse Herald-American*, Syracuse, N.Y. June 22, 1952

"I was well pleased. This is the first time we had a regatta under ideal conditions."

Coach Eriksen personally was satisfied with the success of the IRA Regatta. He was responsible for a great deal of the initial planning and preparation long before Syracuse was selected as the site for the races.

Goes and other Syracusans, however, though happy they appeared on the surface, were saddened by the death of Cy Thurston a few hours before he was scheduled to attend a reunion of his 1913 crew in Syracuse. Former athletic director at the University, Thurston was once treasurer of Wesleyan University in Middleton, Connecticut. At death, he was eastern manager of a company that manufactured industrial lubricants in Columbus, Ohio.

The next year, 1953, Gosta Eriksen served his fourth year as head coach of crew, but the fortunes of rowing were bankrupt. The Orange crew finished far behind in the IRA races.

As the junior varsity race began, heavy winds churned up the placid waters, rain fell and dark clouds gathered. The heat of 100 degrees was stifling. Then as quickly as the storm gathered, it departed. Within a few minutes, the mercury dropped 11 degrees.

Some of the crews asked to row without jerseys due to the oppressive heat, but Referee Goes forbade the requests. He explained his denial by pointing out that the finish judges were unable to identify them.

Princeton oarsmen protected themselves from the heat by wrapping towels around their heads, parts of the towels hanging down the backs of their necks in the fashion of French Foreign Legionnaires.

The 1953 IRA regatta was simply a replay of the previous year for Navy. The Midshipmen extended their victory skein to 20, including in that string their 1952 Olympic victories over Russia, Australia, England and Germany.

However, Navy's varsity triumph did not come as easy as it did the year before. Cornell forced her to produce a tremendous concentration of power for a final spurt. Sanford's Big Red came up fast in the closing yards to shade Washington and almost nip the Midshipmen.

Nonetheless, Washington by its varsity finish and its victories in the other races amassed enough points to capture the Ten Eyck Plaque.

Nevertheless, not all the excitement in the area was confined to the races in the regatta. Four of the Princeton freshman crew that gave Cornell such a battle for second place in the yearling race tried out their skill as hot-rodders on the State Fairgrounds racetrack the previous day. Their station wagon rolled over four times. Fortunately, they escaped serious injury.

Eriksen's crews finished poorly in the IRA regatta the following year, and Cornell saved the honor of Central New York rowing by winning both the junior varsity and freshman races. And once more the Big Red came close, but not close enough to overcome Callow's winning Navy crew in the varsity event.

A few weeks previous to the races, Lew Carr, long-time University baseball coach, while in retirement, was chosen for the Helms Hall of Fame. The honor was announced during the seventh inning stretch of the Colgate baseball game. Then he returned to his seat and watched the Orange team coached by Ted Kleinhans defeat the arch rival 5-3.

REGATTA TIME AROUND THE BOATHOUSE AND QUONSET AREA, JUNE IRA

REGATTA TIME AT ONONDAGA LAKE: VIEW OF FINISH AREA

Tradition: Long Branch bridge decorated with college block letters.

The Hall of Fame to which Carr was named was established some years before by Paul Helms, a Los Angeles baker and one-time substitute coxswain at Syracuse under Jim Ten Eyck.

Little interest or enthusiasm appeared evident on campus for rowing in the sixth year of Eriksen's coaching. The great expectations of five years were shattered by the time of 1955, despite herculean efforts of the former Washington star.

Thin in numbers by comparison to other schools, the squad was largely inexperienced and not particularly heavy in weight. Eriksen, his men, University officials and alumni found little solace in the knowledge that Columbia also wallowed in the same disappointment.

It was Cornell's year at the regatta. They swept the Lake, the first time the Big Red accomplished this feat in Syracuse. And its varsity for the first time in quarter of a century was victorious in the IRA race.

Eriksen's crews raced nobly but were definitely out of their class. The varsity was last, the junior varsity finished seventh. The freshmen were eighth.

It appeared that the time to do something about rowing on Piety Hill was close at hand. Two physicians discussed that same problem after the regatta, while dining in Tubbert's Restaurant in Syracuse.

"What in tarnation is wrong with rowing on the Hill, Tom?" asked Bruce Chamberlain of Syracuse, a former oarsman. His companion across the table was Thomas Kerr, his mate in the 1939 varsity shell.

"I really don't know," Kerr answered. "But let me tell

you something—somebody's got to do something. Right away!"

"I suppose it's a combination of things," Chamberlain mused between chews on a celery stalk.

"Uh—huh—sure," Kerr replied, reaching for roll and butter.

All during that meal the two men searched for an answer, their families tactfully refraining from entering the conversation. Suddenly, Chamberlain stopped chewing and with a burst of enthusiasm exclaimed:

"Listen, Tom. What about the alumni?"

"How do you mean?"

Chamberlain swallowed and hesitated a moment before continuing.

"Why not get the alumni together and find out how we might support rowing on the Hill? They did it years ago!"

"Sure. We might hold a pre-regatta luncheon or picnic for all the gang that rowed," Kerr suggested.

The two stopped eating, all thoughts of food forgotten. Before finishing, they agreed to go to the Alumni office and discuss the proposal with Newell Rossman, then Alumni field secretary, later vice president for University Development. Perhaps, they reasoned, names of former oarsmen could be obtained and invitations sent them for such a gathering.

"We'll write them," Kerr pointed out, "asking them to some sort of a feed before the races."

During the following winter months, Chamberlain and Kerr, Russell Swanson and Edward Otis, the latter two of the 1935 crew, wrote invitations and planned a luncheon for that June. When a large number of rowing alumni attended the luncheon, they were enthusiastic about rekindling interest in rowing at the University. And when Chamberlain and Kerr presented a charter of organization, they hastily appoved. They set into motion what is now known as the Syracuse Alumni Rowing Association (S.A.R.A.).

First president of the new organization was Dr. Gordon Hoople '15, one of the four sons in a famous rowing family. Others elected to serve with Hoople were: Vice president, Bernard Dawson '22; secretary, Chamberlain '41; executive committee, Edward Otis, Kerr, Swanson and Martin Hilfinger '14.

S.A.R.A.'s purpose was clearly defined in its charter:

To support the interest in rowing at Syracuse University, the city of Syracuse and Onondaga County.

Therefore, a group was formed to help, not to interfere; to perpetuate, not to abandon, the noble sport that placed the University on the collegiate map back in 1904.

S.A.R.A. at first was accepted with reservation by a few who thought the members were out to "get the coach fired." Nothing was further from the truth. In time, the group's sincerity in helping the sport dispelled those fears. Today, it is accepted as an important adjunct to the objective which Chancellor Tolley once explained to Kerr:

"We must have a crew at Syracuse of which we are proud!"

Regardless of the enthusiastic plans of S.A.R.A. and rising spirit for crew, Eriksen resigned and returned to his native Sweden to coach the Swedes in the art of rowing.

In conducting a diligent search for Eriksen's successor, the University followed the same direction that it did fifty-five years before when it hired Sweetland. It looked south-west towards Cornell and found its man.

290

COACH LOREN W. SCHOEL

CHAPTER XXXIII

LOREN SCHOEL BECAME

the fifth coach of rowing at Syracuse in 1956. At Cornell from where the University called him, he directed freshman crews to unprecedented glory, his last two winning the IRA titles and his 1954 yearlings the class of the Eastern sprints. His Big Red cubs were unbeaten in dual regattas in the previous four years. Much of the later success of the freshmen as varsity crews under Sanford was attributed to Schoel.

Catching first glimpse of him on campus, students saw a big, six foot, four-inch man. They learned that he was a native of Albany, Oregon, and was an outstanding oarsman under Tom Bolles and Al Ulbrickson, coaches against whom his crews were to compete.

Inking a five-year contract, Schoel ushered in a new era of rowing on Piety Hill. He was fully aware of the pitfalls that faced him in rebuilding the spirit at Syracuse. He promised nothing—or rather nothing other than work, loyalty and dedication. In him was the chemistry of a man to make these possible. His biography supported his philosophy.

After graduating from Washington, Schoel coached the 150-pound crew of his Alma Mater. In the Depression, he served as teacher-athletic coach in several high schools. Pearl Harbor changed all that.

Schoel enlisted in the Navy. During the ensuing years

of war, he was commissioned. Upon discharge, he was a battle veteran with the insignia of lieutenant-commander.

Freed from the Navy, he became athletic director and crew coach and basketball mentor at Marietta College on the Ohio River. He stayed there a year and then was summoned to coach Cornell freshmen.

Sanford, a former Husky himself, regretted losing Schoel, but in characteristic style wished him well:

"Loren made a very important contribution to the Big Red's recent rowing success. And we're going to miss him greatly. However, he has all the qualifications to make good in a big way, and I sincerely wish him well in his new undertaking at Syracuse."

The first thing Schoel did upon assuming the duties as coach was to retain Victor Michalson as mentor of the frosh Next, he instituted an intensified recruiting program on campus.

"No man with potentialities for rowing will get away from us without our trying to sell him first on crew," he declared. And in the following period, he kept a steady eye on male students in search of possible crewmen.

Schoel pretty much exemplified the type of man Chancellor Day found in Jim Ten Eyck many decades ago:

"A man whose aim was to help young men develop character, a sense of responsibility, and a feeling for competitiveness with other young men on the water.

"A man who believed rowing was more than a sport—rather a way of living."

Chomping usually on a dead cigar in practice, Schoel was a man of a thousand faces, but of only one mood and of one thought. He was a different type from Ten Eyck. Where the Old Man spoke quietly, Schoel spoke brusquely. But there the difference terminated. Beneath Schoel's gruff voice was concern and paternal interest that endeared him to his young men. His gesticulating hamlike hands, the heightened color of cheeks and his deep rolling voice were all part of his repertoire for teaching and guiding his students.

Fortified by this climate of enthusiasm, many turned out for crew that first spring of 1956. Pathetically green, they listened to Schoel's greetings and then heroically bent to the task. They knew—

Schoel promised only hard work.

A gruff "well-done, boys," was probably the only reward for them.

But still they knew deep down inside themselves, for some unexplainable reason, that he was to give them more than they gave him, even with their rowing victories—

It was camaraderie!

They took to their shells for the first race of the season against a strong West Side Rowing Club of Buffalo on the Lake. The varsity covered the mile and one-half course in fast time, winning by three-fourths of a length. The junior boat won by six lengths. A four-man varsity crew with coxswain and a ten-second handicap rowed for Syracuse and won by a length. In winning, the freshmen were impressive, too.

The spirit instilled in the men by Schoel was best exemplified by the set jaw of a sophomore, who the year before rowed as a freshman. He insisted on trying to win a seat in the varsity shell despite an earlier attack of polio.

Wan and pale, M. Charles Hatch, Jr., appeared at the boat-house late that spring.

"What are you doing here, boy?" Schoel demanded in amazement.

"I'd like to try out, coach."

"Let's see—you rowed last year in the frosh boat, didn't you?"

"Yessir—I did, coach."

"Didn't the polio bug hit your right shoulder and leg?"

"Yes, coach—but I've been working out since January in the gymnasium. I've been in the rowing tank. I'm ready!"

"Isn't it a little early for you, Chuck?"

"No, sir. I've never wanted to do anything as much as I want to row!" the tall man declared.

That spring Hatch learned rowing anew under the patient eye of the coach. And in time, he became a regular in the varsity boats. Hatch's quiet determination later on was responsible for his continuing interest in rowing and his present duties as race official in eastern rowing competition.

On a similar day that spring, S.A.R.A. was officially recognized, when it became a member of the National Association of Amateur Oarsmen. A familiar face disappeared from the Syracuse boathouse about this same time.

Serving more than three decades as rigger, Charley Keller retired. Coach Schoel took him out in the launch to witness his first complete crew race. Other years, under the Ten Eycks and Eriksen, Keller was always too busy working on the rigging of the shells, much too engrossed to follow any race.

Earl Margeson, former Cornell rigger, succeeded Keller in the post.

First victory for Schoel made him somewhat of a prophet. Speaking earlier in the week before a race at Boston, he told the Cornell Club of Syracuse that "what we really need at Syracuse more than anything else right now is a victory. And Saturday at Boston might be the day for us."

Overhauling Boston and MIT, early pacesetters, the varsity boat won. The first crew rowing under Schoel included:

Bow—Richard Nichols
No. 2—M. Charles Hatch
No. 3—Peter Beckett
No. 4—Walter Howard
No. 5—David Acker
No. 6—Robert MacLelland
No. 7—Robert Angelucci
Stroke—Michael Smyth
Coxswain—John Follis

The freshmen won handily while the junior varsity battled gamely down to the finish line before losing out to Columbia and MIT.

The Eastern Sprint Regatta dampened the optimism of the Schoelmen, temporarily, at least. They failed to qualify for any of the three afternoon finals over the much shorter course than their three-mile run they customarily raced. Cornell in the varsity event raced ahead near the finish line to edge out a strong Yale eight.

Meanwhile, S.A.R.A. was busily assisting crew. Spearheaded by Kenneth Gallagher, the members raised funds and in turn purchased a new eight-oared shell and a four-oared craft for the University rowing fleet. The new shells were christened "S.A.R.A." and "Alumni," respectively.

Against Cornell twice that spring, Schoel's varsity crews fared poorly. However, the frosh caused Michalson and Schoel to smile as result of their race with the Big Red.

The freshmen took definite command at midway of the race on Onondaga Lake and finished a good length ahead of Cornell. It proved to be the first victory for the yearlings in several years, and needless to say, Coxswain Lawrence Wiener was joyously dunked into the water by his mates.

A storm with characteristics similar to the tornado of 1912 swept into Syacuse four days before the 1956 IRA races. Severe thunderstorms and winds blanketed the area, bowling over trees, snapping off utility poles and whipping up ocean-size waves on the Lake. Pennsylvania's junior varsity was caught out on the water when the storm came into the area.

Rowing off French Fort, the Quakers were overturned by a 40-mile-an-hour wind after the shell received a 20-foot gash to its starboard side. A launch picked them up. Schoel in his outboard motorboat towed the shell to the boathouse for repairs.

As quickly as it appeared, the storm departed, leaving devastation beyond imagination. But by regatta day, cooling breezes soothed the brows of some 10,000 spectators at the 54th annual event. The crowd watched thirty crews that were conditioned to crispness for this important meeting on North American water. The oarsmen fidgeted to get started.

Partly responsible for the crews' anxiety was the knowledge that the Olympic rowing trials were to be run on the Lake a few weeks later. Tip Goes, regatta referee, was chairman of the U. S. Olympic Rowing Committee, and on that day he carefully assessed each crew that came to the starting line. Winners of the regatta events might enter the trials and later go on to represent the United States at Melbourne, Australia that December in the Games.

Favored Cornell lived up to prior-race expectations in the varsity race and led Navy by two lengths across the line. Syracuse was eighth out of 12 contestants. The junior crew was seventh in its event.

Michalson's freshmen rowed one of the most amazing races recorded in the past 30 years of IRA history.

The Syracuse freshman boats of the seven previous years were unable to finish any better than fourth in the regatta. But the Syracuse yearlings this season were good, and they knew it. Didn't their time trials prove it? But as Coxswain Wiener questioned, did the others know it?

There is one thing every oarsman experiences in common with competitors of other athletic efforts:

Those pre-race butterflies.

Today before the freshman race, the Syracuse frosh was no different. Tension! Tension! Tension! The very air seemed electrified as if a sudden burst of laughing or loud talking was to send the boathouse up in churlish smoke!

Four of those nine freshmen were Syracuse or area students. Lance Osadchey, bow oar, was from Homer, home of the famed David Harum, the horse trader. William Laidlaw, No. 2 oar, was from Syracuse. Glenn Vatter, No. 3, from Elbridge, and Bruce Baker, No. 7, Minetto.

The horror of tense nerves and flip-floppy stomachs was plainly marked on the faces of the aforementioned as well as on those of their companions, Wiener, James Edmonds, Robert Braue and Nelson Miller.

Schoel and Michalson knew their freshmen, moreover.

They knew that beneath the wedge of tension there was a desire so parched from thirst for victory that these oarsmen were not content to accept anything less than victory. How accurate were the coaches' assessments?

The crews got off to a smooth start and big, beefy Navy took the lead in the first few hundred yards. The shells then settled down for the long pull ahead.

Once the race started, the University crew pulled savagely, all signs of pre-race tension forgotten. Initially, they pulled 36 for the first 25 strokes, then gradually reduced it to 30.

Wiener tore his eyes from the contorted face of Hawkins, his stroke, and searched for Navy. He wanted to carry out Michalson's orders to cling tenaciously to the Midshipmen. Oops—there they were! And at the one-quarter mark,

Syracuse bid for the lead.

Navy answered the challenge by increasing to 36. Soon, Navy increased its lead by half a length. Meanwhile, Syracuse remained a length and a quarter behind at the three-quarter mark, only a length ahead of hard-pressing Washington. Navy. Syracuse. Washington. Cornell. Princeton. Penn.

That was the order of the first six at the start of the final leg home.

Syracuse again moved.

Picking up Wiener's call, Hawkins and his mates increased the beat for a sprint finish. The stroke knew it must go up carefully without destroying the smooth stroking of his oarsmen. Slowly it was increased from a 28, up to 29, to 30, to 31, to 32, and finally to 33.

The Syracuse boat closed up 15 feet on Navy!

1956 FRESHMAN IRA CHAMPIONS

Navy, in turn, desperately increased its tempo to 33.

The Midshipmen, consequently, moved out in front again by a length. It was a short-lived lead, however.

With Wiener pounding the beat on the side of the shell, again Syracuse surged ahead.

Closer. Closer. Syracuse crept up.

Higher. Higher. The stroke went up.

On. On. The two shells came down the course.

The spectators were screaming!

The judges nervously squinted their eyes, nervously adjusted their positions.

—Whoosh!—all of a sudden the men wearing the Orange jerseys swept out in front and won!

Collecting the discarded shirts of opponents afterwards, Wiener admitted:

> "We pulled together as one man for the first time this year, and it was definitely our best race of the year." [18]

In victory, the freshmen gave their coaches and their University the first yearling triumph in the IRA since 1932!

A few days after the dramatic frosh victory, the nation's rowing scribes organized the Rowing Writers of America, picking Allison Danzig of the *New Yok Times* as president of the 21-member group. Bill Reddy of the *Post Standard* was chosen regional vice-president for the Central New York area.

On Independence Day of that year, Charles Mills, Jr., of Syracuse, rowed at No. 2 position with the Kent School eight that won its opening race at the English Henley. Kent eliminated the British Burton Leander Club by half a

---

[18] The *Syracuse Herald-American*, Syracuse, N.Y., June 17, 1956.

length. Mills figured prominently in Syracuse University rowing at a later date.

Rowing lost three by death in 1956:

Ned Ten Eyck, 77, in the Idaho home of his son, a short time after surgery, 17 days after his wife's death.

Charles Whiteside, 62, former Syracuse stroke and Harvard coach, in Oroville, California.

Richard Glendon, 86, "Grand Old Man" of rowing at Navy, in Cape Cod Hospital.

Four former Syracuse oarsmen were chosen that season for the Helms Athletic Rowing Hall of Fame: Jim Ten Eyck, Arthur Osman, Howard Robbins and Clifford Goes.

On the water once known by Hiawatha, Yale, a few weeks later, captured the eight-oared race in the Olympic trials, upsetting Cornell. The Eli victory made possible the appointment of their coach, Jim Rathschmidt, a graying apple-cheeked ex-boat rigger, to lead them as official American representative at the Games in Australia.

For the first time in rowing's history on Piety Hill, two four-oared boats were entered in the Olympic trials by Syracuse. Syracuse did not compete up to this time in any shell smaller than an eight, since 1913 on the Hudson.

Manned by Edward Montesi, bow; Hatch, No. 2; Angelucci, No. 3; Michael Smyth, stroke; and Richard Davenport, coxswain, the entry performed brilliantly. It won its heats and competed in the semi-finals before being edged out later by the Detroit Boat Club by two-tenths of a second.

The other boat, without coxswain, contained Peter Beckett, bow; Robert Beier, No. 2; Thomas Lotz, No. 3; and John MacLelland, stroke.

Not to be outdone by their companion shell with cox-

302

SYRACUSE ENTRIES, 1956 OLYMPIC TRIALS ON ONONDAGA LAKE.

swain, this crew won its preliminary heats, too, but then lost out by one and five-tenths of a second in the semi-finals.

It was a good year for America in the Olympic Games. Yale nosed out Australia in the semi-finals, then upped the stroke to 40 in the final 400 of the 2,000-meter race to defeat the Canadian crew from British Columbia.

The men in blue were the first crew in Olympic history to row in the repechage heats as the underdog and then capture the world's title. Their triumph was the eighth consecutive one for America in the eight-oared races since Navy first turned the trick in 1920.

Two others long associated with rowing at the University died in this period. Mrs. Ten Eyck Brewer died at 85 in Maine. Paul Helms '12, who established the Helms Athletic Foundation as "an investment in youth," died in California.

In 1956, Schoel, assisted by S.A.R.A., the University, and particularly by the enthusiasm of the oarsmen, started the Orange back on the comeback road to national prestige. In the year ahead, a trophy was to be established and the courage of an Orange boat pulled at your heartstrings in an IRA race.

303

CHAPTER XXXIV

THE PACKARD TROPHY

for winner of the Syracuse-Dartmouth race was the result of a conversation in 1957 between two physicians.

To lead up to the point where the idea crystallized, it was necessary to know that there were some gaps in Loren Schoel's long range planning for the rowing program. One of these was open dates in the spring schedule caused by more and more of the Ivy League crews establishing Cup races. Although Syracuse was a part of the Goes Trophy competition with Cornell and Navy since 1955, there were still open dates in the Orange schedule. As the problem became more acute, S.A.R.A. officers pondered over the question with Schoel and University officials. During one of the conferences, someone suggested, "Why not establish a Cup race of our own?" The idea was approved, but who was to sponsor it, and with whom?

Dartmouth College, returning to big-time rowing once more, solved the second part of the question. There was an open date on her spring schedule, since she left the Dad Vail Rowing Association founded some years earlier by Rusty Callow for smaller school competition. And, too, Dartmouth indicated she was keen for competition with the Orange.

One winter day in the hallway of a Syracuse hospital, Dr. Bruce Chamberlain, S.A.R.A. secretary, and Dr. Anthony Ladd were discussing professional topics.

During a pause in the conversation, Chamberlain asked:

"Say, Tony—you're interested in rowing, aren't you?"

"Certainly am," replied Ladd.

"Yes—I imagine you are," rejoined Chamberlain. "Particularly since Dr. Packard's daughter, Ann, is your wife."

"So—?" asked Ladd.

"As a matter of fact," Chamberlain continued, "have you ever thought about paying him tribute?" You know, he was a great Syracuse stroke!"

"Yes, I know," Ladd answered, smiling. "What do you have in mind?"

"When we can, let's get together," Chamberlain suggested. "We might talk about the possibility of establishing a trophy in his honor for the Syracuse-Dartmouth race."

"Fine by me," Ladd agreed.

As result of that first discussion and several meetings. Ladd's gift in honor of his father-in-law electrified Syracuse and its University. The trophy was made of sterling silver. Besides this, individual statuettes were to be given to members of the winning crew in the Syracuse-Dartmouth race. Known as the Edward N. Packard Trophy, it was first awarded in 1959.

Through the significance of the trophy, the name of the 1904 stroke, whom Ten Eyck described as "one of the greatest strokes of all time," was perpetuated. The name Packard, long associated with Syracuse University and with victory, became destined to represent the heights reached by young men in the art of rowing.

The trophy represented more than a tribute from his son-in-law. It stood as a remembrance of a man who devoted

his life in the field of medicine for mankind. After graduation from the University's Medical College, Dr. Packard in-
terned in New York, later establishing private practice and
specializing in chest diseases. In 1915, he was summoned
to Trudeau Sanatorium at Lake Placid, New York, where
he remained except for years of distinguished duty in both
wars until 1950. After serving two years as director of the
Trudeau Foundation, Dr. Packard retired.

Quiet and unassuming, Dr. Packard still prefers to
present personally his trophy to the winner of the Syracuse-
Dartmouth race. His hair may be frosted by the years, but
his gait is still as steady as was his stroke on the memorable
day his crew placed Syracuse on everyone's lips.

Schoel took his men out to the Seneca River for a
workout on February twenty-seventh, 1957. The date for
practice was the earliest in crew history and eclipsed the
previous record set by Ten Eyck's crew on a cold February
twenty-ninth, thirty-two years before.

In May, the Syracuse crews journeyed to the Charles
River but only the junior varsity won from Boston University in its race.

The following week, Syracuse met Cornell and Navy
on the Lake for the annual Goes Cup race, but the Big Red
swept the water. Encouraging to Schoel was the showing of
the freshmen stroked by Charles Mills. They battled and
lost to Cornell by only a length.

Cornell's varsity crew of that race was the same one
that won the 1956 IRA meet, but then lost out in a heart-
breaking finish to Yale.

Schoel's varsity boat competed against Yale and Cornell
on May 11, on Cayuga Lake in the Carnegie Cup Regatta.

Both Yale and Cornell up to this race were the only undefeated eights in the East this season.

Sanford's varsity avenged its Olympic trial loss of 1956 to Yale by leading the Elis over a two-mile course to win. Yale was second; Princeton next; and Syracuse was last.

A few days prior to the IRA regatta, All-American halfback Jim Brown was chosen to the nation's first All-American lacrosse team. As he packed away his collegiate athletic equipment and prepared for later duty with the professional Cleveland Browns, crews raced in the IRA events.

Cornell took the varsity and junior varsity races. Navy won the freshman event. Syracuse placed fifth in the varsity race, second in the junior boat race, and fifth in the yearling race. Nevertheless, these places were the best overall showings for Syracuse since the regatta came to Syracuse in 1952.

There were plenty of rowing exploits in the world that year. In July, Cornell outdistanced Yale on a choppy Thames in England to win the Grand Challenge Cup in the British Henley. The Big Red met Yale after defeating Russia in the semi-finals, while Princeton won the Thames Cup for lighter crews.

The United States carried off the two prestige prizes and Russia won two lesser events, while witnessing defeat of their Olympic scull champion, Vyacheslav Ivanov, in the Diamond Sculls by Stuart MacKenzie, a rugged Australian.

The scythe of time continued to thin out the ranks of those associated with Syracuse crews. Frank Hugo, in his 87th year and trainer for Hill athletics for some 30 years, died. Colonel Rudolph Propst of the 1913 championship crew passed away.

Dean Charles Noble of the University's Hendricks

Chapel best described the character of an oarsman at an autumn crew dinner held by S.A.R.A.:

> Crew men are a race apart. They lead a monastic and austere existence. In fact, rowing constitutes virtually a new and wonderful way of life. A man develops a whole new philosophy of value and discipline when he undertakes rowing. . . . There's something of this spirit in the development of a crew as it faces tremendous obstacles and conquers them in order to bring forth a winner. . . . The honest satisfaction of achievement in the way of life peculiar to an oarsman is worth all the headaches. . . .

While the rest of Syracuse braved the rigors of winter, the varsity oarsmen went to Florida between semesters in late January of 1958, and raced Tampa University, Rollins and Florida Southern Colleges. The trip was the longest one taken by an Orange crew since the 1947 freshmen raced in Seattle.

In a borrowed shell, they defeated Tampa's Spartans by five and one-half lengths on the Hillsborough River. Next, they defeated Florida by seven lengths at Lakeland. On February 3rd, they defeated Rollins by six lengths.

At Annapolis that spring, the sun-tanned Orangemen won the Goes Trophy race for the first time since it was established three years previously. Defeating Cornell and Navy, Syracuse enjoyed the vibrancy and sweetness of long-denied triumph. The win was not easy, however.

Schoel's men got off to a good start on the Severn and managed to lead all the way, but not before they withstood the challenge of a swiftly moving Big Red in the final few yards. Victory was only by two feet.

Another victory was achieved by the Orangemen when on Onondaga Lake in May they took and kept a comfortable lead over Dartmouth and Rutgers on a two-mile course. And the junior boat copped its first win of the season. The yearling boat with Schoel's son, Robert, in it was second to Dartmouth.

Syracuse finished fourth in the strong Carnegie Cup Regatta, which was won by Yale in a record-breaking race.

Enthusiasm for rowing continued to mount on campus, and students formed on their own a 150-pound crew with former varsity men Michael Smyth '57 and Barton Green '56 serving as coaches. They finished third against Cornell and the Detroit Boat Club in a race held on the Lake. Later they lost out to Dartmouth's third varsity boat by only a slim second.

More remarkable about this was the fact that it marked the first and only evidence of light-weight rowing at Syracuse. However, it wasn't a scheduled part of the rowing program and lack of money caused the efforts to fade away at the conclusion of a single season of effort.

Rain fell, followed by a brisk headwind on the Lake the day of the Regatta. At noon, however, the sun peeked through the tumbling clouds as 12,000 spectators filed into the area.

Cornell won the freshman race. Syracuse finished fourth.

When Schoel's junior boat came in front of the launch, he shouted through the megaphone:

"The frosh rowed a great race—yessir, a great race. Got fourth. Now, come on men—give it what you got!"

The crews came up to the stakeboats, those bobbing slits in a long straight line on the water. Hidden from the spectators and other crews was a serious problem in the Syracuse boat.

Captain Peter Gregory, the No. 2 oar, was ailing. Ten

days previous to this race he suffered torn arm muscles that caused him to miss three days of practice. Still in misery from his injury, he told a friend earlier:

"— but I know I've got to go out there and row. There isn't anybody else!" [19]

Of course, Gregory was correct. Bill Laidlaw, regular No. 2 oar in the boat, was missing from the shell due to a severe back injury. Gregory was the regular stroke, but in order to replace Laidlaw he was moved to that spot by Schoel; Charles Mills filled in at the stroke position.

The shell was off to a heavy start in the race due to choppy water, then it lengthened out from the pack as it raced down the course into a strong headwind. For two miles minus one stroke, Schoel's patched-up and battered crew managed to stay ahead by two lengths over Cornell. Mills set a torrid pace, and his coxswain, Robert Miron, directed a brilliant race.

"Cornell's at 28—"

"Navy's at 30—"

"We're at 31—" [20]

Schoel nervously conversed with Michalson in the launch as the latter kept a stop-watch on the leaders.

"That Syracuse boat looks good—whoopie!" exclaimed Schoel.

"Cornell's moving up—" Michalson warned.

Schoel and Michalson soon discovered that something was amiss in their boat. Perhaps it was a hestitation in the former clean sweep of the oars.

"What's the trouble?" wondered Schoel.

---

[19] Bill Clark, "Pete's Finest Hour," the *Syracuse Herald-American*, Syracuse, New York, June 22, 1958.
[20] Clark, *op. cit.*, p. 47.

Then he knew.

"Pete's having trouble!"

"Naw—Pete's still rowing—" reassured Michalson.

"Come on, Pete—come on, boy—come on!" they urged.

Schoel proved correct. The steady punishing pressure of the race sapped away Gregory's strength.

When the beat was increased in the final stages, Gregory's shoulder was afire with pain. His arms didn't respond. His chest felt heavy. He ached badly. He was unable to see for the pain. His head swam, then everything went mercifully black—into oblivion.

Gregory in the last mile was not conscious of anything. Somehow, he kept dipping his oar in rhythm with the rest of the crew. Finally, he only went through the motions.

Meanwhile, Cornell savagely crept up on the slackening Orange boat, leaving yards of water behind it. The two shells swept across the line almost bow to bow. Gregory and the others sat there in the boat, almost in a stupor, too tired to think about anything but their own exhausion. On shore, the officials huddled. Who won? the fans wondered.

Cornell won by a few inches the judges decided. And as his men lay spent over the oars, Schoel in tribute hollered out to them:

"— you rowed the greatest race I've ever seen—you're real men. And I'm proud of you—proud as I can be! [21]

Thirty minutes later Cornell duplicated the junior varsity feat in its varsity race. Syracuse was third.

By its clean sweep, Cornell matched its victories of

---

[21]Clark, *op. cit.*, p. 47.

1955. Its varsity string now consisted of 19 consecutive triumphs.

"Hey, George—we brought home the bacon for you!" shouted the Cornell oarsmen as they dunked their three coxswains. To them, George was the fencing coach, who for the past 15 years doubled as trainer of crew. "Uncle" Georges Cointe was trainer in the 1956 Olympics and known and admired by the college rowing fraternity.

One of the Syracuse junior varsity boat oarsmen, when besieged by reporters after the race, paid his tribute:

"Just say this Syracuse jayvee gang is the greatest bunch of guys in the business . . . we just kept in there with heart!" [22]

During the following days, Coach Charles Logg, who succeeded Ned Ten Eyck at Rutgers, retired. He was replaced by Howard Smith, former Cornell oarsman. About the same time Con Findlay was named Stanford coach, succeeding Lou Lindsay.

That fall Walter Glass, captain of the 1916 victorious Hudson crew, donated a four-oared shell with coxswain in memory of his fellow oarsman Percy Leroy "Pete" Wallis, who died in 1918.

Schoel in 1958 laid the foundation for an exciting season in 1959—a forthcoming time when Syracuse represented the United States in international competition and was triumphant!

---

[22]Clark, *op. cit.*, p. 47.

CHAPTER XXXV

LOREN SCHOEL'S FIRST

victory in 1959 came on the heels of a shocking defeat in a four-school regatta on the Charles River. Up to the time of the Boston races, Schoel hoped his crews were strong enough to compile an undefeated season, something few coaches attained in these days of strong collegiate competition. His oarsmen, he believed, were in good physical condition, experienced in rowing and were high spirited. But the Massachusetts races ended his dreams of an unblemished record.

As time proved, perhaps those defeats were really beneficial, for whatever was responsible, his varsity crew stroked by Charles Mills scored a smashing victory over Cornell, Navy and Rutgers on May 2, at Ithaca.

In winning the Goes Trophy race, Syracuse bested Cornell on Cayuga Lake for the first time since May twenty-ninth, 1937. The victory meant something else. It was Schoel's first triumph over Cornell since he left that university and came to Syracuse.

As if to prove the victory over Cornell, Navy and Rutgers was no fluke, Mills and his mates defeated Dartmouth at Hanover the following week and won the Edward Packard Trophy. Dr. Packard was personally on hand to make the first presentation of the Trophy.

With his varsity progressing rapidly in late season, Schoel took the boat to the Eastern Sprints Regatta at

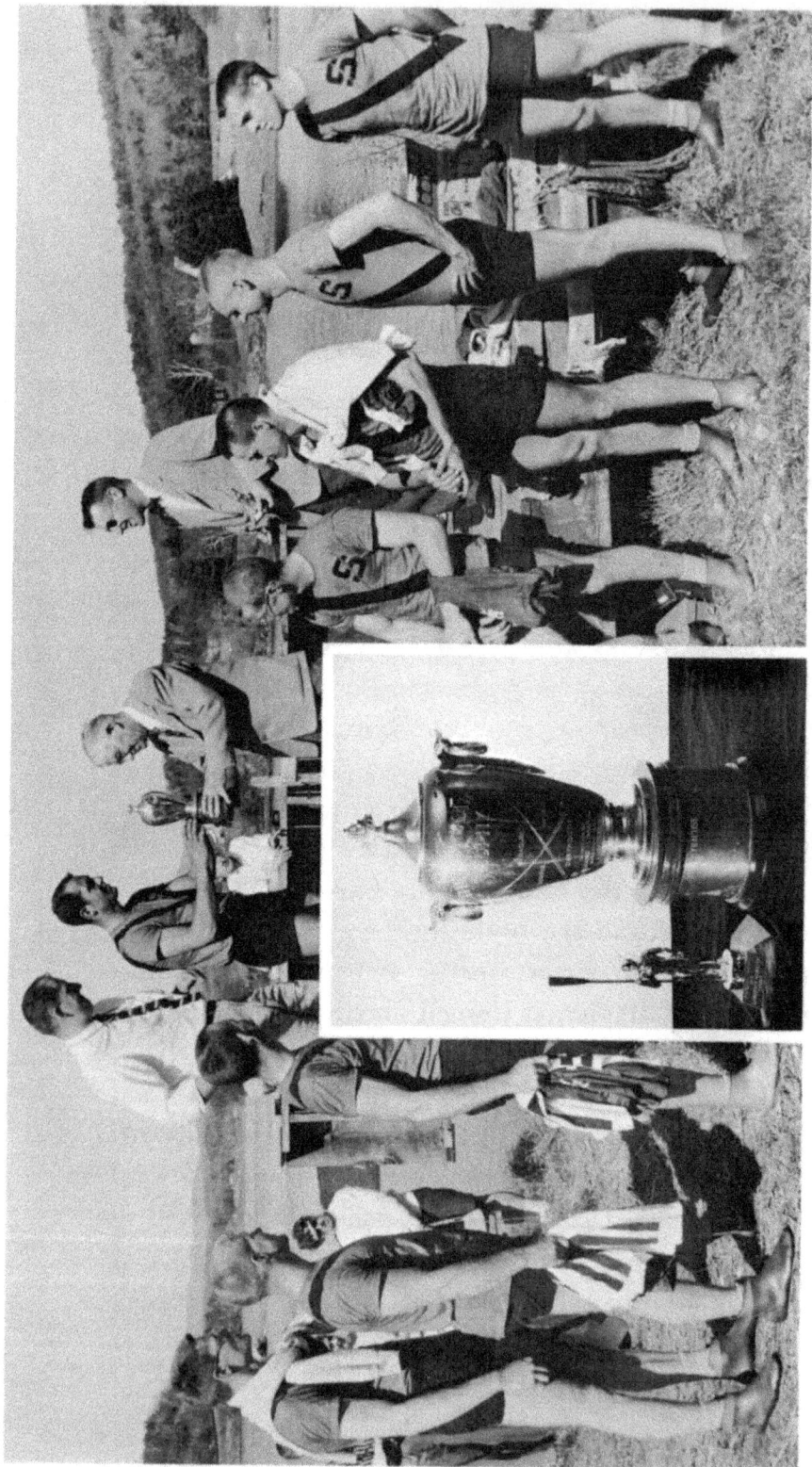

314

Dr. Edward N. Packard makes the first official presentation of the trophy bearing his name to Captain James Kries of the winning Syracuse varsity. Annual Syracuse-Dartmouth Regatta. Dr. Anthony Ladd awards the individual statuettes. Dean Thad Seymour stands by. Inset. Close up of the trophies.

Princeton on May 16. In a furiously rowed race, unfortunately, the crew lost out to Harvard by a scant two feet!

Syracuse's varsity was the pre-regatta favorite that year.

However, there were other things besides the techniques of rowing playing an important part in the 1959 IRA races. Three contenders on Onondaga Lake expected results to surpass the normal this year. They were:

First. California.

Second. Navy.

Third. Washington.

This year's California crew was the last for Coach Ky Ebright. After coaching 35 years, during which time he rescued the Golden Bears from rowing extinction, he was retiring. During his tenure since 1924, he developed more Olympic winners than any other coach; six of his crews won the IRA; and his 1939 boat established the time record for the four-mile course at Poughkeepsie. California deemed it necessary to give Ebright a last victory.

Then there was Navy. The Midshipmen held the same valid reasons for wanting victory. Rusty Callow, ill and tired, was retiring, too.

Finally, Washington was on the same emotionally-pitched plane this year as were California and Navy. They offered two valid and important reasons:

Release from two years' suspension from IRA competition imposed by the National Collegiate Athletic Association.

Their coach, Al Ulbrickson, was also retiring.

These factors were discussed at the S.A.R.A. luncheon and meeting at noon of race day. Marty Hilfinger, during the business meeting, was elected to succeed Bernard Dawson as president and afterwards, the members went out to the races and joined the crowd of 10,000 spectators.

The crowd that day was shocked to learn about Rusty Callow's decision to retire. They recalled his three Navy triumphs in 1952, 1953 and 1954, and knew the collegiate rowing world was poorer without him. Therefore, they stared in disbelief as Rusty turned over the coaching duties to Paul Quinn, his assistant, and settled down in an automobile near the finish line to watch the races.

The varsity race, as predicted, was one of high drama and fury. Off to a bunched start, the crews frantically fought for positions. First Cornell grabbed the lead. Soon Syracuse snatched it from her.

Meanwhile, Wisconsin replaced the fading Cornell boat in second place. Advancing from fifth, then to fourth, Washington came up strong and drew abreast of both the Big Red and Navy at the mile.

While this trio fought for third, the Badgers, with their strong sweeps, passed the Schoelmen. And at the two-mile point, Syracuse was a quarter of a length behind. A few minutes later the smooth-rowing Badgers swept out to a full length.

Only once before triumphant in IRA competition, Wisconsin, half mile from glory, lengthened out its lead. Desperately, Syracuse increased its stroke—29, to 30, to 31, and to 32, and to 33, then to 34, to 35, and finally to 36!

Unmindful of those valid reasons why California, Navy, Washington and Syracuse all desired victory, Wisconsin administered the coup de grace to the threatening Orangemen by increasing its stroke to 40. The Badgers smelled victory, and later they won it by sweeping across the line, stroking a lowered 33 strokes per minute.

While Wisconsin poured it on, things were happening other places on the course. Navy, after fighting off Cornell and Washington, began to move up on Syracuse. And for the second time in the championship race, the Schoelmen were forced to row a killing pace in order to salvage second place. Right down to the final stroke the two battled, but the Orange took second by one and one-tenths of a second.

California was fourth.

Navy was third.

Washington was fifth.

Cornell was sixth.

Followed by Dartmouth, Pennsylvania, Princeton, MIT and Columbia.

Honors of the day were evenly divided by three schools after the races. Wisconsin, of course, proudly took the Varsity Challenge Cup. California's jayvee boat won the Kennedy Challenge Cup. Cornell retained the Steward's Cup for its freshman victory. But Washington accumulated the most points to relieve Cornell of the Jim Ten Eyck Plaque. The Big Red gave it up after holding onto the symbol of supremacy for five consecutive years.

Immediately after the regatta, Schoel and his varsity crew expressed their disgruntlement. They knew they were worthy of victory. Perhaps, they might prove it by entering the forthcoming Pan-American trials? With these trials for eights scheduled for Onondaga Lake, there was no interruption in their training. They entered.

First, in order to do this, the seniors in the crew delayed careers, and others gave up deserved summer vacations. The

317

squad was a closely-knit group, practicing with zeal and devotion. That attitude paid off handsomely three weeks later.

Syracuse defeated the Vesper Boat Club of Philadelphia in the trials on June 28. In winning by a length and one-quarter, the men set a new course record for the 2,000 meter distance. Detroit was third.

Financed in part by S.A.R.A., the crew that was the first University athletic team representing the nation in international competition flew to Chicago for workouts several days prior to the Pan-American games on the Cal-Sag Canal, located eight miles southwest of the Windy City.

They were quartered in a North Central College dormitory in Naiperville, a Chicago suburb. In the practice days that followed Schoel and his men worked on the high stroke so necessary for the shorter course than the one in the IRA.

America was proudly represented. America entered all seven rowing events, either by winning previous qualification heats or by drawing byes for the finals. A temperature of 94 degrees and a cross wind greeted the crews on the water.

In the four-oared with coxswain race, the Lake Washington Club gave the United States its first Gold Medal by more than three and one-half lengths over Argentina, Brazil and Canada.

A second Gold Medal was won by Lake Washington in the paired-oared without coxswain event. Victory was by more than five lengths.

Uncle Sam's Harry Parker of the Vesper Boat Club won the singles event by four lengths from William Biernocks. Uraguay and Brazil followed in that order.

The march to additional medals by the United States was temporarily interrupted in the pair-oared with coxswain event when Uraguay and Argentina finished in a dead heat. A photo-finish camera recorded that Uraguay was victorious. The U. S. boat from the Detroit Club was several lengths behind the winners but ahead of Peru.

A resumption of the march to honors began when America won the final three events of the four-oared without coxswain race by a length over Argentina, Chile and Peru.

In the double sculls race, Jack Kelly, son of the famous Philadelphia sculler, with companion William Knecht of the Vesper Club won over Uraguay, Peru and Canada by five lengths.

Time drew near for the eight-oared race.

Schoel's men paddled up to the starting line dressed in jerseys of red, white and blue stripes. They were ready, they were fighting for the United States, now.

"They're sharp and crisp," Schoel commented eagerly to others in the coaching launch. "No one is going to beat them, today," he admitted.

Competition against Syracuse was forecast as being stiff: Canada boated the nucleus of its 1956 Olympic crew.

Argentina whose 1951 and 1955 boats dominated the Pan-Am Games was as strong and experienced as ever.

Brazil was successfully embarking on a new program of rowing.

The men from Syracuse took lane one. The green shirts with yellow letters of Brazil were next. Canada's crimson jerseys with white maple leaves and oars swung into third lane. Attired in light blue jerseys with white letters, Argentina occupied the last lane.

The gutteral command, "Ready all—row!" a pistol shot, and thirty-two oars, each one measuring 12 feet one-inch long, held by a triangular outrigger swept in and out of the water in immediate unison, propelling the boats forward as coxswains barked orders in *three different languages!*

Ten strokes beyond departure the American crew surged ahead of the others by at least a foot. Brazil and Canada came close behind in challenging sweeps. Both rowed 36 beats to the minute.

Rowing a steady 34 strokes, the Schoelmen were smooth in their motions, their shell uninterrupted in its hang, the oars matching their puddles with finesse.

—Whooosh!—

—Screech!—

—"Keep on!"—

burst the cacophony of noises from the University shell.

At 500 meters. A challenge developed. A battle!

Canada poked ahead of Brazil in second position. And at 1000 meters, the Maple Leafs gained on the American crew. Paced at 34 by Mills, the Americans eagerly answered the Canadian challenge.

Canada increased its beat to 36.

America continued its strong 34.

Canada began to increase its beat again.

America carefully increased its beat to 35, then to 36.

The American boat inch by inch pulled ahead.

Canada's last drive slackened somewhat.

The race was finished! America won by two lengths.

320

With the flag lazily floating overhead and the band playing the National Anthem, the winners from Syracuse mounted the platform. Flanked on each side by the others, they received their Gold Medals.

It was a time of pride and of glory in the affairs of Syracuse rowing. The magnificent victory came during a time when:

Fidel Castro took power in Cuba.

The St. Lawrence Seaway opened.

Hawaii was proclaimed the 50th state.

The University's football team became national champions, undefeated.

Coach Schoel was elected president of the Rowing Coaches of America.

In an unprecedented gesture by the Athletic Department, the oarsmen were introduced to the crowd between halves of the Holy Cross football game that following October.

Rowing to victory in the Pan-American Games were:

Bow—James Edmonds, Penn Yan, N.Y.
No. 2—Robert Schoel, Syracuse
No. 3—Thomas Rouen, Erie, Pennsylvania
No. 4—Michael Larsen, Honeoye Falls, N.Y.
No. 5—Edward Montesi, Amityville, N.Y.
No. 6—Nelson Miller, Gooding, Idaho
No. 7—Capt. James Kries, Rockville Center, N.Y.
Stroke—Charles Mills, Jr., Syracuse
Coxswain—Jerry Winkelstein, Syracuse

The campus was highly elated over the crew's performance in the Games. The men were guests at a dinner held by the Alumni Association in Graham Hall. During ceremonies a victory banner was presented by S.A.R.A. to the University in honor of the crew. Besides this, the names of

THE SYRACUSE CREW WHICH WON THE PAN AMERICAN GAMES EIGHT OARED EVENT FOR U.S.A. IN 1959.

Included above are Coach School, Louis Buhrmaster, Ferdinand Geiger, Monte Bower and Rigger Earl Margeson.

322

Dr. Gordon Hoople presents the SARA victory banner to Syracuse University. Assisting is Arthur Gabriel, Alumni Secretary. Dr. William P. Tolley is seated (below) Coach and Mrs. Schoel accept the Joslyn Trophy Award for his celebrated crew.

the crew were placed on the hand-carved William L. Joslyn Trophy for outstanding service to the University, state and nation.

In the following two years after all this excitement, four former Orange oarsmen crowded the local scene of history: two outstanding figures on the national rowing level retired from active duty, another was tapped for high national honors, while a fourth was chosen to head the trustees of his Alma Mater.

CHAPTER XXXVI

"MISTER ROWING" OF

the United States chose 1960 as the year to retire from active
duty with the collegiate and Olympic crew activities of the
nation. In his sixty-seventh year, Clifford Goes formally and
graciously surrendered the baton of leadership and all that
went with it:

Respect.

Excitement.

Satisfaction.

Responsibility.

The road to that significant retirement began when
Goes came to Syracuse University from a hop farm on the
Cherry Valley Turnpike in upper New York State. From
the day he entered in 1910 until he was graduated in 1914,
he supported himself through college. Probably the happiest
day of his young life came when he was chosen by national
newspaper writers as the "All-America Coxswain," following his 1913 crew's amazing victory at Poughkeepsie. After
graduation he was athletic director, football coach and business manager at Rutgers Preparatory School. Then in 1917,
he joined a Syracuse hospital unit that went to France in
the first World War. While overseas, he was commissioned
in the Quartermaster Corps.

After the Armistice, Goes returned to Syracuse and

worked in a lumber company, but in his spare time he assisted Jim Ten Eyck with rowing duties.

Ambition caused him to form his own contracting business in the next few years. At the same time he headed the city's assessment and taxation bureau. He became an enthusiastic member of the U. S. Olympic Committee. Four years afterwards he became its chairman.

He was the logical choice to run off the sprints of the Eastern Association of Rowing Colleges one spring day at Annapolis. Soon he was refereeing the IRA regatta in Marietta, Ohio. His splendid handling of 32 crews from 13 competing schools on the turbulent Ohio River earned him the sobriquet, "Mr. Rowing."

Besides all this, Goes' love for the Old Man caused him to spearhead the drive for the Ten Eyck boathouse. It was his personal support that persuaded the IRA to transfer the regatta to Syracuse, and in 1956, the Olympic trials.

Goes is remembered for his gift in 1939, the time of his 25th class reunion. He presented a beautiful permanent plaque for the University's Trophy Room. Each year the name of a junior oarsman, who is chosen the most improved, is engraved on it. John More of Texas in 1938 was the first one honored.

In addition to this gift, Goes presented another to the University in memory of his wife and brother. Called the Goes Memorial Bequest, it is used in "non-sectarian work at Hendricks Chapel for religious and cultural benefit of enrolled Syracuse students regardless of race or creed."

One of the most notable gifts to collegiate rowing other than his own devoted service and work was his donation of a trophy in 1955 to commemorate three grand old coaches:

Clifford "Tip" Goes holds the trophy he donated in honor of the three old men of rowing. Inset: The Goes Award presented in 1939 to the University honoring an outstanding junior oarsman each year.

Charles Courtney of Cornell.

Richard Glendon of Navy.

James Ten Eyck.

The Goes Trophy goes to the winner of the race among the crews of these three institutions.

A tribute to Goes, written by his personal friend, Allison Danzig of the *Times*, perhaps describes best the Syracusan's profile of dedication to young oarsmen:

> . . . But nothing gives him the pleasure of standing in his launch, with the wind and sun on his face, his megaphone to his lips and a dozen boatloads of rangy athletes awaiting tense and expectant for his "ready all, row!" to send their delicate shells flying over the water. . . .

About the same time in 1960 that Goes retired, another member of the 1913 crew and beloved figure in collegiate rowing—Howard Robbins—quietly left the active life of collegiate refereeing.

To know this figure, we turn back the clock and the pages to another era, in 1911 to be exact, in circumstances similar to those present in the day of freshman Edward Packard. As in 1903, Jim Ten Eyck's eyes swept over the freshmen hopefuls this year.

"Hey, young man—what's your name?" the coach asked.

"Howard Robbins, sir—" he answered.

"Well, now—you ever rowed before?"

"No, I haven't," answered Robbins.

Then Ten Eyck stepped down into the gig in the water.

"Come here, please," he ordered. "Take No. 4 position and let's try out this combination."

Ten Eyck thus tapped Robbins for the freshman boat and in the forthcoming four years of crew Robbins was never replaced. It must have been Ten Eyck's wonderful insight responsible for picking Robbins, for the youth's physique was not imposing. Lithe he was, but his height was only five feet, nine inches, and he scaled only 164 pounds. Perhaps it was his burning eyes. Or perhaps it was the set of his jaw. Anyway, the Old Man chose Robbins for reasons known only to himself.

The fact that Robbins was out for crew was by accident rather than design. Interested only in football and baseball, he came to crew because of a University regulation. He became involved in rowing that first winter because the institution was concerned about the health of its students. Robbins and the others were given a choice: either take what we today call physical education classes or workout on the rowing machines and in the rowing tank. He chose the latter, and by spring, luckily for rowing, his interest was hooked by crew. He never reported for baseball.

How Robbins came to Syracuse is quite another story. One of six children of a farmer in Ashby, Massachusetts, Robbins early in life knew farming was not for him. He thought it might be law, but this, of course, required a college education. Where was he to obtain money to finish high school to say nothing about college?

Robbins solved the problem by working at the thing he liked best: trapping. Snaring skunks and muskrats, he sold their pelts and worked his way through Cushing Academy. In his spare time he played football and ran on the track team. It was his prowess and ability that caught the attention of others and he was offered a scholarship at Syracuse. He accepted.

As Goes, Robbins was named "All-America" oarsman after the 1913 victory on the Hudson. That next summer

329

before entering Harvard Law School, he and "Chris" Mahan, the 1913 bow oar, rowed with the professional Duluth Boat Club. The fact that Jim Ten Eyck, Jr., was coach didn't hurt his chances a bit. After an active summer of competition, Robbins and Mahan rowed with Duluth in the National Regatta at Boston.

At law school, textbooks and studies did not keep Robbins from the long narrow oars and the slender cedar boats. He stroked and captained the Law School's crew, composed of former undergraduate oarsmen from Yale, Harvard and Princeton.

A short time after graduation, he was admitted to the Massachusetts bar, but when America entered the first World War, he enlisted in the Army as a buck private. By Armistice time, he was captain.

Chosen as U. S. Commissioner in Boston, Robbins continued his rowing. He stroked the No. 2 position with the Union Boat Club. At a time when men of his age began to thicken in the midrift, a lean Robbins captained his crew in the Grand Challenge Cup race in England. And even more amazing, eight years later while still pulling an oar, he was named coach of the Union Boat Club crew. Almost a quarter of a century after Syracuse, he stroked the Union boaters in the national regatta!

Ready for retirement due to pressing business rather than to physical condition, Robbins was held away from the spectator's armchair by officials of intercollegiate rowing. They appointed him official referee of the IRA regatta as well as of the Olympic trials. If this did not seem tribute enough, they made sure he refereed the Yale-Harvard race continuously for 19 years. And during those years he started every race held on the Charles River. Upon retirement in 1960, he was named honorary referee of the Yale-Harvard race.

However, he did not forget his Alma Mater. Back in 1938, he served as Syracuse's representative on the IRA Board of Stewards. He was then re-elected to another three-year term, but resigned after Pearl Harbor. During the second war he was regional director of Civil Defense for all six New England states and was decorated for meritorious service.

Thus, Howard Robbins, who much preferred baseball and football originally in his freshman days, gained stature and prestige in rowing over the years; in turn, he gave these same attributes to a sport, which will always excite the pulses of young Americans as they answer the call to send their fragile boats across the waters.

In the first test for 1960, Schoel's crews swept Onondaga Lake against an eager but inexperienced St. Joseph's College crews.

Aside from the remarkable showing of Syracuse, everyone saw for the first time the famed "Italian Rigging."

The boats were rigged differently. Instead of the customary American port, starboard alternating placement of oarsmen, Italian rigging consisted of the bow oar on the portside; the 2 and 3 oars to starboard; 4 and 5 oars on the portside; the 6 and 7 oars to starboard. Stroke was on the portside.

St. Joseph adopted this unusual rigging because Allen Rosenberg, its coach and veteran coxswain of the Vesper Boat Club of Philadelphia, saw it used by the Italians in the 1958 European championships. He argued that the boat with this rigging pulled more evenly, and the coxswain didn't employ the rudder as much.

On the Seneca River in May during the Goes Cup race the Orangemen and Cornellians tried to overcome Navy's early lead but were unsuccessful. The race was transferred from the Lake and reduced to five-eighths of a mile because of high winds and heaving water. Cornell's junior varsity and freshman crews, however, were victorious.

In the Eastern College Sprints at Worcester, the Cornell varsity eight won. Harvard was second and Navy took third place. Schoel's crew was fourth.

To win the Packard Trophy the Syracuse varsity defeated a strong Dartmouth crew by three lengths. The freshmen won their event, too, but the junior varsity lost a close one to the Indians.

Dr. Edward Packard on June seventeenth, 1960, was named to the Helms Rowing Hall of Fame. His selection was announced at the annual Stewards' Dinner on the eve of the IRA regatta. The sixth named from the ranks of former Orangemen, Dr. Packard joined Tip Goes, Howard Robbins, James Ten Eyck, Arthur Osman and Ned Ten Eyck in the Valhalla of rowing.

California's Golden Bears presented victory the next day to their new coach, Jim Lemmon, in the 58th varsity run of the famous classic. In the IRA event they rushed up in the last half mile to win in a thrilling finish before 15,000 spectators. Navy was second. Syracuse was ninth.

About the same time Harvard was defeating Yale in their annual race, their Ivy League colleague, Brown, finished fourth in the IRA varsity event and became known as the "Cinderella Crew."

The name was given Brown's crew in this way.

Without financial assistance or formal recognition by its institution the crew came to Syracuse and the regatta without its volunteer coach. Gordon Helander '56, former Syracuse oarsman under Schoel, coached the inexperienced oarsmen that spring. He was absent from the regatta, serving on military duty. A Navy coach, David Pratt of the lightweight crew, saw Brown's predicament and graciously offered help. He gave the green crew helpful suggestions on how to row the grueling three-mile race.

The Brown crew's finish startled the rowing fraternity and the crowd. Enthusiastic over their showing, the crew entered the Olympic Trials the following week. They were eliminated on the second day, but they gave Pennsylvania a close race before losing on Onondaga Lake.

Navy's big crew won the right to represent the United States at Rome, Italy, during the third day of the Trials. Favored California in the race finished more than a length behind the future Admirals.

A Syracuse crew consisting of undergraduates and alumni sponsored by S.A.R.A. won its preliminary heats. In the finals the crew led most of the way before losing out to the Navy oarsmen whom they defeated the previous day.

Two of the crew in the "Alumni" boat, Edward Montesi, No. 3 oar, and Nelson Miller, No. 6, were veterans of the 1959 Pan-American championship group. They were graduated in 1959; consequently, they did not row all that

334

FINISH OF THE FIRST HEAT OF THE SEMIFINALS IN THE 1960 OLYMPIC TRIALS, ONONDAGA LAKE.
SYRACUSE BY THREE QUARTERS LENGTH.
Below: The crew sponsored by SARA, positioned as they are rowing.

Annual Sprint Regatta Reunion luncheon.

President's Citation Plaque presented to Martin Hilfinger by President-elect Russell Swanson.

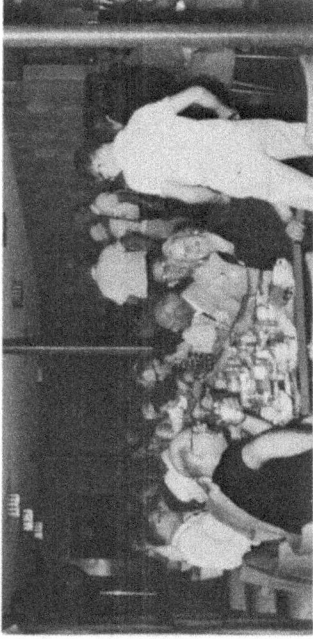

Annual Regatta Day meeting and reunion luncheon.

Alumni old oars have a splash reunion.

GLANCES AT OTHER SARA ACTIVITIES WHICH CONTINUE THROUGH THE YEARS.

335

Christening of the "Bernie Dawson", second SARA president. Miss Ronnie Dawson does the honors.

SARA Exec. Comm. 1962-63 (Blocher, Morrison, Dunham, Mills, Stratton, Swanson, Chamberlain).

Annual ceramic awards to winning crews of the autumn regatta.

SARA Blanket award to Seniors Gregory, Smeltzer, Howard, Mittlestaedt.

GLANCES AT OTHER SARA ACTIVITIES

season with the undergraduate men who made up this crew in the Trials.

However, Montesi and Miller came back to campus for graduate work and kept in shape by daily workouts on the Lake. When the crew was entered in the Olympic Trials, they were eligible and eagerly volunteered for duty.

Rowing with them were Ferdinand Geiger, bow oar; Gary Gardner, No. 2; Michael Larsen, No. 4; Bryan Collier, No. 5; Thomas Rouen, No. 7; Charles Mills, stroke; and Jerry Winklestein, coxswain.

Later that summer Navy lost to Canada in the heats. In the championship race it followed Germany, Canada, Czechoslovakia and France across the finish line. Navy's defeat terminated America's long winning streak for eight-oared crews, a skein initiated in 1920 by a crew from the same institution.

Nineteen sixty-one was an up and down season for the Orange. Schoel's oarsmen lost the varsity and junior varsity races to Harvard and Brown, but the freshmen won. All three crews were triumphant against Dartmouth and Boston University on the Connecticut River.

The freshman crew continued its winning streak by copping the Charles Courtney Trophy at the Eastern Sprints on Lake Quinsigamond at Worcester. It was the first University crew to win in the Sprints.

Washington won the 59th IRA freshman race. Syracuse was third. Cornell took the junior varsity event. Syracuse finished last. California won the varsity race. Syracuse was ninth.

Cornell with its junior varsity victory and two second places was awarded the Ten Eyck Plaque.

338

FRESHMAN EASTERN SPRINT CHAMPS, 1961
With inset of Coach Victor Michalson holding the Courtney Trophy, Worcester, Mass. Str. Dan Hogan, Paul Eckhardt, Ed Kakas, Steve Galdstone, Don Dick, Jerry Haslach, Giles Vanderbogert, Dave Norris, Dick Hersh, Larry Hopcraft, Charles Lee.

That autumn and winter the freshman coach and former Orange oarsmen took their places in collegiate rowing:

Victor Michalson became coach at Brown University.

Ferdinand Geiger was named Dartmouth freshman coach.

Eugene Perry, No. 7 oar in the 1947 Orange freshman crew that was dubbed "best in the East," became Syracuse freshman coach.

Thomas Rouen was named rowing coach at Liverpool (N.Y.) Central School. Phenomenally successful, he directed his crew to second place at Poughkeepsie in the high shool regatta on the Hudson in June, 1962.

The University's board of trustees at its annual meeting in November of 1961 chose a former oarsman as its chairman. Dr. Gordon Hoople '15 was named after serving several years as board vice chairman.

Dr. Hoople's high honor was in keeping with his long tradition of exemplary service and dedication to his Alma Mater. One of a famous rowing family in Orange history he gave unselfishly of himself to the sport of rowing. And through the years he also devoted himself to the affairs of the University.

New York City born, he went to China after graduation from Medical College and internship. A co-founder of the philanthropic Syracuse-in-China program, he served in the Orient in 1921. Back in Syracuse several years later he inaugurated the present student infirmary system at the University.

An outstanding specialist in Otolaryngology, Dr. Hoople served in World War II and later founded the speech and hearing center at the University's Department of Special Education for the Handicapped.

In 1951, his Alma Mater honored him with the Arents Pioneer Medal for outstanding service to mankind and to the University.

Although busy with professional duties, Dr. Hoople in the spring of 1962 found time to inspect the boathouse area, watched with interest the young men in training, and talked with Coach Schoel about the posture of rowing on Piety Hill. His long association with the sport and with young men made him a valuable friend to Syracuse rowing.

A few days before Dr. Hoople's selection as trustee chairman, Earl Margeson, 57, rigger of Syracuse shells since 1955, died. Widely known for organizing the Intercollegiate Rowing Riggers' Association, he served as the group's first president. And among the rowing fraternity of the world Margeson was fondly remembered for his superb rigging of Syracuse shells in the Pan-American Games in 1959.

Cornell dominated the 1962 IRA regatta, capturing both the varsity and freshman races. Only a belated rush by the Navy junior varsity kept the Big Red from a clean sweep. In victory Cornell retained the coveted Jim Ten Eyck Plaque.

Tip Goes was succeeded as chairman of the U. S. Olympic Rowing Committee by Tom Bolles, former Washington Husky and Harvard coach. At the time of the appointment, Yale won its first crew victory over Harvard in four years.

From the humble beginning of professional crew races on Onondaga Lake in 1873, and then the introduction of college rowing at Syracuse University in 1900, the sport through the years was a strong thread in the fabric of University history. Achievements of yesteryear presented the guidelines for young men of tomorrow. These oarsmen created and handed down a heritage of richness and of meaning. They shaped the pattern of crew life at the University and gave it meaning and a sense of dedication.

The outlook for rowing at Syracuse in the years ahead is bright. With Coach Loren Schoel's guidance, the monarch of all collegiate sports is definitely on its way back up the ladder on Piety Hill. Another golden era in rowing takes time. As Henry W. Clune wrote in the Rochester (N.Y.) *Democrat and Chronicle* in 1935:

> The crew coach, working with more fundamental materials, is unable to resort to hocus-pocus systems or new fangled schemes, since these would have no value in a . . . race. . . . There is nothing very new about rowing a boat. The crew man simply applies the tried and true principles he knows to the material that is given him and strives to do the best he can.

341

Supported by a new spirit as exemplified in part by the Syracuse Alumni Rowing Association, Syracuse's eager young men of today and tomorrow will carry on the fine tradition, have no fear.

Meanwhile, those of the past, be they oarsmen, coxswains, coaches, riggers, trainers, alumni, University officials, or just plain followers of rowing, in their own way have taken their places in

Mark   of   the   Oarsmen.

BIBLIOGRAPHY

I *Correspondence*

Alumni Association. U. S. Navy
Blomquist, Albert
Buff, Ernest
Busch, George
Bush, L. M.
Conderman, Joseph
Davis, Darius
Davis, Gerald H.
Day, Dr. James Roscoe
Donaldson, Harold
Eldredge, Frank
Eller, Rear Admiral (Ret.) USN Historian
Emery, Robert
Fairman, Kenneth, Princeton University
Follis, John
Frink, James
Gallagher, Kenneth
Glass, Walter
Goes, Clifford
Gramlich, J. Edward
Gregg, Mahlon
Harriman, Gov. W. Averell
Hoople, Howard C.
Keefer, Ralph
Kerr, M.D., Thomas
Laidlaw, John
Lombardi, Thomas
McDougall, William
Mang. Sidney
Marcham, John. *Cornell Alumni News*
Olsen, Olaf
Park, Robert
Rice, Ted
Richardson, H. H.
Robbins, Howard
Schiefer, Frederick W.
Schoberlein, George
Scobell, George
Smart, Wayne D.
Sprague, Lloyd
Stone, Robert R.
Thayer, Donald
Toch, Leo
Tollerton, Harry
Tolley, Howard
Van de Water, Gerald
Van de Water, Jerome
Weibezahl, Harold

II *Newspapers*

Boston *Globe*
New York *Herald-Tribune*
New York *Post*
New York *Times*
New York *World Telegram*
Poughkeepsie *Courier*
Rochester *Democrat-Chronicle*
Syracuse *Herald*
Syracuse *Herald-American*
Syracuse *Journal*
Syracuse *Post-Standard*
Syracuse *Standard*
Worcester (Mass.) *Times*
Syracuse University *Daily Orange*
Syracuse University *Herald*

III *Books, Pamphlets and Periodicals*

Alumni News, Syracuse University.
Clark, Bill, Syracuse *Herald-American*, June, 1958.
Evans, Arthur, *Fifty Years of Football at Syracuse University*, Syracuse University Football History Committee, 1939.
Danzig. Allison. The New York *Times*.
Encyclopedia Brittanica, Library Research Service, Chicago, V. A. Stenberg, Director.
Galpin, Dr. W. Freeman, Vol. I, II, *History of Syracuse University*, 1952, 1960, Syracuse University Press.
Kelly, Robert, *American Rowing*, G. P. Putnam's Sons, New York, N.Y., 1932.
Gallico, Paul, *Further Confessions of a Story Teller*, Doubleday and Company, Inc., New York 22, N.Y., 1961.
Outlook, The New York, N.Y., 1924, 1926, 1927 Intercollege Rowing Association souvenir programs.
Newsletter, Syracuse Alumni Rowing Association.
Onondagans, Syracuse University yearbooks.
Sports Illustrated.
Trace, James Dale, Vignettes of History. 1961-1962.
Reddy, Bill, Syracuse *Post-Standard.*
Woolever, Frank, Syracuse *Herald-Journal.*
World Book Encyclopedia.
Young, C.V.P., *Courtney and Cornell Rowing*, The Cornell Publications Printing, Co., Ithaca, N.Y., 1923.

343

BIBLIOGRAPHY

IV *Interviews*

Brewer, Mrs. Edna Ten Eyck
Chamberlain, M.D., Bruce
Hoople, M.D., Gordon
Hilfinger, Martin
Hatch, M. Charles
Dworshak, Louis
Kerr, M.D., Thomas
Ladd, M.D., Anthony
Michalson, Victor
Mills, Charles
Packard, M.D., Edward
Perry, Eugene
Roth, A. Brohman
Rouen, Thomas
Schoel, Loren
Stratton, Hubert
Sundstrom, Donald
Swanson, Russell

V *Personal sources* (scrapbooks, photos, souvenirs, etc.)

Blomquist, Albert
Brewer, Mrs. Edna Ten Eyck (personal scrapbook and letters of James A. Ten Eyck)
Brown, Ancil
Chamberlain, M.D., Bruce
Conderman, Joseph
Crowley, Francis
Curtiss, Henry
Davis, Darius
Davis, Gerald
Donaldson, Harold
Dunham, Thomas
Ellis, Eric
Ellis, Leon
Emery, Robert
Evans, James, Jr.
Fisher, W. Claude
Frink, James
Gregg, Mahlon
Grimshaw, Wesley
Hilfinger, George
Horlacher, Herman
Horstmann, Richard
Hrushesky, William
Hutton, John
Irvine, Philip
Jennings, William
Johnson, Robert
Keefe, Webster
Keefer, Paul
Keefer, Ralph
Kerr, M.D., Thomas
Klock, Karl
Laidlaw, John

LaMonte, John
Lombardi, Thomas
Loring, Robert
Love, Ronald
MacLelland, John
Mang, Sidney
McFadden, M.D., Samuel
Meacham, Edward
Mills, Charles, Jr.
Morrison, William
Packard, M.D., Edward
Page, Chamberlain
Palmer, John
Perry, Eugene
Phi Gamma Delta Fraternity
Poole, Sidney
Schiefer, Henry
Schoberlein, George
Schoel, Loren
Schoolcraft, Earle
Scobell, George, Sr.
Shepherd, Edward
Sprague, Lloyd
Stark, Harry
Stimson, James
Stone, Robert
Stratton, Hubert
Stuhlman, Frank
Summerville, Orin
Sundstrom, Donald
Swanson, Russell
Syracuse University:
    Alumni Association
    Athletic Department
    Audio-visual Center
Tau Epsilon Phi Fraternity
Thayer, Donald
Weibezahl, Harold
Wetherell, William
Winter, John

Special acknowledgement goes also to
Alumni Associations of
    Columbia
    Cornell
    Naval Academy
    Pennsylvania

Sports Departments of the
    Syracuse *Herald-Journal*
    Syracuse *Post-Standard*

Photographers
    Dan Owen and Bachrach
    And the photograph section of
    the U. S. Veterans Hospital at
    Syracuse, New York
    The University Audio-visual
    Department

INDEX

345

INDEX

348

INDEX

349

INDEX

INDEX

351

INDEX

INDEX of PICTURES

355

CREW ROSTER

This alphabetical list of names includes all who made a mark in rowing history at Syracuse University. Even though one had not rowed for a complete season, his name will be found here. The information given is as accurate as it could be obtained from the records reviewed.

Key to symbols and abbreviations:

The years enumerated indicate actual participation in crew.

Parenthesis ( ) denotes the class year if the individual participated during that year; if he did not, his class may be marked by CL.

Capt.: CAPTAIN, Comm.: VARSITY MANAGER or COMMODORE. "S": Varsity letter award.

**: Received the Frederick Plumb-Ten Eyck Trophy for the most valuable crewman. (1929-1941).

*Awarded the Clifford "Tip" Goes Award as most improved and outstanding Junior crewman. (1939-).

Abberger, William M., '11, '12, Cl. '14 S
Abigail, George W., '26, Cl. '29
Abrams, Prentice, '29, '30, '31, ('32) S
Acker, David P., '54, '55, '56, Cl. '57 S
Ackerman, John M., '55, ('57) S
Ackert, Bruce, '56, '57
Ackley, Earle L., '02, ('05)
Adams, Thomas R., Jr., Cl. '37
Alcorn, Everett M., '62, Cl. '65
Aldridge, Albert H., '12, Cl. '15
Allen, Andrews, '42, Cl. '44 S
Allen, Harry B., '31, '32, '33, ('34) S
Allen, Murray, '29 S
Allen, Richard E., '57, '58, ('60) S
Alonge, Anthony, Cl. '26
Alvord, Vincent, '36, Cl. '38 S
Anderson, Richard A., '54, '55, ('56) S
Anderson, Ross, '04, '05, ('06) S
Anderson, Russell E., Cl. '35
Andrews, Thomas, '58, Cl. '61
Andrews, V. E., '20, '21, Cl. '23 S
Andrews, Willard W., '04, '05, '06, ('07) S
Andrews, William A., ('32)

Andrus, William E., '47 Comm., Cl. '48 S
Angelucci, Robert G., '55, '56, ('57) S
Angwin, Lester E., '20, '21, '23, ('24) S
Antrim, Doron S., '52, Cl. '55
Aradine, A. W., '06
Archoska, Julius, '24, '25, Cl. '27 S
Armstrong, Albert M., '04, '05, '09
Arps, Edward H., '23, '24, '25, ('26) S
Ashcroft, Sterling H., '29, '30, '31, ('32 Capt.) S
Avery, Floyd B., '13, '14, '15, ('16) S

Babbitt, Grover C., '09, '10, '11, ('12 Capt.) S
Bagg, Linus H., '02
Bailey, B. Mart, '02
Baker, Alva P., Cl. '22
Baker, Bruce E., '56, '57, '59, Cl. '60 S
Baker, Leonard, '30, '31
Balent, Andrew, '53
Ballard, Frederick A., Cl. '23
Baltensperger, Casper V., '22, '23, ('24) S

Banks, D. Eugene, '06, ('09) S
Barber, Arthur S., Cl. '23
Barber, Walter C., '60, '61, '62, Cl. '63 S
Barge, Henry F., '37, '38, Cl. '40 S
Barlow, Ralph S., '27, '29, ('30) S
Barnard, Edward S., '39, Cl. '40 S
Barnes, Stanley G., '41, '42, Cl. '44 S
Barnhart, Gilbert R., '36, ('37) S
Barrett, Philips N., '50, '52, ('53) S
Barron, Elwyn L., '09
Bassett, Richard O., '13
Bates, Thomas C., '55, Cl. '58
Batzer, Bryce, '40, '41, Cl. '43
Bauer, Harold P., '26, '27, '28, '29, Cl. '30 S
Bauer, Richard H., '58, Cl. '61
Baule, Gerhard M., '52, '53, '54, ('55) S
Bayer, Peter F., '57, Cl. 60
Bebout, Lawrence E., '24, '25, Cl. '27 S
Becker, Clarence H., '02, '03, ('05)
Becker, J. Edmund, '33, Cl. '35
Beckett, Peter E., '54, '55, '56, ('57) S
Beebe, Richard L., Cl. '50
Beier, Robert J., '54, '55, '56, ('57) S
Belden, Willard N., '23, '25, ('26) S
Belko, John H., Jr., '36, '37, '38, ('39) S
Belluz, Primo, '50, Cl. '54
Belnap, James R., '55, Cl. '59
Beltz, Edward, '27, ('28 Comm.) S
Bennett, Edward, '27, Cl. '30
Bennett, Milton A., '19, ('21)
Bennett, Robert, '52, Cl. '55
Benson, Frank H., Jr., '60, '61, '62 S
Benson, Harvey S., '08, Cl. '11
Bergsten, Carla, '37, ('38)
Berkey, Robert A., Cl. '41
Bertram, Kenneth E., '42, '47 Capt. S
Bessant, William T., '12 ('13 Comm.) S
Bettinger, Sterling, '34, '35, '36, ('37 Capt.) S **
Bettinger, William H., '51, Cl. '55
Biggs, Carl S., '24, Cl. '26
Birnie, James J., '18, ('21)
Blake, O. William, '47, '48, Capt., Cl. '49 S
Blakeley, Bryce D., '18, '19, ('20 Comm.) S
Blanchard, Ernest M., ('18)
Blanchard, Harold F., '15
Blanchard, Orlo D., '01, Comm. S
Blessing, David A., '57, '58, '59, Cl. '60 S
Bliss, Craig C., '34, Cl. '36
Blixt, Karl K., '54, '56, Cl. '57 S
Blocher, Ackley E., '05
Blocher, Howard N., '34, '36, Cl. '37 S
Blomquist, Albert E., ('29)
Bluhm, Richard F., '41, '42, Cl. '43 S
Blum, George A., '36, ('37) S

Bogart, Loyal K., '39, '40, '41, ('42) S
Bogdan, Louis J., 40, '41, Cl. '43 S
Bohr, Frank M., '02, Cl. '05
Boldizar, Robert, '47, Cl. '48 S
Boles, Harold E., '32, Cl. '35
Bonney, George, '40, '41, '42, Cl. '43
Boone, Charles E., (41) S
Borst, Jacque B., '33, Cl. '36
Borst, Kenneth J., '47, '48, ('49) S *
Bowen, Roy H., '07, ('08) S
Bradley, Gerald T., '37, '38, '39, ('40) S
Bradley, Harvey E., '03
Brady, Eugene J., '01, '02, '03, Cl. '04 S
Brady, William G., Cl. '15
Braue, Robert W., '56, '57, '58, ('59) S
Braun, Ellsworth J., 22, '23, Cl. '25
Breckheimer, Herbert C., Jr., ('52 Comm.)
Brewster, Harold, '23, '24, '25 S
Brewster, Neal, '01, Cl. '02
Broadway, Kenneth E., '14, '15, '16, ('17) S
Brockett, Roy R., '04, ('05 Comm.) S
Brogan, William E., '26, ('27) S
Brooks, Joseph H., '53, '55, Cl. '57 S
Brower, Egmont G., '56, '57, '58, ('59) S
Brower, Ernest E., '29, '30, Cl. '32 S
Brower, Paul L., '21, '22, '23, '24 S
Brown, Alex, '39, Cl. '42
Brown, Ancil D., '00, '01, ('03) S
Brown, Fred H., '04, '05 S
Brown, Harold H., '08, ('09) S
Brown, James A., '02
Brown, Robert M., '53, ('54) S
Bruce, John R., '18, Cl. '21
Brunish, Thompson P., '30, '32, ('33) S
Brust, Norman C., '29, '30, ('31 Comm.) S
Bruster, Harold G., Cl. '25
Buchanan, Harold F., '15, Cl. '18
Buckley, Bruce W., '62, Cl. '64
Buckley, Frederick H., '09
Buckley, Kenneth P., '19, ('21 Comm.) S
Buff, Ernest D., '30, '31, '32, Cl. '34 S
Buff, Ernest D., Jr., '62
Buhrmaster, Kenneth E., '36, ('37 Comm.) S
Buhrmaster, Louis H., '58, '59, '60 Comm., ('61 Comm.) S
Bump, Guy A., '03, Cl. '06
Bunch, T. Hooper, '25, Cl. '28
Burnham, Robert A., '53
Burns, Bernard M., '14, Cl. '17
Burns, Frederick T., Cl. '04
Burns, William J., '23, Cl. '26
Burwell, Gerwood N., Cl. '50
Busch, George P., '18, '19, ('20 Capt.) S

358

Bush, Edgar J., '38, '39, Cl. '40
Bush, Lucius M., '08, '09, '10, Cl. '11 S
Bushnell, George K., Cl. '16
Butler, James A., '47, Cl. '48 S
Butler, M. Griffith, '11, '12, ('14) S
Butterworth, J. Raymond, '31, '32. Cl. '33
Butz, C. Edwin, '05. '06. '07, ('08 Comm.) S

Cabesas, Erol, ('53)
Cacavo, F. Arnold, '37, Cl. '40
Cadin, Francis J., '22, '23. Cl. '25
Cady, George A., '30
Cain, Alden B., '61, Cl. '64
Cagwin, Douglas P., '38, '39, Cl. '41 S
Calkins, John T., '48 Comm., ('49 Comm.) S
Camp, Samuel H., '09, '10, Cl. '12 S
Camp, Steven E., '38, Cl. '41
Campbell, Howard J.. Jr., '51, Cl. '54
Capano, Richard F., '49
Capron, Wilbur W., '13, '14, Cl. '16 S
Carney, Lyster T., '49
Carr, William C., '14, '15, (Cl. '17) S
Carter, L. E., '01, Cl. '02
Carter, Sam, '36, '37, ('38)
Castle, John F., '47, '48, ('49) S
Castle, Lewis S., '11, '12, ('14) S
Castonguay, Samuel J., '24, Cl. '27
Cathers, Calvin B., '19, Cl. '23
Cecot, Felix, ('41)
Chadsey, Bradford, '39, Cl. '42
Chaffee, Frank W., '22, '23, Cl. '25 S
Chamberlain, Bruce E., '38, '39, '40, Cl. '41 S
Chambers, Leon S., '16, Cl. '18
Champlin, E. G., '08, '09, Cl. '12 S
Chapman, Charles R., '49, Cl. '51
Chapman, John W., '29, '30, ('31) S
Chapman, Ralph, '39, Cl. '42
Chase, Richard D., Cl. '57
Cheney, C. C., '09
Cheney, Harold L., '09, Cl. '12
Chesbro, Robert C., Cl. '41
Chester, Frederick, '28. '29, '30, ('31 Capt.) S
Childs, Richard J., '37, Cl. '38
Christie, Thomas E., '54. '55, ('57)
Cibelli, Gennard, '62, Cl. '65
Cimino, John, '47
Clark, Albert A., '53, '54, '55 S
Clark, Leonard H., Cl. '43
Clark, Paul C., Cl. '27
Clarkson, Roy K., '38, '40, ('41) S
Clary, F. Ware, '01, ('02 Comm.) S
Clash, Harwood G., '20, '21, Cl. '23 S
Clearwater, James B., '19, ('20) S
Clingen, Donn H., Cl. '52

Coburn, Robert W., '48, '49, '50, ('51) S
Cochran. J. Rowland, '22, '23, '24, Cl. '25 S
Cockrell, Robert A., '26, '28, '29, Cl. '30 S
Cole, Clare L., '28, ('29) S
Colella, Robert D., '52, '53, '54, ('55) S
Collier, Bryan J., '58, '59, '60, ('61 Capt.) S
Collins, James T., '15, Cl. '18
Collins, Robert W., '34, '35, '36, ('37) S
Compson. Wilber C., '25; '26, '28, ('29) S
Conan, Mark E., '33, '34, '35, ('36) S
Conderman, Joseph, '18, '19, ('20) S
Connell, George L., '00, '02
Connell, Harry W., '00, '03 S
Connell, Harvey F., '00, ('03) S
Connelly. James F., '51, '52, Cl. '55
Converse. Howard, '56, Cl. '60
Cook, John F., '22, '23, Cl. '24
Cooper, John R.. Jr., '52, '53, ('54) S
Cooper, Lewis K.. '08, Cl. '11
Correy, Al H., Cl. '43
Cornwall. Leon H., '04, '05, '06. Cl. '07 S
Corp, David T., '05, '06 S
Corrigan. Bruce J., Cl. '35
Corrigan, Edward B., Cl. '51
Corry, Al H., Cl. '43
Corson, Raymond F., '47, Cl. '49
Cosgrill, Jack W., '29, '30 S
Costello, William J., '00
Cotrell, Gerald, '51
Cottrell, Edward, '12, '14, '15 S
Coulter, Richard G., ('35) S
Cox, Glenn H., '19, Cl. '22
Craig, John P., '51, '52, '53, ('54) S
Cramer, Kenneth F., '25, '26, Cl. '28 S
Crapo, George W., '07, Cl. '10
Crawford, Herbert W., '11, '12 S
Creegan, Charles C., Jr., '00
Cregg, Frank, Jr., '26, '27, ('29)
Crichton. Edward M., '48, ('51) S
Crimmins, John D., '10, '11, '12, Cl. '13 S
Cromwell, Robert M., '50, ('51) S
Crosby, Charles A., '54, Cl. '57
Crosley, Dorr E., '08, Cl. '11
Crosson, Frank A., '42, Cl. '45
Crowell, Robert K., '41, '42, Cl. '47 S
Crowley, Francis E., '33, '34, '35, ('36) S
Cuddeback, William, ('32 Comm.)
Cumings, Orville E., '04, '05, '06, ('07) S
Cummings, Ernest M., '19, Cl. '21
Cummings, Malcolm E., '21, Cl. '24
Cunningham, Charles, Jr., ('25)
Cunningham, John P., '57, '59, ('60)

361

Jackson, Robert S., '62, Cl. '65
Jacobs, Joseph, '34, ('35) S
James, Herbert T., '12, Cl. '15
Jappe, Paul E., '20, Cl. '24
Jayne, George G., '14, '15, '16, Cl. '17 S
Jeffery, Stanley C., '27, ('28) S
Jeffords, Harrison M., '10, ('14) S
Jenkins, Horace S., '25, Cl. '28 S
Jennings, Warren D., '16, ('19)
Jennings, William H., Jr., '09, Cl. '12
Jennison, Lynn E., '00, Cl. '02 S
Jeschke, Robert L., '60, '61 S
Jewert, Russell J., '51
Johnson, Benjamin R., '18, '19, Cl. '20 S
Johnson, Evan S., '18, Cl. '20
Johnson, Kenneth P., '48, Cl. '50
Johnson, Philip A., '59, '60, '61, ('62) S
Johnson, Robert P., '31, '32, ('33) S
Johnson, Russell, '58
Johnston, Alonzo S., '35, '36, Cl. '37 S
Jones, Arthur, '28, Cl. '29 S
Jones, Rollin L., '29, '30, ('31) S
Jordan, Robert W., '19, '20 S
Jordan, William C., '15, '16, Cl. '17 S
Joslyn, William L., '12, '13, Cl. '15 S
Justice, Howard H., '25, Cl. '28

Kakas, George J., '62, Cl. '65
Kakas, Edward F., '61, '62, Cl. '64 S
Kaley, Lester J., '07
Karkut, Emil J., '38, Cl. '41
Kearney, Edward F., Cl. '36
Keefe, Webster W., '29, '30, '31, ('32) S
Keefer, Paul B., '42, Cl. '45
Keefer, Ralph O., '14, ('17)
Keim, Addison, Cl. '37
Kehm, Walter H., '56, '57, '58, Cl. '60 S
Keller, Charles, Rigger
Kelley, Eugene E., '47, '48, '49, ('50) S
Kelsey, Charles E., '35, '36, ('37) S
Kemp, John R., ('51) S
Kengott, Alfred G., '06, ('08)
Kerr, Thomas ,Jr., '36, '37, ('39) S
Kessel, John J., '51, '55
Kevin, Herbert, Cl. '50
Kimball, G. Dene, '57, Cl. '59
Kimberly, Oscar S., '03, '04, Cl. '06 S
Kimmell, Claude L., '03, '04, ('05) S
King, Albert J., '16, Cl. '17
Kingsley, Carroll E., '18, Cl. '20
Kirkwood, George, '32, '33, '34, ('35)
Kitchin, Bernard L., '11, Cl. '14
Klassens, Henry, '57
Kleinhans, Richard C., Cl. '43
Kline, Roger B., '58, '59, '60, '61, ('62) S
Klinger, Allan H., Cl. '50
Klock, Karl T., '09, '10, ('11) S
Knapp, Robert P., '07
Knight, F. Robert, ('50)

Kniskern, Floyd B., '13, '15, ('16) S
Knoff, Frederick H., '00
Koerner, Norman H., '33, Cl. '34
Kowall, John R., '14
Kozelek, Frank F., Jr., '50, '51, ('52) S
Kratina, K. George, '29, '30, '31, ('32) S **
Kries, James S., '56, '57, '58, ('59 Capt.) S
Kuehn, Martin H., '12, '13, '14, ('15 Capt.) S

Ladage, Howard H., '39, '41, ('42) S
Laduke, William J., '57, '58, '59, ('60)
Laidlaw, John E., '26, '27, '28, ('29) S
Laidlaw, William F., '56, '58, Cl. '59
Lakin, James R., '42, Cl. '46 S
Lamb, Lester S., '15, Cl. '18
Lamonte, John C., '47, '48, Cl. '49 S
Lanckton, Clark S., '00, Cl. '03
Land, Percy A., '28, '30, Cl. '31
Landers, Everett J., '13, ('14) S
Lang, William N., '18, Cl. '20
Langford, Harold, '29
Lapham, William G., Jr., '21, '22, '23, ('24) S
Larsen, Michael J., '57, '58, '59, ('60) S *
Larson, Alan W., '57, Cl. '60
Lathrop, Henry, '33, Cl. '36
Laussier, Culver, '56
Lawrence, Richard, '25, '26, '27, Cl. '28 S
Lea, Richard V., '39, '40, '41, ('42) S *
Leagans, John P., Jr., '58
Lee, Charles, '61
Lee, George W., Jr., '41, ('42) S
Lee, Robert P., '49, '50, '51 S
Lehman, Norbert, Cl. '52
Lehmann, Douglas K., '59, '60, ('61)
Leis, David, '61
Lesher, Robert S., ('38 Comm.)
Leonard, James, '59, Cl. '60
Lester, Howard W., '15, ('18)
Levy, Charles M., '57, '58, '59, ('60) S
Lewis, Glendon R., '12, '13, ('15) S
Libbey, Charles F., '18
Lieberman, Stanley I., '53, ('54) S
Lincoln, Ivory M., '08, ('09)
Livingstone, Theodore M., '42, Cl. '45
Lloyd, David A., ('51) S
Lobo, Walter R., '49, ('51) S
Loizeaux, Elie T., '27, '28, '29, ('30) S
Lombardi, Thomas A., '30, '31, '32, ('33 Capt.) S **
Loomis, Leslie, '61
Loring, Robert B., ('37) S
Loskamp, Alvin P., '18, '19, '20, ('21) S
Loskamp, Charles L., '20, '21, Cl. '23 S

Lotz, Thomas M., Jr., '54, '55, '56, ('57) S

Love, Ronald J., '52, '53, '54, ('55 Capt.) S

Love, Thomas W., '13, Cl. '16

Lowery, Thomas J., ('21)

Lowry, Bruce D., '19, ('21) S

Lowther, E. A., '01, Cl. '02

Lucas, Jack, '18, ('21)

Lucy, Henry D., '18, '19 Comm., ('20) S

Lyon, Claude, ('25)

Lyons, Leroy F., '23, ('24) S

Maas, Jerry, '48

Mabie, Roger W., '37, ('39) S

Mace, Robert, '48

MacCallum, Daison, '27, ('28) S

MacFarlane, James, '29, Cl. '30

Machold, Earle J., Cl. '27

MacInnis, Harold B., '22, Cl. '25

MacLelland, John R., '54, '55, '56, ('57 Capt.) S

MacVittie, Joseph C., '49, ('51) S

Magee, Edward B., '48

Magoon, Herbert A., '03

Mahan, C. T., '10, '11, '12, ('13) S

Mallery, Roger H., '50, Cl. '53

Maloney, Martin F., '61, Cl. '63

Mang, Sidney, '22, '23, '24, ('25) S

Mantegna, Alfred C., '42, ('47) S

Margeson, Earl, Rigger

Marinus, Lucien D., '16, Cl. '19

Marmo, Carmen, '38, '39, Cl. '40

Marsden, George P., '48, '49, '50 ('51) S

Martineau, Daniel L., '21, '22, Cl. '24

Marvin, Raymond F., '20, '21, '22, ('23) S

Marvin, Robert S., '08, ('09 Comm.) S

Matasavage, Vincent P., '32, '33, '34, ('35) S

Mawhinney, Donald M., '18, ('21)

McCabe, P. A., '47, Cl. '49 S

McCormick, Floyd R., '47, '48, '49, ('50) S

McCully, Donald T., '30, Cl. '33

McDonald, James H., '24, '26 S

McDougall, William J., '39, '40, '41, ('42 Capt.) S

McDowell, Alexander, Cl. '45

McDowell, Robert A., ('40 Comm.) S

McFadden, Samuel D., '50, '51, '52, ('53) S

McKaig, Alan N., '39, Cl. '41

McKaig, Murray, '30, '31, '32, ('33) S **

McKean, Herbert B., '30, '31, '32, (33) S

McKee, James, '36, Cl. '38

McKee, McCormick H., '21, '22, '23, ('24) S

McMurray, Charles F., '01, '02

McNamara, Dennis, '62, Cl. '65

McNeil, Gomer T., '36, '37, '38, ('39) S

McNulty, Roland J., 23, '24, ('25) S

McRae, David, '52, S

McTiernan, John C., '41, '42, Cl. '44 S

Meacham, Edward D., '30, '31, '32, ('33) S

Mead, Thomas C., '62, Cl. '65

Meier, Emil F., '20, ('21) S

Meloney, Henry F., ('18)

Meloy, William C., Jr., '36, ('37) S

Menner, William G., '49, ('50) S

Merk, Harvey J., '34, ('35) S

Merriam, Spencer H., '18, Cl. '21

Merrick, Richard H., '42, Cl. '46

Merrill, M. Chester, '19, ('23) S

Messinger, William, '59

Metz, John R., ('41 Comm.) S

Meyer, Daniel, '54, Cl. '55 S

Meyer, Richard H., '21, Cl. '24 S

Michalson, Victor, Coach

Middleton, James A., '03

Millard, John T., '02, '03

Miller, C. W., '15, Cl. '18

Miller, Charles E., Jr., '03, '04, ('05) S

Miller, Nelson T., '56, '57, '58, ('59) S

Miller, Robert, '47, Cl. '49

Mills, Charles E., Jr., 57, '58, '59, ('60) S

Milne, Maurie, '38, Cl. '41

Minard, C. W., '13, '14, '15, Cl. '16 S

Miron, Robert J., '57, '58, '59, ('60) S

Mittlesteadt, Arthur H., '55, '57, ('58 Comm.) S

Moecker, Herman, '33, Cl. '36

Moffet, Thomas E., ('42)

Monstrastelle, William F., '48, Cl. '50 S

Montesi, Edward N., '56, '57, '58, ('59) S

Moore, John H., '51, Cl. '52

Moore, Paul J., ('23 Comm.) S

Moore, Robert B., ('37)

More, John W., '37, '38, 39, ('40 Capt.) S *

Morey, Robert W., '18, '19, ('20) S

Morris, Louis P., '02, '03, Cl. '05

Morris, Myron B., '02, Cl. '04

Morris, William, '42, Cl. '48

Morrison, William A., '47, ('48) S

Morse, J. Edwin, '53, '54, ('55) S

Morton, George, '59

Mulford, Robert M., '32, '33, Cl. '35

Mulholland, Francis P., Cl. '39

Mulholland, Malcolm M., '32, '33 S

Mulroy, Thomas, '48

Munger, Harlan D., '36, Cl. '38 S

Munro, James G., '28, Cl. '30

Murphy, Charles B., Jr., '49, '50, '51, ('52 Capt.) S *

Murphy, Lawrence, '57, Cl. '60

Murray, Albert K., '27, '28, '29, ('30) S

Murray, Bertram E., '06, ('07)
Muser, C. Joseph, '21, '22 S

Nash, Crosby C., '49, Cl. '53
Neasmith, John I., '16. ('17 Comm.)
Nelson, Alan C., Cl. '51
Nelson, Brooke, '58
Nelson, G. Merle, '24, '25, '26. ('27) S
Nelson, Harold, '47, Cl. '48 S
Nelson, Mark W., '01, '02 S
Nelson, Ray S., '06, '07 S
Newell, Dean W., ('24)
Newell, William B., ('24)
Newport, Floyd D., ('30 Comm.) S
Nichols, Richard A., '53, '54, '55, ('56) S
Nicholson, Charles A., '13, Cl. '16
Nicholson, Lowell S., '18, '20. ('21) S
Nitka, William E., '41, Cl. '44
Nix, Leon A., '10, Cl. '13
Nixon, John M., '38, '39, '40, Cl. '41 S
Northrup, Leverne E., '31, Cl. '34
Norton, Frank L., '48. Cl. '51
Norris, David M., '61, '62, Cl. '64 S
Noxon, James A., '10, '11, '12, ('13) S
Nunan, James D., ('35)
Nye, Richard. '57

O'Brien, W. Smith, '33, '34, ('35 Comm.) S
O'Connor, Charles J., '26. '28, ('29 Capt.) S
O'Hearn, Bart J., '32, '33. '34, ('35 Capt.) S
Okey (Okolowicz), Raymond, '39, '40, '41, ('42) S **
Okrepkie, Ralph G., Cl. '51
Oles, Wilbur S., Jr., '41, '42, ('43) S
Olp, David W., '58, Cl. '61
Olsen, Harold G., '38, ('40 Comm.) S
Olsen, Olaf LaCour, '20, '21, '22, ('23) S
Olver, Arthur G., Cl. '50
Olzsewski, Sigmund V., '55, '56, ('58) S
Osadchey, Lance M., '56, '57, '58, ('59) S
Osborn, William, '39. Cl. '42
Osman, Arthur J., '14, '15, '16, ('17 Capt.) S
Osthus, Kenneth L., '51, ('52) S
Otis, Edward T., '35. '36, '37, ('38 Capt.) S **

Packard, Charles A., '05, Cl. '07 S
Packard, Edward N., '03, '04. '05, ('06) S
Paddock, Albert E., '05
Page, Chamberlain A., '19, '20, '21, ('22 Capt.) S
Palmer, Charles B., '25, Cl. '28
Palmer, John E., '47, '48, ('49) S
Palmer, Sidney W., '12

Pangmon, Willard T., '00. '01, ('02) S
Pappas, George L., '39
Parfitt, Roger T., '51, '52, '53, ('54) S
Park, Ernest R., ('24 Comm.) S
Park, Robert, '02, Cl. '05
Parlatto, Carl A., '60, '62
Parrish, Jason B., '01
Parry, Irwin, '52
Parsons, George B., ('29 Comm.) S
Partridge, Gordon S., '24, Cl. '28
Partridge, Everett G., '50, ('56)
Pattyson, Brewster, '41, Cl. '44
Paul, Roland A., '57, Cl. '60
Pease, Floyd H., '19, '20, '21, ('22) S
Peck, Richard W., '39, ('41)
Penchos, Kenneth L., '62, Cl. '65
Pendill, Willoughby C., '09, '11 S
Percy, Earl, '39, Cl. '42
Perkins, Charles N., '37, Cl. '39
Perrin, Arthur R., Jr., '41, '42, '47, ('48 Capt.) S *
Perry, Eugene H., '47, '48, '49, ('50 Capt.) S, Coach
Peskin, Michael, '59, Cl. '61
Pessel, Thomas, Cl. '50
Peterson, R. A., '08, '09, ('10) S
Phelps, Duane Forest, '00, '02, ('03) S
Phifer, John E., '22, '23, '24, ('25 Capt.) S
Phillips, Crandall, '18, Cl. '22
Pigott, John W., ('51)
Pierce, Reginald F., '19, Cl. '22
Pinder, Thomas F., '10, ('11 Comm.) S
Pitcher, Bert, '61
Planck, Wesley S., '25, ('26 Comm.) S
Poole, Sidman P., '14, '15 S
Port, Ephraim G., '22, ('23)
Port, John T., '15, '16 S
Porter, Harold G., '12
Post, Charles D., '01, Cl. '02
Pranikoff, Howard L., '61, Cl. '64
Prescott, Allen S., '25, Cl. '28
Preston, Donald L., '58, Cl. '61
Price, Charles W., '33, Cl. '35
Price, David A., '60, '61, '62, Cl. '63 S
Prime, Raymond C., '11, ('14 Comm.) S
Prindiville, Thomas, '62. Cl. '65
Priory, Frank D., '14, ('15 Comm.) S
Pritchard, Thomas A., '36
Propst, Rudolph W., '12, '13, ('14) S
Puls, Irving, '31, '32, '33, ('34) S
Purick, Robert J., '50, '52, Cl. '53
Putelo, Michael C., '42, Cl. '45
Putnam, D. F., '08, '09, '10, Cl. '11 S
Putnam, Ronald W., ('10)

Quigg, August H., '21, '22, Cl. '24 S

Racht, Leon E., '18, Cl. '21
Rader, J. Walter, '32, '33, '34, Cl. '35 S
Rainbow, Harry J., '19
Rammi, August W., '18, '19, '20, ('21 Capt.) S
Rapelje, John A., '09, Cl. '11
Rayfield, Charles W., '60, '61 S
Raynor, Emerson M., '18, ('21)
Raynor, James, ('50)
Redman, Gladstone E., '14, '15, Cl. '17 S
Redway, Brayton S., ('22)
Reed, John B., '61, '62, Cl. '64
Reed, Neil C., ('25 Comm.) , Cl. '26 S
Reichert, Donald E., '47, ('48) S
Reifsnyder, William E., '42, Cl. '46
Reilly, Wayne, '49
Resen, Kenneth, '53
Resnick, Robert J., '59, '60, '61, ('62) S
Reswick, Bernard S., ('16)
Revelle, Richard B., '51, '52, '53, ('54) S
Rice, Charles, '36, Cl. '38
Rice, Edward A., '39, '40, ('41) S
Rice, Frank B., '36, ('37) S
Rice, Frank S., '03, '04, '05, ('06) S
Rice, George, ('24)
Rice, Leon C., '04, '06, '07, ('08) S
Rice, Orion E., '23, ('24)
Rice, Robert S., '38, '39, Cl. '41
Rich, C. A., Cl. '25
Rich, J. Harry, '11, '12, '13, ('14 Capt.) S
Richards, George D., '47, ('48) S
Richards, Melbourne K., '34, '35, '36, ('37) S
Richards, Oliver C., Jr., '52, '53, '54, ('55 Capt.) S
Richardson, Alfred R., '36, '37, ('38) S
Richardson, Daniel J., '02, Cl. '03
Richardson, Harry H., '09, '10, '11, ('12) S
Riddell, Fred J., '62, Cl. '65
Rigby, Judson L., '47, '48, ('49 Capt.) S
Robbins, Howard W., '11, '12, '13, ('14)
Roberson, William D., Jr., '58, Cl. '61
Roberts, Charles B., Jr., '58, '59, '60, ('61) S
Roberts, Eugene C., Cl. '09
Robinson, Edward S., Cl. '37
Robinson, Herbert A., '04, '05 S
Robinson, John E., '36, '37 S
Robinson, Paul H., '25, '26, Cl. '28
Robinson, Roy S., '06
Robinson, Thomas R., '05, '06, Cl. '08
Robinson, William G., '41, Cl. '44
Rockwell, Ford A., '26, Cl. '31
Rogers, Kenneth, Cl. '25
Rogers, Raymond H., '22, '23, '24, ('25) S
Rogers, Raymond M., '53, '54, '55, ('56) S

Rogers, Vincent J., '16, ('20)
Romer, Paul, '59
Roney, Robert E., '21, ('22 Comm.) S
Root, Stanley R., '52, ('53) S
Rosenau, Gary, '41, Cl. '44
Rosser, Milburn C., '24, '25, '26, Cl. '27 S
Rothman, Albert, Cl. '35
Rouen, Thomas M., '56, '58, '59, ('60) S
Rowell, Charles F., '53, '54, '55, ('56) S
Rowner, Robert H., '26
Roy, William R., '50
Ruhlman, Jack, '39, Cl. '43
Russell, Henry F., '02, '03
Russell, Maurice C., '24, ('25) S
Rutan, F. Guy, '11, '12, '13, ('14) S
Ryan, John F., '15, Cl. '18
Ryan, Joseph F., ('18)
Ryan, Roger B., '50, '51, '52, Cl. '53
Ryder, Loren J., '38, '40, Cl. '41
Ryerson, William, '37, '38, '39, ('40)

Salin, John W., '18, '19, '20, ('21) S
Salisbury, Jay W., '03, '04, '05, ('06 Capt.) S
Salm, Paul R., '62, Cl. '65
Sammon, Leo J., '48, '49, '50, ('51 Capt.) S
Samson, Nelson, '39, Cl. '42
Sanders, Robert A., '41, ('42) S
Sanfilippo, August A., Cl. '39
Sanford, Scott A., '61, '62, Cl. '63
Sanford, William E., '60, '61, '62 S
Santilli, Thomas L., '55, '56, Cl. '58
Sawyer, Robert A., '58, Cl. '61
Saylor, William B., '57, Cl. '60
Sayre, Russell P., '27, Cl. '30
Scalise, Andrew J., '58, '59, Cl. '62
Schermerhorn, Floyd T., '11, Cl. '15
Schermerhorn, John G., '30, '31
Schiefer, Henry J., Jr., '05, '06, '07, ('08) S
Schiffrin, Stuart A., '62, Cl. '65
Schmidt, Bernard, '33, Cl. '36
Schneider, J. Karl, ('27 Comm.) S
Schneller, David J., '62, Cl. '65
Schoberlein, George A., '31, '32, '33, ('34) S
Schoel, Loren W., Coach
Schoel, Robert L., '58, '59, ('61 Comm.) S
Schoenberg, Rolf G., '53
Schoolcraft, Earl L., '18, '19, Cl. '20
Schoonmaker, Floyd D., '18
Schopfer, Ralph, '39, '40, Cl. '42
Schubert, Glendon A., Jr., '38, '39, '40, Cl. '41 S
Schutt, Carl S., '16, Cl. '19
Schutts, Ronald R., '48, Cl. '52

Schweizer, Bruce, Cl. '45
Scobell, George A., Sr., '20, ('21) S
Scobell, George A., Jr., '51, ('52) S
Scofield, Era D., '35, ('36)
Scott, Harry C., '25, Cl. '28
Seager, Edward W. L., '50, Cl. '53
Searles, Lynn J., '34, Cl. '37
Segaloff, James H., '62, Cl. '65
Semple, Robert W., '22, Cl. '25
Serafini, Aldo, '34, ('35) S
Shaw, Charles R., '16, '19, ('20) S
Shaw, Kennedy, '48, '49, ('50 Comm.) S
Shaw, Walter E., '15, ('16 Comm.) S
Shea, Timothy J., '06, '07, ('08) S
Shephard, Edward J., '50, '51, '52, ('53) S *
Shephard, Edgar T., '24, Cl. '27
Shetron, John H., Jr., '15, '16, ('18)
Shimer, Mason C., '07, '08, '09, ('10 Capt.) S
Siegfried, Defois H., '32, '32, ('33) S
Silvanic, George, '48, Cl. '50
Silvernail, Charles D., '33, ('35) S
Simon, Lee K., Cl. '50
Simpson, Robert E., '49, '50, '51, Cl. '53
Simpson, Robert F., '50, ('51) S
Singer, William H., '26, '28, '29, ('30) S
Slingerland, Richard C., '54, '55, ('56) S
Slingham, J. Al., '55
Sloane, Martin A., '59, Cl. '61
Sloat, Benjamin F., '24, Cl. '27
Slocum, Robert H., '18, Cl. '21
Smart, Wayne D., '28, '29, '30, ('31) S
Smeltzer, William S., '55, '56, '57, ('58) S
Smith, Bruce H., Jr., '37, ('38)
Smith, David C., '40, '41, ('42) S
Smith, David L., '07, Cl. '10
Smith, F. Gordon, '08, '09, Cl. '10 S
Smith, Francis P., '48, '49, '50, ('51) S
Smith, Hugh R., '02, Cl. '05
Smith, Lyman C., Pres. SU Navy. '01
Smith, Myron E., '47, Cl. '49 S
Smith, Oliver J., '10, '11, Cl. '13 S
Smith, Roy L., '03, Cl. '04
Smith, Walter J., '13, '14, Cl. '16 S
Smyth, Michael P., '55, '56, ('57) S*
Sowers, Frank, '01, '02, Cl. '04
Spafford, Robert A., '57
Spencer, David C., '06
Spencer, Henry J., '04, '05, '06, ('07) S
Spiegel, Steven R., '62, Cl. '65
Spieker, Francis J., '29, '30, '31, Cl. '32, S
Spontowicz, Derek, '55
Sprague, Lloyd D., '14, '15, '16 ('17) S
Spry, Richard G., Cl. '39
Spurgeon, George W., '36, Cl. '38
Squires, Augustus J., '03, '04, '05, ('06) S

Stankiewicz, Stanley J., '54, '55, ('56) S

Stanley, H. Sumner, '36, '37, Cl. '39
Stark, Harry O., '32, Cl. '35
Steigerwald, Jerome, '55, '56, Cl. '58
Stein, William, '62, Cl. '65
Sterling, Kenneth, '41, Cl. '44
Stevens, Harold D., ('07 Comm.)
Stewart, George D., ('50) S
Stolberg, William, '41, Cl. '44
Stone, Dwight G., '04, '05, ('07) S
Stone, Robert R., '01, '02, '03, ('04 Capt.) S
Stratton, Hubert C., '23, '24, ('26) S
Straus, Michael, '51, '52
Strauss, Michael I., '58, '59, Comm. Cl. '60
Streeter, Charles M., '29, Cl. '32
Strickler, Donald S., '59
Strickler, Richard, '40, '41, Cl. '43
Strife, Cyril F., '16, '18, ('19)
Stringer, Richard, '59
Strong, Donald W., '55, Cl. '58
Struthers, Alfred M., '40, '41, ('42) S
Studer, Carl J., Jr., '40, '41
Stuhlman, F. Wilbur, '36, '37, '38, ('39 Capt.) S
Stumpf, Frank M., '42, Cl. '45
Sturim, Howard S., '51, '52, ('53) S
Sturtevant, George D., '21, '22, '23
St. Germaine, Paul, '39
Suholet, David, '48, Cl. '51
Sullivan, Richard, Cl. '51
Summers, Ronald J., Cl. 52
Summerville, Allen H., '11, '12, '13, Cl. '14 S
Summerville, Orin R., '15, '16, Cl. '18 S
Sumner, Ernest H., '00, '01, ('03) S
Sundstrom, Donald I., '50, ('51) S
Sundstrom, Edward A., Cl. '38
Susi, Ronald A., '58, Cl. '61
Sutor, Emmett C., '25, ('26)
Sutter, Harlow E., '16, Cl. '17
Swanson, Russell S., '31, '33, '34, ('35) S **
Swenning, Earl A., '18
Swift, Charles, '39
Sweetland, Edwin R., Coach
Sze, Ping N. H., '07, Cl. '10

Tainter, Bernard P., '37, '38, '39, ('40) S
Tate, Charles H., Jr., '25
Taylor, John F., '57, Cl. '60
Taylor, Raymond H., '48, Cl. '51
Taylor, Robert C., '36, '37 S
Tedesco, Andrew R., '51, '52, Cl. '53 S
Ten Eyck, Edward Hanlon, Coach
Ten Eyck, James A., Jr., '06, '07, '08 S
Ten Eyck, James A., Sr., Coach
Thayer, Donald R., '47, '49, ('50) S

367

Thomas, Donald R., '27, ('28) S
Thorne, Richard J., '59, '60, '61, ('62) S *
Thompson, Charles, ('41) S
Thompson, Edward, '31, ('33 Comm.) S
Thompson, John, '26
Thompson, Robert C., '36, ('37) S
Thompson, Stanley J., '49, ('50) S
Thompson, Syndor, Cl. '45
Thomson, Winslow E., '23, '24, '25, ('26) S
Thurston, George B., '10, '11, '12, ('13 Capt.) S
Tinklepaugh, Glen I., '19, Cl. '22
Tobin, Robert A., '58, '59, '60, Cl. '61 S
Tobin, Robert M., '53
Toch, Leo, '27, ('28) S
Tollerton, Harry, '26, '27, ('28) S
Tolley, Howard B., '25, '26, '27 Capt., ('28) S
Tompkins, John H., '53, Cl. '56
Topping, Harry R., Cl. '12 S
Topping, John H., '53
Tracy, Robert E., '48
Tracz, William J., '60
Travis, Alanson R., '24, '25, Cl. '28
Treat, Merritt W., '42, Cl. '45
Trigg, Joseph E., '13, '14, '15 S
Tripp, John E., '60, '61, Cl. '62
Trnavsky, Benjamin D., '28, '30, '31, ('32) S
Tucker, Henry R., ('23)
Tuft, Richard, ('51)
Turnbull, Howard F., '12, '13, '14, ('15) S
Turner, Egbert S., Jr., Cl. '36
Turner, Richard H., '59, '60, '61, ('62 Comm.) S
Turner, Robert, '62, Cl. '65
Twombley, Gray, '41, Cl. '44
Tyler, H. Johnson, '35, Cl. '38

Uffelman, Dale, '40, '41, ('42) S

Valentine, John P., '55, Cl. '58
Van Auken, Gilbert L., '11, '12, ('13)
Van deArnum, H. Robert, '34, '35, ('36) S
Van deWater, Donald B., '30, Cl. '33
Van deWater, Jerome T., '59, '60, '61, ('62) S
Van derBogert, Giles Y., Jr., '61, '62, Cl. '64
Van Dusen, William R., '48, '49, ('50) S
Van Ness, Harold W., '20, ('23)
Van Nostrand, Charles, '28, '29, ('30) S
Van Vost, Horace, '48
Van Winkel, Richard S., '60
Vatter, Glenn A., '56, Cl. '59

Vaughn, H. B., 13, Cl. 16
Vaugn, Samuel G., '10, '11, ('13) S
Vay, Michael D., '62, Cl. '65
Ventre, Frank, '59, Cl. '62
Veseley, Vincent M., '30, '31 S
Vincent, John B., '31, Cl. '40
Vogeler, Edward C., '34, Cl. '37
Von Berg, William G., '38, Cl. '39

Walberg, Milton A., '62, Cl. '65
Waldorf, Lynn O., '22, '23, '24, Cl. '25 S
Walker, John, '59, Cl. '62
Wallis, Percy L., '15, '16 S
Walter, Carl, '27, '28, '29, Cl. '30 S
Ward, Thomas F., '22, '23, '24, Cl. '25 S
Ward, Vernon G., '40, '41, Cl. '43
Wardwell, Charles R., '37, '38, ('40) S
Warren, Harris C., '42, Cl. '49 S
Warren, John C., ('39 Comm.) S
Warren, Thomas C., '08
Watson, Leon A., '07, '08
Waugh, Rogers V., '38, '39, '40, ('41) S
Weatherup, Watson A., '10, ('14) S
Weaver, Robert C., '06, Cl. '09
Weber, Jack A., '27, '28, '29, ('30) S
Webster, George, '32, Cl. '35
Weed, Walter F., Cl. '21
Weeden, Morris S., '40, '41, Cl. '42
Weeks, Howard, '20, Cl. '23
Weeks, Wilmot L., ('42) S
Weibezahl, Harold E., '49, '50, ('51) S*
Weiler, Milton C., '29, '30, '31, Cl. '32 S **
Weinberger, Richard A., '53, Cl. '55 S
Weiss, John, '42, Cl. '45
Weitsman, Allen W., '59, '60, Cl. '62
Wells, Lawrence L., '35, '36, '37, ('38) S
Welton, Robert Q., '48
Wengrovius, John E., ('37)
Went, David, '37
Weston, Ralston A., '34, '35, '36, '37 S
Wetherell, William P., '27, '28, '29, ('31) S
Wharff, Edward M., '05, ('06 Comm.) S
Wheaton, James H., '52, Cl. '55
Whelan, Ande G., '21, '23, '24
Whisman, Donald E., '61, Cl. '64
Whitebread, Floyd B., '14, '15
Whitehead, Bruce E., '37, '38, '39, ('40) S **
Whietside, Charles J., '15, '16, S Coach
Whiteside, John M., '26, '27, Cl. '28 S
Whitmore, Benjamin, '48
Whitney, Miles S., '05, '06, '07
Wiener, Lawrence H., '56, 57, 58, Cl. '59 S
Wilcox, Arthur T., '37, '39, ('40) S
Wildman, Gilbert H., 01, ('02) S

Wilkinson, Robert E., '48, '49, '50, Cl. '51 S
Will, Eric W., Cl. '17
Willenborg, Richard L., '40, '41, '42, ('43 Capt.) S
Williams, Frank R., '15, '16, Cl. '18 S
Williams, Randolph B., '08, '09, '10, ('11 Capt.) S
Williams, Richard E., '49, Cl. '52
Willner, John, '26
Willoghby, Earle S., '31, '32, '33, ('34) S
Wilson, James H., '08, Cl. '10
Wilson, William D., Jr., '47, '48, '49, ('50) S
Winans, Albert, '55
Winklestein, Jerome A., '58, '59, '60, ('61) S *
Winter, John R., '19, '20, '21, ('22) S
Winter, Thomas, '50
Wirsig, Carl F., '08
Wise, George E., '42, Cl. '50
Wise, Milton A., '21, '22, '23, ('24 Capt.) S
Wisner, Benjamin S., '29, '30, '31, ('32) S
Withers, Lloyd M., Cl. '28
Witzel, August E., '10, '11, '13 S
Womer, Marcus D., '18, Cl. '20
Woodrow, William, '52

Woods, Arthur L., '35, '36, '37 S
Woodworth, Hugh, '23, '24, '25, ('26) S
Wooler, Alfred G., '39, Cl. '42
Woolsey, Royal D., '00, '01, ('02 Capt.) , '03 S
Worden, Leslie J., '15, '16, '22 S
Worden, Robert W., '36, ('37)
Wright, Dexter H., '20, Cl. '22
Wright, Edward G., '12, '13 S
Wright, Robert M., '26, '27, Cl. '29
Wuerch, Reinhold, '14, Cl. '17
Wykoff, Lynn B., '00, ('01 Capt) , '02, ('03) S

Yager, George J., '25, Cl. '28
Young, Peter, '39
Young, Richard I., '57, Cl. '60
Young, Robert C., '47, '48, Cl. '49 S
Young, Ward R., '42, Cl. '45
Young, William, Jr., '18, ('21)
Youngs, Truman, '22, Cl. '26
Yull, Paul C., '16

Zeh, Dale W., '58, Cl. '61
Zeldis, Louis J., Cl. '37
Zeller, Alfred G., '08, Cl. '11
Zerner, Stuart E., Cl. '50
Zimmer, Fred G., '50, Cl. '54

369

HISTORICAL COMMITTEE

Ernest Buff

Dr. Bruce Chamberlain

Thomas Dunham

Eric Ellis

Leon Ellis

M. Charles Hatch, Jr.

Martin Hilfinger, Sr.

Dr. Gordon Hoople

Richard Horstmann

Benjamin Johnson

Robert Johnson

Dr. Thomas Kerr

Dr. Anthony Ladd

Robert Loring

Ronald Love

John MacLelland

Sidney Mang

Charles Mills, Jr.

William Morrison

John Palmer

Eugene Perry

Thomas Rouen

August Sanfillipo

George Schoberlein

Edward Shephard

James Stimson

Hubert Stratton

Russell Swanson

370

GENERAL PLAN I.R.A. REGATTA
SYRACUSE, N.Y.

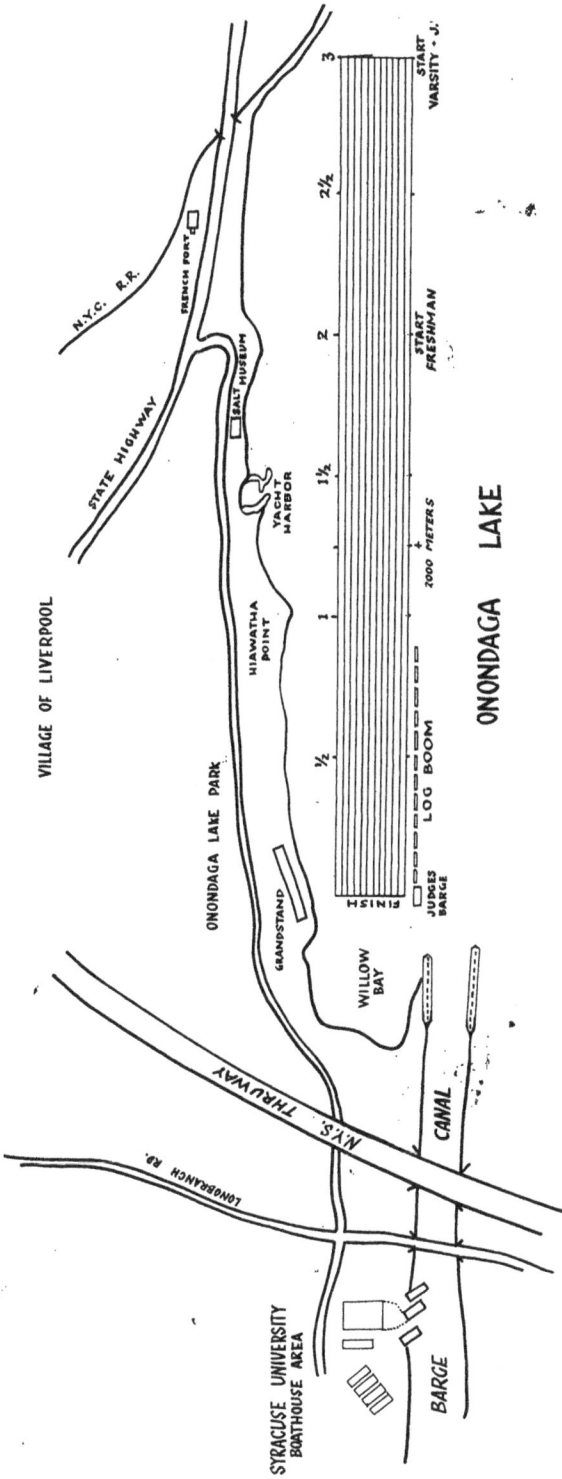

N

VILLAGE OF LIVERPOOL

N.Y.C. R.R.

FRENCH FORT

STATE HIGHWAY

SALT MUSEUM

YACHT HARBOR

ONONDAGA LAKE PARK

HIAWATHA POINT

GRANDSTAND

WILLOW BAY

SYRACUSE UNIVERSITY BOATHOUSE AREA

BARGE

N.Y.S. THRUWAY

LONGBRANCH RD.

CANAL

FINISH

JUDGES BARGE

LOG BOOM

2000 METERS

½   1   1½   2   2½   3

START VARSITY + J.

START FRESHMAN

ONONDAGA   LAKE

www.ingramcontent.com/pod-product-compliance
Lightning Source LLC
Chambersburg PA
CBHW030254100426
42812CB00002B/433